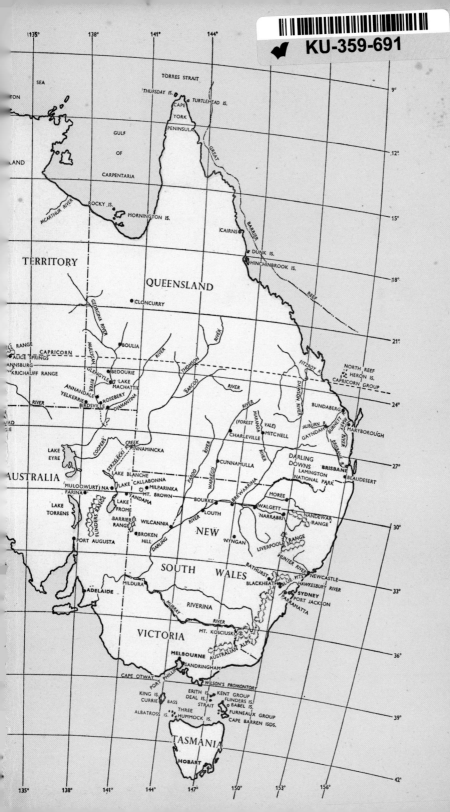

WANDERERS IN AUSTRALIA

By the Same Author

BIOGRAPHY

In Mortal Bondage: The
Strange Life of Rosa Praed

GENERAL

The Australian Novel
Twenty Australian Novelists

BELLES LETTRES

An Introduction to Australian Fiction

To Alick

With warmest love from
your old Aunty Holly
June 1957

KANANGRA WALLS, BLUE MOUNTAINS

"A spot of earth which defies you to touch it"

Photograph by David D. Stead.

WANDERERS IN AUSTRALIA

A BOOK OF TRAVELS

Edited by
COLIN RODERICK

ANGUS AND ROBERTSON
SYDNEY · LONDON

First Published 1949
Reprinted 1950

SET UP IN LINOTYPE JANSON

PRINTED AND BOUND IN AUSTRALIA BY

HALSTEAD PRESS PTY LTD, NICKSON STREET, SYDNEY

REGISTERED IN AUSTRALIA FOR TRANSMISSION THROUGH THE POST AS A BOOK

TO

Miles Franklin

ACKNOWLEDGMENTS

IT is with pleasure and gratitude that I acknowledge the ready co-operation of the following authors and publishers in the compilation of this anthology, the extracts of which are taken from the books named:

ANGUS & ROBERTSON LTD

C. E. W. Bean: *On the Wool Track*
A. M. Duncan-Kemp: *Our Sandhill Country*
Francis Birtles: *Battle Fronts of Outback*
Sir Albert Ellis: *Adventuring in Coral Seas*
T. C. Roughley: *Wonders of the Great Barrier Reef*
H. H. Finlayson: *The Red Centre*
R. H. Croll: *Wide Horizons*
Francis Ratcliffe: *Flying Fox and Drifting Sand*
P. G. Taylor: *Call to the Winds*
Ion L. Idriess: *The Great Boomerang*
Elyne Mitchell: *Australia's Alps*

OXFORD UNIVERSITY PRESS
JONATHAN CAPE LTD
GEO. G. HARRAP & CO. LTD
JARROLDS; and HUTCHINSON & CO. LTD (Melb.)
ROBERTSON AND MULLENS
MACMILLAN & CO. LTD
ERNEST BENN LTD

Dr Thomas Wood: *Cobbers*
C. Price Conigrave: *North Australia*
Fred Blakeley: *Hard Liberty*
M. Barnard Eldershaw: *My Australia*

Malcolm Uren: *Sailormen's Ghosts*
Richard Semon: *In the Australian Bush*
E. J. Banfield: *Confessions of a Beachcomber*
E. J. Banfield: *My Tropic Isle*
A. Buchanan: *The Real Australia*
Jack McLaren: *My Crowded Solitude*

GEO. ALLEN & UNWIN LTD
MELBOURNE PUBLISHING CO.

Myrtle Rose White: *No Roads Go By*
Charles Barrett: *In Australian Wilds*

All the photographs in this book, with the exception of the frontispiece, were kindly supplied by the Commonwealth Department of Information. The frontispiece is by David D. Stead, of Sydney.

I would add a word of tribute to that thorough-going Australian, Miles Franklin, inasmuch as this book originated in discussion with her.
—C.R.

PREFACE

As far as I am aware, no book of this nature has hitherto been published in Australia. There are English anthologies of travel literature from which readers derive pleasure and instruction. The Australian can travel with Drummond in Africa, with Kinglake in the Middle East, with Mungo Park and Speke, even with Marco Polo and Hakluyt's heroes. But before reading books that reveal life under alien skies, surely he ought to read about his own country. Only by first knowing the travel literature of a familiar environment can he really begin to appreciate this sort of writing.

Through the travel book the novel becomes more meaningful: the casual reader perceives that the novel is set in a real country. The characters do not move in a world of pure fancy; they are seen against a known or familiar background.

Thousands of people know at least some of the places written about in this book, and the scenes painted come to life because of the reader's previous knowledge. These writings help him to measure the degree of his own intimacy with the life about him, to realize that literature has its roots in life.

In Australia any approach to literature should first be through Australian works. They provide the natural starting-point for a journey into the world of books. The vast range and amazing variety of natural life in Australia make it unnecessary to apologize for proclaiming this self-evident fact. And what is true for the student, whose reading is directed, is equally true for the general reader, whose literary entertainment is largely a haphazard affair.

Wanderers in Australia has been compiled to provide a jumping-off ground for literary experience. Here are extracts from books written by travellers in our own country. Many of them were sojourners; others came to Australia and adopted it as their home; the remainder are native-born. All have a vital impression to record.

Each extract is typical of the book from which it was taken. Since the literature of travel should be a source of delight and instruction, I hope this collection will help to awaken interest in such writing, guiding the reader to the books which reveal his own country, and arousing a desire for closer acquaintance with its literature.

CONTENTS

ILLUSTRATIONS

ANTHONY TROLLOPE

ANTHONY TROLLOPE, author of the "Barchester" novels, visited Australia and New Zealand in 1871-2. He went first to Queensland, then to New South Wales, Victoria, Tasmania, Western Australia, South Australia, and New Zealand. His impressions are recorded in the two volumes of *Australia and New Zealand* (1873) from which the following passage is taken.

SCENERY IN NEW SOUTH WALES

I HAVE said in the preceding chapter that the scenery of the bush is monotonous. It is the complaint that has been made generally of all Australian landscape, so generally as to have reached England, and to constitute one of the few facts that are supposed to be known about the country. The "everlasting gum-tree" has become proverbial. Consequently no one visits Australia to see its scenery, and comparatively few of those who go there in pursuit of business, or to see men and women, make a search after the beauties of nature a part of their programme. The same feeling prevails with permanent settlers and with natives. It is taken for granted that Australia is ugly, and that the touring in quest of the picturesque, which forms so great a part of the delight of an Englishman's holiday, would be altogether time wasted and money misapplied if attempted at the Antipodes. Nevertheless, there is grand scenery in, I believe, all the Australian colonies. It is certainly to be found in Queensland and Victoria. Tasmania is one of the prettiest countries I ever visited. And in New South Wales I came across wonders almost as magnificent and charms as lovely as any that I have seen in Europe. As yet the localities are unknown, as yet the means of communication are unfrequent and uncertain, as yet popular taste has not settled herself in the direction of scenery, directing people to go here or to go there,—and by her potency providing the means of encouraging them, feeding them, and amusing them. But the time will come in which Australian men and women will find that they need not go to Europe to delight themselves with mountains and rivers.

Of the extreme beauty of Sydney Harbour I have already spoken, and will only say of it further that its extent is so great as to require days for its examination. It is not a sheet of water which can be seen from one spot,—and then be ticked off from the list of sights as a thing completed, and numbered among the lions which have been killed. That lion will demand four or five days before it can be killed to satisfaction, and will then bear to be rekilled by those who really take delight in natural loveliness.

The Australian Alps, whence springs the river Murray, or Hume,—for the upper part of this river was called the Hume in the early days after the explorer of that name,—stand on the south-eastern corner of New South Wales, forming a part of the great range which divides the narrow eastern strip of the continent from the vast bulk of the interior. Of the beauty of these mountains I can only speak by hearsay, having seen no more than their snowy tops at the distance of forty miles. Mount Kosciusko stands just on the borders of New South Wales and Victoria, and is 7,300 feet high. It is the monarch of Australian mountains as Mont Blanc is of those of Europe. From what was told to me, I was very anxious to visit the district, and made plans with that purpose. But I found that Australia was too big and my time too limited to enable me to see everything; and as the life of the men and women around me was more essential to my object than scenery, I was obliged to leave Kosciusko unseen. The district is difficult of access, and must be visited either on horseback, or, by those who are strong enough, with much greater facility on foot. The starting-point should, I am told, be from the little town of Tumberumba*, from whence the mountains are distant about forty miles. From the description I have heard of them, I imagine the country to be wild and fine, but I doubt whether the summits ever rise in sharp inaccessible peaks. I feel bound to apologise to

* Tumbarumba.

Above: HAWKESBURY RIVER *"Scenery as lovely as any which I ever beheld"*

Below: CERATODUS *"An uncommonly dull, slow, and lazy fish"*

COLLINS STREET, MELBOURNE

"A clear, unbroken passage for the Arctic wind"

my readers for attempting even so far to describe a region
I did not see; but on the other hand, an apology more humili-
ating would have been due to Mount Kosciusko, had I written
a book about Australia and not mentioned him.

The railway from Sydney to Bathurst passes through the
Blue Mountains, which form a portion of the same dividing
range. They presented a cruel, awful barrier to the earlier
settlers, and for a long time debarred them from the land
beyond, which they hoped to find flowing with all the re-
quisites for milk and honey. The eastern strip, where Sydney
is built and Paramatta,* was singularly barren, though a little
farther to the north and west there were river valleys, the soil
of which was as singularly rich. It was felt by all the settlers
that the Blue Mountains hemmed them in, making, as it were,
a prison for them on the shores of Port Jackson. With infinite
suffering and indefatigable energy, a way was at last found
through the dark defiles of the hills, and the colonists made
their way down to those plains, which are now called the
Plains of Bathurst. Now a railway passes up and down
through the wildest parts of the mountains, crossing their
very summit, and passengers go from Sydney to Bathurst,
thinking nothing of the struggles of their forefathers,—and
thinking very little of the wonders around them.

Close to the highest part of the range, with a fall to it so
slight as to be hardly more than perceptible, and at a distance of about two miles from the railway, there is a ravine
called Govat's† Leap. Mr Govat was, I believe, simply a
government surveyor, who never made any leap into the
place at all. Had he done so, it would certainly have been
effectual for putting an end to his earthly sorrows. I had
hoped, when I heard the name, to find that some interesting
but murderous bushranger had on that spot baffled his pur-
suers and braved eternity; but I was informed that a government surveyor had visited the spot, had named it, and had
gone home again. No one seeing it could fail to expect better
things from such a spot and such a name.

It consists of a ravine probably more than a mile wide. I

* i.e., Parramatta.
† i.e., Govett's.

had no means of ascertaining the distances or heights of the place,—but the whole was on so gigantic a scale as to deceive the eye greatly at the first sight. The only approach to it from the railway leads the visitor to the head of the ravine, at which he is stopped by a precipitous wall of rock, which runs round, in various huge curves, till on each side it loses itself in the distance. As you stand there, looking down, you see a world below you,—a valley, but certainly not a happy valley, dark, awful, and inaccessible. Nowhere round these curves and lines of the rock can the eye find a spot at which it would be possible to descend. It is as though the ocean were below, and you were standing on the edge of a lofty cliff;—but in lieu of the ocean there is this black valley, densely filled with forest timber, filled so densely that you see nothing but the continuous tops of the black foliage, which, though the wind is blowing hard above, never seemed to move. In looking down from cliffs upon the sea, one is conscious that the foot of the rocks may be reached. A boat, at any rate, will place you there, if the weather be fair. But here the mind becomes aware of no mode of entering the abyss. On reaching the edge it seems as though you had come upon a spot of earth which defied you to touch it, and which forbade the possibility of escape should you succeed in doing so. The idea is common to us when we look up at snowy peaks— and is not the less common because we know that men have learned the way to climb them. But to look down on a place which cannot be reached,—into a valley full of trees, through which a stream runs, a green, dark, crowded valley,— and to feel that you are debarred from reaching it by a sheer descent of four or five hundred feet of cliff all round, is uncommon. I would say double that descent only that I do not quite believe in their entirety some accounts of the place that I have heard. I never saw before so vast a gaping hole on the earth's surface.

At about half a mile to the right, as you reach the edge, a stream of water very much like the Staubach, near Lauterbrunner, in Switzerland, falls precipitously over the rock. I was there in winter, after rain, and there was water in plenty.

I heard different altitudes named for the fall, ranging up to very high figures indeed. I believe it to be about 900 feet. From the spot whence it is seen it appears that the water is broken nowhere by striking against the rocks, and that therefore the descent is perpendicular; but this, no doubt, is a fallacy of the eye, caused by the distance. As we lay on the rock gazing at it, the wind would every now and then catch the long silver thread and sweep it away into the bend of the curve, so that it would disappear from sight. The forest trees above were wild with the wind, but the interminable thickets below were never stirred. I have said that we could not descend. There was not a spot at which we could think of making the attempt;—but there was an easy track down to a jutting rock, about 200 feet below the top, and this we found to be the proper spot from whence to look down upon the awful grandeur of the scene below us.

As I have already said the place is to be reached by railway from Sydney, from whence it is between forty and fifty miles distant.† The nearest station, or stopping place, is Blackheath;—at which the trains are pulled up if there be passengers. But there is no inn at this place. We,—the young squatter of whom I spoke in the last chapter and myself,— left the train at Mount Victoria, a station four miles distant from Blackheath, where we found very good accommodation at the house of one Mrs Perry,—whom we knocked up at two o'clock in the morning, and who took our somewhat noisy intrusion in perfect good humour. I would advise any stranger who finds himself at Sydney to make a visit to Govat's Leap, and to stop at the inn at Mount Victoria when doing so.

Govat's Leap astonished me very much,—but not, I think, so much as the scenery of the Hawkesbury River. A great portion of this is within forty miles of the town of Sydney, and might be as easily reached and much more quickly and cheaply seen than the Rhine,—if only people knew of it, so that an hotel or two might be built on its banks, and a steamer built to ply upon it. A trip of two days from Sydney, at a

† Trollope wrote "four and five miles"—an obvious mis-reading of his notes.

B

cost of 30s. a head, might make the river known to every pleasure-seeker in Sydney,—and if the expedition were customary, the Hawkesbury would soon be as much to Sydney as the mouth of the Clyde and the Kyles of Bute are to Glasgow. And yet who has heard of the Hawkesbury? As it is altogether unknown in Sydney, it is hardly surprising that the river should not have been much talked about in England. Had it been known in Sydney, it would have been talked about in England. I must own that when I was invited to join a party to visit the scenery of the river, I myself had never heard of the Hawkesbury, except as one of the first-named rivers on the Australian continent,—so called many years ago when Lord Liverpool was young.

The party which I was kindly invited to join was a very august party, consisting of nearly all the cabinet ministers, and a very considerable minority of the House of Assembly. The premier was at the head of it, and no man fitter for such an occasion ever held absolute dominion over hampers. It was by no means a partisan party; for I observed on my return to Sydney six months afterwards, when that premier had, alas, succumbed to the fate of premiers, and another head of the government reigned in his stead, that two of the most lively of our politicians on the Hawkesbury trip were sitting on the treasury bench. And we had been all so friendly then! I must confess that when I saw those two gentlemen on that bench, and saw that former premier opposite, turned out into the cold, partly no doubt, by their efforts, I could not but say to myself that there could be ingratitude in New South Wales as deep as among the older nations of the earth.

We went by railway to the little town of Windsor, to which a branch line runs from the Sydney and Bathurst line; —a quaint little place, inhabited by old settlers who came to this district as being singularly fertile. Very fertile it is; no land in the Australian colonies is perhaps more so; hardly any soil in any country is perhaps more so. But for this great gift it has to pay a proportionate penalty. Every now and then, perhaps once in six or seven years, it is so absolutely flooded by the Hawkesbury and its tributaries, that the farmers are forced to fly for their lives. And there have been floods so sudden and so high that all the farmers have not been able to fly with their lives. Windsor is built upon the Hawkesbury,—here so called; but up above this it has another name and is called the *Nepe-an*;—for it is the fashion in New South Wales to divide what with us at home would be the last syllable. From Windsor we went five miles down the river in open boats, and there found a steamer waiting for us. I must confess that during the first part of our journey I was disposed to think that I had been enticed away by false representations. Immediately below Windsor the river is not beautiful. It passes through a rich country, which gradually becomes narrower as the hills are approached;—but for an hour or two the fertility of the land and the specialities, such as they might be, of its productiveness were the chief attractions. But gradually as we reached the bluffs and high banks of the lower reaches, the scene was changed, and as the afternoon wore itself away we steamed down among river scenery as lovely as any which I ever beheld.

There can I think be no doubt that among rivers the Rhine has the highest character for sustained beauty. There may be special points on other streams which have endeared themselves to the world,—such especially as the Falls of Niagara,— such as the Inn at Innsbruck, or the Rhone at Geneva,—or the Upper Lake at Killarney, which is, in truth, a river. But for continued scenery the Rhine stands first. There is a river, or rather a portion of a river, known to very few tourists, which I think beats the Rhine. This is the Upper Mississippi, for about 150 miles below St Paul. It is not my business here to describe the Mississippi,—but I mention it with the object of saying that in my opinion the Hawkesbury beats the Mississippi. I should not make the contrast unless there were many features in the two which are similar. At all of them the beauty consists in the breaking of the land on the very margin of the river, and is not carried far back into the interior. At all of them the banks rise suddenly, sometimes covered with timber and sometimes bald,—sometimes sloping and sometimes precipitous,—but at all of them the banks are broken here and there into lateral valleys, which give to the imagination the idea that the glory of the scene is far spread, and would repay pursuit. Unless it can convey this vague feeling of distant, unapproachable, and almost mysterious delight, scenery loses half its charms. On the Rhine, on the Mississippi, and on the Hawkesbury alike, there is created an idea that if the traveller would only leave the boat and wander inland, he would be repaid by the revelation of marvellous beauties of Nature,—beauties which have perhaps never yet met the eyes of man. The Rhine has its castles and its islands—and it has, too, in its favour the bright colour of its waters. The Upper Mississippi has no castles, nor are its waters bright; but it has islands, and innumerable bluffs and headlands and varied valleys, and park-like timber, and its own fast-running rush of waters,—which are to me more than compensation for the castles and the colour. The Hawkesbury has neither castles nor islands, nor has it bright clear water like the Rhine. But the headlands are higher and the bluffs are bolder, and the turns and manoeuvres of the course which the waters have made for themselves are grander, and to me more enchanting, than those of either the European or American river.

It took us two days to descend the Hawkesbury to Broken Bay, and during the night our steamer lay at a bend in the river called Wiseman's Ferry,—where there is a large dilapidated and unused church, showing how soon ruins may be instituted in a new country. Along the banks, at intervals from each other of a few miles, whenever a bit of alluvial soil gave an opportunity for cultivation, settlers had placed themselves, and lived by growing maize, potatoes, and fruit. These people, or their fathers, were among the earliest colonists of New South Wales,—as the banks of the Hawkesbury had been soon reached. But civilisation had passed by them and gone beyond them,—and they were left now much in the condition in which their fathers were sixty or seventy years ago. Great portions of the banks are not approached by any road, and are accessible only by water. Small luggers from Sydney ply up and down the stream, taking the produce of the settlers to market, and bringing them back flour and tea in return. There can be but little intercourse even between families at ten miles' distance from each other,—as a river is, after all, but a poor road for the purposes of familiar intercourse. Life there must be very solitary and cheerless,—but at the same time independent and plentiful. We saw children about, amidst the garden patches,—but I fear that they were often out of reach of any school.

The lower part of the river, that between Wiseman's Ferry and Pitt-Water,—which is a large inlet of the sea, running southward from Broken Bay,—is very much finer than the upper reaches. There are various spots, especially at Mangora Creek, Berowat Creek, and Mullet Creek, at which the expanse of water assumes the appearance of a lake, and from which the stream escapes under banks almost perpendicular, and, as we calculated, from four to six hundred feet high. At Broken Bay, after having steamed up to the head of Pitt-Water, we got out into the sea, and within an hour and a half were in Sydney harbour.

Up along the river banks there were numberless sites fit for private houses or for hotels,—all of which might be reached within a few hours from Sydney. We saw but one house of any pretence,—which, I was told, was occasionally inhabited by a gentleman's family. But residence here, except to a cockatoo farmer, or to a hermit, is at present impossible. Though the place be no more than forty miles from Sydney, it is altogether beyond reach,—as many parts of the highlands of Scotland were some few years ago. In another space of a few years there will probably be daily means of getting to the Hawkesbury; and there will be villas dotted on its banks, and hotels of all descriptions for the accommodation of Australian tourists.

As of Australian scenery, so also is it generally said of Australian country houses, that they are without the charms and prettiness which are thought so much of at home by our squires and their wives and families. I do not know that I had many preconceived opinions as to country life in the colonies,—but I certainly did think that the surroundings of

† Now called Berowra.

it would be ugly. It is a matter of course that finished beauty at a homestead cannot be achieved to order by any given time. The surroundings of a house want years for the full creation of their charms. In England many an old ruined house is lovely, but who has ever succeeded in making a new country mansion pleasing to the eye? On this account landscape beauty of the domestic kind must be less frequent in a new than in an old country, and is, of course, less frequent in Australia than in Europe. But, nevertheless, it is to be found,—and I saw the preparations for it frequent in many of the colonies. I think that Coombing Park, in New South Wales,—the property of Mr Icely, one of the oldest settlers, and now the residence of his son,—is as pretty a combination of hills, river, and woodland as ever I saw round a gentleman's house in any country. The house itself is but of one story,—as a squatter's house should be,—straggling, with a long verandah and varied appurtenances here and there, over much ground. But it was covered with flowers, as I never saw a house covered before, and the garden was a wilderness of loveliness. The herbage on the cleared ground about the place was richer than any other herbage; and the hills, timbered up to their summits, formed an amphitheatre round the back, which at home would have made the site invaluable.

I beg my reader, therefore, to believe that in spite of the everlasting gum-tree there is scenery in Australia which would repay a visit. That of which I have spoken in this chapter is the scenery of New South Wales alone.

RICHARD SEMON

RICHARD SEMON, the eminent German naturalist, came to Australia in 1891-2, and spent twelve months in Queensland studying Australian mammals and marsupials and, especially, the Ceratodus, or Queensland lungfish. His scientific work appeared in fourteen volumes. Many of his personal experiences and observations find expression in a delightful travel book, *In the Australian Bush* (English edition, 1898), much of which is of perennial appeal.

BIRDS OF THE UPPER BURNETT

THE deep solitude surrounding me during those days, and often enough in after times during Dahlke's absence, or when I made long excursions by myself, was by no means dull or tedious, but most enjoyable. It is very difficult to find solitude to such perfection upon earth nowadays, and I had never known anything like it before. Even in the desert or on an uninhabited island you are rarely quite by yourself, there always being either the members of the caravan or the crew of the boat about you. In the depths of the primeval forests you generally have companions, and the natives of the country will be in attendance. The immense Australian bush offers *genuine* solitude, by allowing a man to exist in its interior as long as it pleases him, without his undergoing any dangers or difficulties by being alone. Such solitude cannot be compared with the sort which the stranger experiences when staying in a great metropolis, the language of which is unknown to him, still less with the terrible loneliness of a prisoner in his cell. At first the solitude of which I speak was new and interesting to me, and it used to bring me lonely hours and a sense of abandonment, but finally I felt it like a great and mighty revelation, a thing as vivid and intense as the witnessing of the most varied scenes amongst foreign lands and nations. It gives a man time and a chance to look into his innermost self, to see himself, not as he appears in the eyes of his neighbours, but in his relation to great, ever-creating, ever-destroying Nature. No other circumstances favour an intimate relationship with Nature like this, the living free and alone among her works, without a house, without any vestige of human culture about the place, without any human society. The observing of animals and plants, the aesthetic pleasure I felt in watching land and water, rocks and trees, and their ever-changing hues and moods were my only enjoyment; but how much more intensely and purely did I enter into this than under ordinary conditions!

On first coming to Australia one is inclined to find the eucalyptus woods rather strange than beautiful, being used to admire in a tree its fresh verdure and its rich and dense foliage. The latter serves to give a relief to the tree, to make it stand out from among its environs and against the sky, to give it an individually distinct shape and character. The beauty of eucalyptus lies in another direction. If its foliage lacks force and freshness of colour, its mild tender tints produce charming effects in contrast with the more vivid green of the meadows, or the silvery sands of the river banks, particularly so when the whole scene is bathed in the slanting rays of the evening sun. The growth of the trees is always noble and stately, sometimes quite gigantic, but the narrowness of the leaves and their vertical position make the foliage seem much thinner than it really is, so that the appearance of the tree becomes less strong and vigorous than its size would seem to warrant. On the other hand, the tenderness and transparency of the foliage is hardly equalled by any other tree, and once used to the peculiarity of its character I never tired of admiring the daintiness of its design. There are only two European trees one might compare with it— our birch in its spring garment, and the olive tree. Both show something of the eucalyptus character, but on a much feebler scale, being puny dwarfs compared with the gigantic, though so exquisitely shaped Australian tree. It is quite an exception that the eucalypts form handsome groups, and the endless park landscape with its isolated trees offers—so I must own—rather a monotonous aspect. The greater is the delight of the lonely traveller at the sight of a river bank, if on the height of it the beautiful blue-gums stand out like lofty sentinels. From afar he will see the shining white bark of their trunks, and their dainty crown of tender green leaves, the deep-blue sky shimmering through their foliage in a thousand little spots and dots.

Charming and picturesque is the sight of the silver-white bed of the river itself, its sides fringed with dense Casuarinae and tea-trees, its surface marked here and there by fallen trunks, stretching their branches like so many arms out of the water, in various and fantastic attitudes.

The water of the rivers, at all events during the dry season, plays a subordinate part in enlivening the landscape, except where wide water-holes or rapids, like those of the Burnett at Ideraway, give it a more prominent position in the scene. Wild and imposing, however, is the sight of the Burnett in times of flood, when its bed, even though it be more than half a mile broad, does not suffice to hold its overflowing waters. Then the river will come rushing along, foaming and bursting its banks, laden with uprooted trees, and filling the air with its roaring far and wide. All these impressions, however, are not such as to captivate a traveller at first sight, and force him to enthusiasm and admiration like the radiancy of Southern Italy, the severe grandeur of the Alps, or the luxuriance of the tropical forests. He must know them intimately before he will arrive at a real enjoyment of their charms. He who is sensible to the peculiar, and who enjoys to search after the beautiful, will find himself rewarded, and gather many a pearl amongst these remote scenes and sights. He, on the other hand, who is sensible to those beauties only which have been proclaimed to him as such from his childhood, and who will see no charm in a landscape devoid of picturesque form, vivid colouring, and luxuriant vegetation, will regard the Burnett district "a country as utterly uninteresting and monotonous as can well be imagined", an expression used by one of its describers.

Poor Australia is often exposed to most unjust criticisms, sometimes in jest, sometimes in earnest. She is called the land of extremes, and reproachfully accused of having nothing

just as it ought to be. Her climate, they say, is either too
warm or too cold, too dry or too hot, her flowers without perfume, her birds without melodies, even her swans are black
instead of white. But black swans may be also beautiful! And
as to the climate, that of South and Middle Queensland is
the finest and healthiest imaginable, though floods and
droughts may sometimes inconvenience the owner of flocks
and fields. And at times, when the melaleuca-shrubs adorn
the river banks with their white, and the acacias deck the
scrub with their yellow blossoms, the country is filled far
and wide with the sweetest perfume. Singing birds like our
finches, nightingales, and sedge-warblers you will indeed
seek in vain in the interior of Australia. But neither will the
coasts of tropical Africa, nor the woods of Ceylon and Java,
the banks of the Ganges and Yumna, ever offer you a birds'
concert equalling that which can be heard on any fine spring
morning or evening in our German woods and meadows, or
along the banks of our modest streamlets. I, at least, have
never heard the like anywhere else. But still within the Australian bush the morning is greeted by glad songsters, and
one only has to rise betimes to hear them, since the sub-
tropical sun, hastening towards the zenith, silences them
earlier than the sun of our latitudes.

How oft was I awakened by the loud peculiar tunes of the
"leather-head", of Ptilotis and other Meliphagidae. Really
beautiful, however, is the joyous morning song of a bird belonging to the crow tribe, *Gymnorhina tibicen*, the flute-
like notes of which make the silent bush resound every morning. The feathers of this bird are of a deep black, contrasting
vividly and agreeably with the white design on its neck,
wings and tail. Like our jay it is forward and lively, not in the
least afraid of man. Its food consists of insects, particularly
of grasshoppers and locusts of all kinds. But it will also
attack small reptiles, and become dangerous even to young
nestlings. The song of the birds, taken individually, is not
equal as to melody and force. There are bunglers and artists
among them. Up to this day I can recall the tune, which a

particularly accomplished bird sounded every morning close to my tent at the Auburn junction.

This charming melody, delivered with much fervour, and in clear perfect notes, and repeated with ever fresh enthusiasm, delighted me anew every morning, and made me love the joyous little songster.

For hours after sunrise the neighbourhood of the rivers and stagnant pools used to resound with the dull decoying call of longtailed birds, called by the colonists bush-pheasants. They mostly keep near the ground, hidden among dense grass and shrubs. When scared, they fly clumsily to the low branch of some tree, and hopping from twig to twig, take a long time to reach the top, whence they take flight. This bush-pheasant is by no means a pheasant, but a cuckoo, even though its call does not resemble the cuckoo's in the least. Real pheasants, as well as the real finches, woodpeckers, and vultures, are quite lacking in the Australian region. The real cuckoo's call is, however, often heard in the bush, but almost exclusively during night-time, and is not produced by a cuckoo, but by an owl, the cuckoo-owl. A wonderful country indeed! Her mammals lay eggs, her cuckoos look like pheasants, and her owls call out "cuckoo".

After sunset, sometimes even after the final setting-in of darkness, I used to hear a loud shrill call. Dahlke referred it to the Australian curlew; but I never had a chance of shooting this bird.

The most singular sound heard within the bush is an infernal laugh, resounding near the river at sunrise and sunset with the regularity of a clock. Rare till now are the settlements of man within the bush, rarer still are churches and chapels, and never in these regions have I seen a church-clock or heard one strike. The "settler's clock" is a bird, the laugh of which opens and closes the day. Beside the just mentioned name, it bears that of "laughing jackass", whilst scientifically it is termed *Paralcyon (Dacelo) gigas*.

The laughing jackass belongs to the family of kingfishers, and is one of its biggest members. Unlike the common kingfisher, it seeks its booty on land, and not by diving and thrusting its beak into the water. The same habit I noticed in another kind of kingfisher inhabiting the Burnett region, *Todirhamphus sanctus*, whilst the handsome ultra-marine *Alcyone azurea* coincides in all its habits with our well-known European kingfisher. The laughing jackass is a great devourer of reptiles, not only killing lizards, small and big poisonless snakes, but even attacking the numerous poisonous reptiles of Australia, the "black snake", "brown snake", and the "death adder", the most dangerous of all. Both courage and caution distinguish his mode of attack. This part of the jackass's doings ensures him forgiveness, even though he happens from time to time to pounce upon a poor little chicken, and makes the heart of the housewife lenient towards these latter misdeeds. He is a cunning, acute fellow, full of humour, who follows the doings of men from the high standard of a eucalyptus with interest and benevolent condescension, and who occasionally accompanies his observations by a hearty laugh. This is so infectious that a second, a third, a whole dozen birds immediately begin to join in, and soon the silent bush resounds with a merriment you seldom hear outside a House of Parliament or a theatre, during the performance of a favourite comic actor.

THE QUEENSLAND LUNGFISH

With the view of furnishing myself continually and conveniently with full-grown specimens of Ceratodus, I stretched a long stout string from one side of the Auburn to the other, in a place known to abound with fish. To this string I attached, at fixed intervals, lines with strong fishing-hooks, long enough to hang pretty deep into the water. Usually I kept about twenty of these fishing-hooks in action, baiting them with snails, worms, crawfish, meat, and, better still, with small fish.

Every morning, noon and night the hooks were examined, such fish as had been caught were secured, and the bait renewed. Besides, we used another method. A fishing-hook attached to a long line and weighted by a heavy stone was flung out into the river, and left at the bottom till either a fish had been caught or the bait had been eaten. In this way we caught many fish, numerous Ceratodus, many Percoids, and three kinds of sheath-fish, the "jewfish" and two sorts of "catfish". The fins of the latter are furnished with strong pointed spines, the sting of which produces violent inflammation. The spines of the pectoral fins possess in their joints a special mechanism, by which, if raised at the will of the fish, they remain in that position and cannot be pressed back. This contrivance gives them a splendid weapon of defence, and one does well to handle captured specimens with the greatest precaution. Our fishing was often disturbed by three kinds of tortoise very frequent in the Burnett district, *Emydura Krefftii* and *E. latisternum*, and the long-necked *Chelodina longicollis*, which cannot draw in its head *straight* under its shield, but has to hide it by bending the neck sideways. Specimens, with shields measuring sixteen inches in diameter, were not rare on the Burnett. These turtles vied with each other in robbing our fishing-hooks of their baits. They were sly and clever enough almost always to avoid getting caught in the process, and it was quite an exception that they paid for their theft by their life. Dahlke declared to have heard that they would avoid baits of turtle flesh, and in consequence, we began to use the latter, but were none the less robbed by the greedy cannibalistic reptiles, and we even caught some of them with the flesh of their brethren. Our table was richly supplied with fish at that time. Still it is remarkable, and was for us a great pity, that all the Burnett fish, with one exception, furnish a very indifferent food. This one exception is represented by a kind of mullet, *Mugil Cunnesius*, called by the blacks Ngaria. The handsome and lively creature, which attains a length of more than a foot, is difficult to catch, since it does not take the usual baits. Certain

algae, however, which develop in the hot season in parts
of the river sheltered from the rapid current, are in its eye
the greatest delicacy, not so much for their own sake as on
account of the numerous little water-insects which haunt the
hairs of the plant. All those parts of the river which are
rich enough in water to be accessible to the mullet, will soon
be razed, while in the flat parts, which are inaccessible to the
fish, the algae thrive most opulently. Here and there the
water-current tears off a bunch of algae from these places
and carries it down the river. One can easily see the fish
assemble below such profitable spots and await the morsels
which the current carries down to them. If you take your
stand near a place of this kind—so that the fish cannot see
you, they being quite able to observe what is going on above
the water, and very much afraid of any shadow shown on
the surface—and if you bait your hook with a cluster of
algae and let it float into deeper water, you may be sure to
catch a fish at each fling of the rod. At a particularly favourable spot I once caught twenty big mullet in the course of
half an hour, and only left off because I did not know what
to do with so many. When we had no algae, we secured this
excellent fish by shooting it in the water with shot. This is
by no means very easy, as one has to stand almost vertically
above the water to get a successful shot, and is easily detected
by the fish in this position. If the shot enters the water at
an acute angle, it is considerably diverted from its aim.

Another quality of this famous fish is its wonderful skill
in leaping. During the evening hours the mullet often dart
out of the water to a height of several feet, apparently more
for their own amusement than to evade pursuit or to catch
insects flying above the surface. This talent for leaping is
the reason why it is difficult to catch them with nets, which
they simply avoid by jumping over. When disturbed, they
produce a queer growling noise, and dart away with the
rapidity of an arrow.

Now and then our baits of meat or molluscs attracted a
Ceratodus, and this proved that the Australian lungfish is
by no means a vegetarian, as has hitherto been thought. On

opening the animal, the intestinal canal will indeed almost always be found filled with green vegetable matter, partly composed of leaves and blossoms of gum- and tea-trees, carried into the river by the wind, partly of genuine water-plants. But noting that Ceratodus took so well to animal bait, I grew doubtful whether the above-mentioned plants are eaten for their own sake, or for the sake of the many little animals: crawfish, worms, snails, shellfish, and insect-larvae, which they harbour. On examining the contents of the intestines, I found that the tough fibres of the plants are not digested, but leave the body in an almost unchanged state. They are, so to say, but the vehicles of the food itself, which is of essentially animal character. Quite tender plants, as, for instance, the filamentous-algae favoured by the mullet, may be digested; the firm and tough tissue of the higher order of plants is, however, proof against its digestive powers. Altogether I found that errors about Ceratodus abound in scientific literature, the principal reason for this fact being that the fish is confounded with another. The settlers call the Ceratodus the "Burnett Salmon" on account of its reddish flesh, and another fish, appertaining to the Fitzroy-Dawson, a river district north of the Burnett, "Dawson Salmon", on account of its taking the fly like a salmon. William Forster, the discoverer of Ceratodus, committed the trifling error of describing it as "Burnett *or* Dawson Salmon", and from this one mistake there arose a multitude of others. The Dawson Salmon, *Osteoglossum Leichhardti* by its Latin name, is called Barramunda by the natives of the Dawson. This name was erroneously applied to Ceratodus, which is nowhere so called on the Burnett, where the natives term it "Djelleh". The fish was, moreover, considered an inhabitant of brackish water, while, on the contrary, it limits itself to fresh water, and keeps beyond the influence of the tide. False, likewise, is the statement that it will take the fly, and quite erroneous are the notions about its geographical extension. This was considered as comprising the farthest north of the Australian continent, regions which are indeed inhabited by Osteoglossum, but not by Ceratodus. The fish dwells exclusively in the two little rivers, Burnett and Mary, neither north nor south of them, while the Barramunda does not extend further south than the Dawson. The watershed between the Dawson and the Burnett marks at the same time the limit between Ceratodus and Osteoglossum.

In former geological periods the genus of Ceratodus inhabited the wide world. Remains of its teeth have been found in Europe, America, Asia, and Africa, and fossil records prove that it extended over a far greater portion of Australia than nowadays. It is therefore very curious that the fish has survived only within these two rivers, the Burnett and the Mary, which show no essential difference from their neighbours to the south and to the north. What may have determined the extinction of the fish in those much greater rivers, what its survival in these two?

In the first place, one has to take into consideration the appearance of an enemy, which may have destroyed Ceratodus in a number of rivers. Crocodiles are indeed found down to the Fitzroy-Dawson, but not further southward, and are entirely absent in the Middle Burnett and Mary. This might lead us to believe that Ceratodus, an uncommonly lazy and indolent fish, has been exterminated by the crocodiles in the rivers north of the Burnett. Still its disappearance from the rivers south of the Burnett remains unexplained. In these it certainly existed formerly, and they contain neither crocodiles nor any other enemy that might have proved dangerous to the big-mailed Dipnoam. The circumstance that fossil remains of crocodiles and Ceratodus are found together in the Darling Downs, likewise disproves this theory.

To my belief, the explanation has to be sought otherwise, and I am inclined to see it in the great difficulty of the transmigration of Ceratodus from one river to another. The climate and meteorological conditions of Australia are such at present that a single drought of several years' duration can, and often does, exterminate all the aquatic inmates of a river. Few rivers have a lake-reservoir which they could feed upon in times of drought. The lack of water-treasuring mosses is likewise a prominent feature of the Australian bush.

A drought setting in—and the short history of Australia tells us of periods, when not a single raindrop has fallen for three or four years in a district known as commonly subject to rains—a whole river area is liable absolutely to dry up, and its animals will be exterminated, with the exception of such as withstand desiccation in either their fully-formed or embryonic state. To these latter Ceratodus, however, does not belong.

When the drought is at an end and the river fills with water once more, it will be peopled anew from the adjacent regions which have suffered less by the calamity. For though the droughts occur over extensive districts, their intensity varies locally.

Concerning the means by which fish are able to migrate from one river region to another, we can state the following as most conspicuous; firstly, a flood will enable the inmates of one river to wander to another in the neighbourhood of their respective sources. This is particularly the case when the sources lie in a tableland, and also with the tributaries near the mouth of a river. Secondly, the sea along the coast forms a passage for such fresh-water fish as can bear a passing sojourn in salt water. Thirdly, some few fish (Siluridae, Labyrinthici) are capable of journey across the country. And last, but not least, the transport of fish-eggs by water-birds and insects may be considered a means of their trans-location from one river-area to another. The carrying along of fish by storms and whirlwinds is so rare an event that we need not take it into consideration.

All these methods, however, which I have described as possible for the passage of fish from one river to another, are closed against Ceratodus. The latter avoids the river heads, and consequently there is no prospect of its migrating into another river that way. It is very easily affected by sea water, so that migration through the mouths of streams proves likewise impracticable. The journey by land is an impossibility for Ceratodus, and lastly, its eggs are extremely frail and tender, as I noticed hundreds of times. They do not bear the most transient drying. If the water, in which I kept the

c

eggs for breeding purposes, became too warm, or there happened to be too many in one vessel, or if I did not take care to remove every dead egg immediately, all the eggs died off rapidly. This circumstance formed a great hindrance to my embryological collecting. Taking all this and the large size of the eggs into consideration, transport by water-birds and other aquatic animals seems excluded.

By all this we see that if Ceratodus, by some reason, most likely by prolonged drought, were exterminated in one river, it would have far less chance to recruit anew from a neighbouring stream than other fish. This is my own theory concerning its limited range of distribution in Australia. The diminution of the water reserves which the Queensland rivers in geologic times possessed in the lakes and swamps of the Darling Downs, the greater chance of the streams drying out, and perhaps a general increase of barrenness may have all played a part in the defeat of Ceratodus. Its survival in the Burnett and Mary rivers may be owing to the presence of some particularly extensive water-holes, and to some fortunate concurrence of circumstances that, from time immemorial, prevented its dying out. Should a particularly fierce drought dry up the Mary river today but spare some of the water-holes in the Burnett, the fish would become limited to the Burnett and remain so for an immeasurable time. If, on the other hand, a naturalist or private person were to take the trouble of depositing living specimens of Ceratodus in the middle course of the Brisbane river, I believe these would be sure to thrive splendidly, and soon cover the entire river system.

As already mentioned, I caught in the Burnett many specimens of Ceratodus with the fishing-rod, the ground-angle, and the trimmer-hook. On returning to the district the year after, I took a pair of big drag-nets with me, and tried several draughts, but with little success. The blacks know the best method of catching the fish by the use of small self-constructed hand-nets. One of these they take into the right, the other into the left hand, and shut in the fish between their semicircular frames. The fisherman begins by diving to the bottom of a water-hole, which he supposes alive with Ceratodus, and tries to make sure of the position of the fish by eyes, hands and feet. The fish is generally found lazily lying upon the river bottom. Having thus ascertained its whereabouts, the fisherman returns to the surface to take breath, whereon he makes another dive, shuts up the fish in his net, and pulls it up. This method can only be used with an uncommonly dull, slow, and lazy fish, a character we may well give to Ceratodus. By exercising caution, one may even touch it under the water without its changing its position, and, even if disturbed by the touch, it will but swim a short distance with a jerk, when it will rest again and let you repeat the game. In this its behaviour very much resembles that of a newt. By means of its great strength it sometimes succeeds in freeing itself from the net, or in breaking the fishing-rod; once out of the water, however, it becomes perfectly helpless.

The circumstance that I succeeded in catching the fish by day and by night, in the morning and evening, proves it to be neither a day nor a night animal, and showed me that it seeks its food heedless as to the hour of the day. It is, however, very capricious as to taking the hook. Sometimes not a single fish was hooked for weeks, at other times several in the course of one day, and once, at the beginning of a rainy period, ten were caught during only two days.

Entirely false is the statement that it goes on land or crawls upon tree-trunks projecting from the water to sun itself. These are pure fantasies, arising from mistaking this fish for another, or originated by people who have never watched Ceratodus. In reality Ceratodus is more helpless when out of water than most other fishes, and incapable of progression. It is not even able to jerk itself on for a small space by its tail. A further fable, pervading all the literature about Ceratodus ever since its discovery, is the statement of its embedding itself in the mud during periods of drought.

Ceratodus has an ally in tropical Africa called by its Latin name *Protopterus annectens*. This is known to bury itself in the mud during the dry season, and to form a sort of cocoon out of its own slime. Thus protected from drying, it is able to outlive the drought, till the humidity of the first rain dissolves its cocoon and awakens it from its summer sleep. When Krefft, the first describer of Ceratodus, examined it, he immediately detected its near affinity to Protopterus, and conjectured that the newly-found Australian fish might spend its summer in a similar way to its African cousin. What he expressed as a mere surmise, was transcribed by others as a positive statement!

As soon as I came to the Burnett, I tried to get acquainted with every detail concerning the fishes' summer-sleep, the supposed formation of cocoon and burial in the mud, for it seemed probable that the frequent drying up of the Australian rivers might cause it to adopt a method analogous to that of its African ally. But the result of my enquiries proved quite negative, and, on the ground of my own observations, I must absolutely deny the existence of a summer sleep and the formation of a cocoon.

All the year round Ceratodus can be caught with net or hook within the river. The time of the lowest water naturally coincides with the end of the dry season, and this latter with the spawning time of the fish. That it should simultaneously spawn and pass through a summer sleep seems, at least, improbable. Moreover, cocoons never having been found by the blacks, whose sharpened senses overlook nothing, we may definitely cast aside this hypothesis.

As aforesaid, Ceratodus is a representative of the almost exterminated class of Dipnoi or lungfish, that is to say, fish possessing gills by which they breathe like other fish, but also an air-bladder, the construction and function of which very much resembles that of a lung. What does Ceratodus use this lung for, since it does not go on land, and therefore is not forced to adapt itself to extra-aquatic conditions of breathing and living like the Protopterus? That the fish uses its lung for breathing I noticed hundreds of times. Near the river area it haunts, one occasionally hears a dull groaning sound. This is produced by the fish, which comes up to the surface at certain intervals to empty the breath from its air-bladder and to take in fresh air. I readily proved Ceratodus to be the author of this strange noise, when later on I kept the fish alive in great barrels and self-dug water-holes. I then saw them appear at the surface every thirty or forty minutes and lift the tip of their snout above the water, at the same time uttering the afore-mentioned grunting noise. Still I was unable to make out whether it is produced by the expiration of the foul air or the inspiration of the fresh, and how or where it originates.

At the same time, like any other fish, Ceratodus makes use of its gills, and is by no means able to exist on land. If taken out of the water and prevented from getting back, its gills soon dry up and the animal dies. Nevertheless its lungs are of great importance to the fish during the dry season, for when the water evaporates over a wide area, and the river gets reduced to some few water-holes, the dimensions of which naturally decrease from day to day, an immense accumulation of river-inmates takes place within these last havens of refuge. The water thus rapidly becomes foul and putrid by rotting animal and vegetable substance, and the fishes die in numbers.

Mr W. B. Maltby of Gayndah told me that he had once emptied a big but not very deep water-hole which was approaching dryness. The little water at its bottom was filled with dead mullet, perch, and other fishes, and the whole was putrid with fish corpses. Some Ceratodus, however, which were contained in this pool were perfectly lively and at their ease, and not in the least disturbed by finding themselves among these most unsanitary surroundings.

This is the occasion when Ceratodus enjoys the advantage of its lungs. Not on land, not during a summer sleep in the mire, or in a cocoon are they most serviceable, but in an extremity of this kind, when they furnish the only means by which the fish manages to outlive the most unfavourable conditions of its native rivers.

ALFRED BUCHANAN

ALFRED BUCHANAN, novelist and dramatic and literary critic, gave an account of his impressions of Australia in *The Real Australia* (1907). Although his experience was limited to personal acquaintance with city life, he shows acute insight into the movement of political and social affairs of the day. Much of his book is concerned with Australian literature, journalism, and the. theatre.

TWO CITIES

Where, O Earth! is a fairer city
Than this by night, when the Quay's half circle
Lights the dusk of the city's face?

MISS MACK's verses to Sydney are the kind of tribute one would wish to pay to a lover of happier days. For that reason they may awake some kind of echo in the breasts of many hundreds of persons who will confess to a fondness for Sydney, but who are indifferent to the ways and methods of the lofty rhyme. For the place has a strong personality. One never thinks of it as merely so many houses and so many people. An entity, a living thing, a friend, a consoler, a woman with soft breath and warm-tinted hair, a queen of men and yet their servant—it is any or all of these, and much besides.

The new-comer should arrange to enter Sydney by night. If he does this he will experience the strong and always remembered sensation of emerging from Cimmerian darkness into the blaze of a lighted arena. The waters of the Tasman Sea are usually cold and stormy. If you have been ploughing across them for the best part of a week, if you have been beset with bad weather, or sea-sickness, or boredom, or with the three combined, you will hail as one of the pleasant sounds of a lifetime the news that there is visible a glimmer from South Head. Thereafter the transformation is rapid. Sydney by night does not *grow* upon you; it *bursts* upon you, and the impression is not soon forgotten. Whatever you have read and whatever you have dreamed of Eastern cities by the Tigris; whatever you have seen of lime-light effects on a brilliant, gaily coloured, thronged and animated stage; whatever you have pictured to yourself of islands and gardens and palaces by the water's edge—all these and more are around you and in front of you as the ship winds past promontory after promontory, island after island, on its passage towards a mooring place in Darling Harbour. The panorama has an unreal and fairy-like splendour. For a minute or two, perhaps for half an hour, you expect that everything will presently dissolve, and the conditions of blackness and vacancy reassert themselves. But the boat passes on, and the picture remains. You realise after a while that it is the city itself welcoming you, beckoning to you, smiling at you with all its arcs and crescents and its glittering phantasmagoria of lights.

In the daytime all this is changed. Sydney by day is the real Sydney, the working Sydney, and like every other place in which men work and congregate, it has its dull and drab and depressing features. But the strangely marked personal characteristics are there still. They have taken on new phases, and they make a different kind of appeal. Your mistress has no longer the sparkle in her eyes and the diamonds on her brow; she no longer scintillates to dazzle you, and no longer challenges you to admiration by her life and movement. She has grown languorous as the land of the lotos-flower, enervating as the Island of Circe. True, she has her marts and her merchandise, her busy streets, her ships, and her people who toil and spin. But they are a people on whom she has set her imprint, and who have drunk the wine of love and of laughter at her hands. The fact is that neither by day nor by night, neither in summer nor winter, can Sydney look consistently hard or repellent. Now and then a bracing wind blows up from the waste places of the Pacific and talks menacingly of storm and stress and shipwreck. But it loses itself or dies to nothing when in the heart of the city, or when endeavouring to make its way along such good-tempered, well-protected thoroughfares as George and Pitt

Streets. Sometimes it rains, sometimes it blusters a little, but only with an amusing semblance of anger. In an hour or two the sun is shining again.

A city that has grown has always an advantage, in point of attractiveness, over one that has been merely made. It is easy to understand the reason. No one cares for the display of qualities that seem to be the result of artificial training. Every one admires spontaneity, or rather the appearance of spontaneity. The thing itself may be a product of the finest art. But that matters nothing. As it is with individuals, so it is with a city. The straight, uncompromising lines which appeal to the draughtsman are of interest to no one else. It is a mistake to cultivate a prim demeanour or to attempt to keep a straight face if Nature has in view something else. The friend who keeps calling "Duty, duty, duty" in your ear is not really wise, and is always certain to be disliked. Equally tedious is the architect, or the surveyor, or the mathematician, who says dogmatically that certain streets should always meet at such and such an angle; that there should be certain spaces for parks and certain widths reserved for traffic; that there should be buildings modelled on particular lines, and conglomerations of houses arranged after a particular fashion; that there should be a scientific method observed in building the thing to be called a city, just as there are particular rules for turning out a baker's oven or for making a carpenter's box.

Sydney, as it does not take long to discover, has grown up after a careless and wilful fashion of its own. It is neither consciously straight, nor consciously irregular. Of modern improvements it takes what it pleases, and leaves what it does not want. Buildings cluster round the harbour and bedeck themselves with red-tiled roofs and flaunt their pleasant inertia in the sun. Some of the more recent structures—hotels, warehouses, public markets and the like—are showy and even magnificent. But the main streets make no pretence to symmetry or modernity, and are strongly reminiscent in their narrowness and grime of second- and third-rate towns in France and England. The resemblance would be more

striking did not Australia lack the pointed, old-world architecture that gives historic quaintness and interest even to the
dirtier and more tumble-down villages of Europe. Sydney is
suspicious of new inventions, and would prefer that the disturbing, scientific spirit of the age left it alone. Until lately
it knew of no better means of locomotion than its steam
trams. It is only within the last year or two that it has had
its electric cars. The energy with which these gigantic structures rush to and fro and disturb traffic is quite out of keeping
with the atmosphere of the place. There are numerous acci-
dents, because so many of the Sydneyites have not the
energy to get out of the way.

The people, as a rule, are not ambitious. They have not
the restless unquiet temperament associated with the Anglo-
Saxon race in other and less pleasant parts of the globe. For
that reason they are often excellent companions. They know
how to enjoy life, and they are willing to share their knowledge with the stranger. They have no cast-iron formulas,
either of etiquette or of morals. They have not yet succeeded
in reducing orthodoxy to a fine art. It matters comparatively
little to them, before or after they have made your acquaintance, whether your education was finished at Oxford or in
Lower George Street, whether your father was a pawn-
broker or an admiral, whether your nearest relations keep a
grocer's shop, or are something connected with the Established Church. Are you an agreeable person? Have you a
pleasant humour? Do you know how to make life entertaining? Can you help others to pass the time? If the answer
to any of these questions is in the affirmative, the gates of
many desirable places will be thrown open to you. You will
be allowed to tread the primrose path to the music of lutes,
to the sound of soft voices, to the rustle of silk and satin
embroideries, to the rhythm of Government House waltzes,
to the popping of Vice-regal champagne. The possession of
wealth is an advantage, but it is not indispensable. The Sydney
creditor is as accommodating as most creditors. Even this
class is not absolutely proof against the influence of climate
and surroundings.

Among the men who do the mental work of Sydney—
the writers, the scholars, the financiers, the preachers, the
politicians, the social reformers, and the rest—you find this
lack of ambition and of sustained effort particularly noticeable. A degree of ability is common enough. But it is not
husbanded and utilised with that fierce concentration of
purpose which marks the North of England man when he
packs his bag for London, or the Western American when
he sets out for New York. The journalism of Sydney is
intermittently clever, sometimes brilliant, never consistently
good. It may be that a man has a vein of humour, a descrip-
tive faculty, a sense of colour in words. It is little use telling
this man that if he works and waits, and waits and works
—if he denies himself the cheap laurels of newspaper favour,
and the thin rewards of journalistic achievement—he may
ultimately win a place in the inner circle of approved and
recognised authorship. He knows that he can get a guinea
for a couple of hours' application. What is the advantage,
then, of going elsewhere? A guinea is a guinea; and Sydney
is an excellent place in which to spend it. Thus he reasons
in act, if not in words. The consequence is that the intellectual tone of the city, as set by the writers and thinkers, is
for the most part a blend of opportunism and of *laisser faire*.
If you want to learn something, if you want an incentive
to act, if you want to live the strenuous life, you must leave
Sydney and go somewhere else.

The women of Sydney are in a class by themselves. They
are as distinctive in their way as the city in which they
live is distinctive in its way. There is little doubt that in a
measure they obtain their character from the place, though
it is also true that they assist to give the place its character.
To think of them, after the lapse of years, is to conjure up
pleasant memories. There is reason to believe that the
Cytherea of the ancient Greeks was born in Sydney, or at
least lived there in prehistoric days, long before settlement
crowded the approaches to the harbour, long before Governor Phillip sighted the Heads, long before the country
knew anything of modern habitations, and while it still

slumbered in the embraces of the Golden Age. The waters still smile when they remember the vision that once rose from them; and to this day they impart something of the warmth and colour of the foam-born Aphrodite to the women who dwell by their fringing shores. Not that the daughters of Sydney are classical, or Grecian, or faultless in form and feature. The symmetry of the marble statue is no part of their equipment. They are deficient, for the most part, in correct outlines. Such charm as is theirs is mainly the result of manner, of temperament, of suggestion, of look. They convey the impression that their sympathies would not soon be alienated, that their welcome would never be ungenerous, that they could, if they wished, make of existence a pleasant thing.

The character of the people has been a subject for uneasy speculation. It is darkly hinted that the city is a refuge ground for many strange sins. The majority of the residents do not trouble about these matters. But there are a few estimable people who do. The women belonging to the W.C.T.U., and the I.O.G.T., and the I.O.R., and the rest of the alphabet devoted to temperance and the higher life, work consistently hard. In their display of zeal they almost make up what they lack in numbers. They are troubled voices calling in a moral wilderness, but they do not despair. They have one friend and confidant—the Colonial Secretary for the time being. The tales of depravity that are poured into the ears of this patient individual each month would fill many volumes. His official life is a round of dreadful discoveries. He begins his Ministerial career a cheerful optimist, and ends it with every vestige of illusion gone. Virtuous and estimable women belonging to every reforming agency in the metropolis are constantly at his elbow, are constantly telling him of fresh detachments of young children found in opium dens, of fresh batches of drunkards picked up in the gutter, of new contingents of women discovered on the street. The Colonial Secretary is asked, entreated, and commanded to do something. Exactly what it is his auditors do not know, but *something*, he is told, must be done. The unhappy man listens, shudders, sympathises, and protests that he is passionately grateful to the earnest women who have thought fit to lighten his mental darkness. He agrees that something must be done, and knows in his heart of hearts that nothing can be done. Meantime the social life of Sydney goes on, and the place, with its agreeable men and graceful women, is a place to be desired and pleasant to the eyes.

It is always pleasant—pleasant to linger in, pleasant to look forward to, pleasant to look back upon. Not very intellectual, not very strenuous, not very inspiring, it has all the aids to enjoyment that have been discovered in the last twenty centuries, and all the ingenious devices that have ever been invented to make time pass. A city that has from its birth been cradled in soft airs; a city that spreads against the storm and stress of dissatisfied ambition the protection of mild and lulling wings; a city intended by Nature to please the artist and bring the practical man relief and rest; a city that rescues humanity from the stern and unlovely asceticism of a gray and narrow school; a city that is indifferent to morals, and cares for religion only on the picturesque side; a city that holds always with the Persian poet and tells its people to enjoy themselves, for to-morrow they may be with yesterday's seven thousand years.

To leave Sydney and to go to Melbourne is to enter a new world. Instead of resemblances there are contrasts. In place of Australianisms there are Anglicanisms, Americanisms, and foreign "isms" of various kinds. Climate may have something to do with the difference, and topographical conditions may have something more. The reception that Sydney gives you is that of a woman in a luxurious room, with soft lights falling on rich curtain hangings, with glitter of glass and silver ornament, with lavish display of elegance and outward charm. The woman rises seductively, looks at you languorously and invites you, not so much by word as by gesture, to make yourself at home. It is delightful; but yet there is something wanting. The reflection comes that you are not being specially favoured; that this is the manner of the hostess to all and sundry; that there may be something unhealthy in this mellifluous atmosphere. . . .

The reception you get from Melbourne is of quite another character. The woman this time is cold and calm, and superbly indifferent. If she seems to smile it is probably the reflection of your own hopefulness. She offers you nothing; she barely acknowledges you; she does not want you; it is certain that she is not anxious to know you. All her panoply of architectural ornament is arrayed against you. And yet the thought supervenes that this cold woman may be better worth knowing in the end than the other one; that her harder outlines may conceal a more genuine worth; that her good opinion may be better worth striving for than that of the other—the one with the redder lips, and the flaunting, unchanging smile.

But the wide streets and the flat unoccupied spaces of Melbourne are an outward semblance calculated to strike the newcomer with a shuddering sense of chill and desolation. More especially if they are encountered for the first time on a winter's afternoon. For the winter that merely dallies and trifles in Sydney, and makes but a pretence of bringing with it cold weather, is genuine in the Southern city. There is no bleaker thoroughfare on earth than Collins Street or Burke† Street on a blustering July day. From Spring Street to the railway station there is a clear, unbroken passage for the Arctic wind. The occasional tramcar and the infrequent pedestrian are cheerless objects around which the Sou'-Wester disports itself, seeking always, in return for some ancient grievance, a grim and unnecessary revenge. If the day happens to be a Saturday, or a public holiday, the outlook is rendered ten times more dismal by the deathly appearance of the streets, from which all but an unreal semblance of life and movement has departed. A wilderness of grim-looking window shutters, and a Sahara of pavement—that is all. The wind drives the dust in front of it, then follows on shriekingly. When it has finished playing with the dust it brings in the rain. And Melbourne, with

† That is, "Bourke".

its wide, shelterless streets swept from end to end by a rain-storm—Melbourne with its blank spaces and its vanished crowds—is the one place on earth where the new arrival would choose *not* to be.

But this appearance and mannerism of the Queen city—it clings to the name, though the boom era which gave the name a meaning has departed—must be lived through, and lived down. Presently the sun will shine again. Presently the holiday will be over; and the people who have been abroad in the suburbs, or cultivating their garden patches, or hiding themselves in their own houses, will be once more visible, and the pavement will once more echo to the sound of feet. By a seeming miracle the streets have become almost full. Melbourne has become an intelligible place to live in. The shops, now that the window shutters are down, are seen to be beautifully fitted up. The buildings are for the most part new, and they are never grimy. One remembers that in the heart of Sydney there are pervading evidences of smoke and grime. One must give Melbourne its due. It has something to boast about. It has been magnificently laid out. Its measurements are on a generous scale. It is fine and large and bracing. One forgets the chill sensation left by those deserted streets and those grim-looking window shutters. The Block has become a centre of bustle and animation. Again the thought presents itself that this place may have a heart of its own, that it may have a personality, even a warmth, concealed behind those set features and those formal lines.

Further acquaintance with Melbourne increases the respect felt for it. One gets to like it for the same reason that the Londoner gets to like London. It is not a question of beauty, or simplicity, or gentleness of form and feature. One gets to like it because of its greatness, and because of its strength; perhaps also, in the case of the older residents, because of the thought of the splendid life and animation that were part of it fifteen or twenty years ago, and that may be part of it again. The Melbourne man, after a certain lapse of time, acquires a personal feeling for his self-contained, self-respecting city. He learns to recognise its various moods—

for even Melbourne has moods—and to enter into them all. He would not care for it if it were flashy and volatile like other places. He can admire it for its reserve and its silences. He knows that, go where he will, he will not find a cleaner, wider, more spacious city to dwell in. And he is fully aware that for him Melbourne reveals much of what she keeps hidden from the stranger; that she will show to him as to one of her lovers a warmth and friendliness that are the more satisfying because not universally shared.

Commercially, Melbourne is not what it used to be. It has lost the sparkle, the animation of other days. Yet, whatever else it has lost, it has retained its consciousness of former prosperity. It is as proud as ever; in fact more proud than in the days when people were pouring into it by thousands, and when fortunes were being made every five minutes in its principal streets. Diminished prosperity has caused it to hold its head higher. And at stated times, like some proud but impecunious beauty, it insists on recalling itself to the mind of the world. On Cup Days and *fête* days it scores a triumph: it arrays itself in the festal garment of the early 'nineties, and queens it to the admiration of the stranger within its gates. On these occasions Melbourne is incomparable. It has no need to be envious, because it is the admired of all admirers. When the cheering is over, and the crowds have departed, and the lights are being put out, Melbourne retires moodily into itself, goes about its daily business with an abstracted air, and consoles itself intermittently by talking of the long deferred prosperity which it insists must come.

For if the place fails in this or in that respect, it never fails to keep its expectations high. It has been doing this for the past dozen years or more. It has long outgrown its happy-go-lucky, red-shirted, soft-collared, mining, pioneering days. It has no wish to recall these outward symbols of an earlier and a vanished generation. With the memory of many losses and many disappointments, there is still the determination to put the best face on everything. Though the crowds no longer hum and vibrate round its chief thoroughfares, it retains its streets and its houses, its spacious theatres and commodious public buildings; its magnificent Houses of Parliament, its squares and gardens, its network of railways and tram lines, its villa residences at St Kilda and its mansions at Toorak. The outward shell of things is still there. Every now and then there is a sign of movement, an agitation as of returning life. The people are convinced that something is going to happen. The period of depression, they say, cannot last for ever. In imagination they can see the Golden Days ever returning.

Meantime, the business of keeping up appearances goes on. Melbourne has become accustomed, through sheer force of insistence on its individual merits, to regard itself as everything that a modern city ought to be, and as most things that other cities are not. It prides itself on a great deal—on its music, its art, its culture, its architecture, its good looks, and its intelligence. In the matter of dress it aspires to set the fashion for Australia. Men and women join in this amiable rivalry. The girl of the Victorian capital is more severe in demeanour, more classic in pose, and more punctilious in attire than her Sydney sister. She takes herself more seriously. She has few *negligé* airs and graces; she does not cultivate the irresponsible freedom of the gown of Nora Creina; she arrays herself for the Block with a firm resolve to compel critical admiration. And in this she generally succeeds. The men of Melbourne live in starched shirts and expensive broadcloth. They cling tenaciously to that fading relic of an earlier civilisation—the bell-topper hat. Social life in the city would be impossible without one. The University keeps up its quota of students, whether the parents can afford to pay or not. The theatres can attract audiences even for a performance of Wagner, or a revival of Shakespeare. The city fathers set an example of dignity to the rest of Australia. The politicians rarely call each other bad names, and never indulge in free fights on the floor of Parliament.

Behind all this outward seeming there is, it need hardly be said, a great amount of make-believe. Melbourne is only the temporary capital of the Commonwealth, but it is the permanent centre of—to use an ecclesiastically sounding word—attitudinarianism. Its mental life is more the expression of a desire to be thought superior to others than the outcome of any set of inborn predilections. Its intellectuality has the motto, *videri quam esse*. There is not one of its learned pundits or its *littérateurs* or its native born poets who has won much outside reputation. Its scrupulous regard for dress is the screen for much actual poverty. Its vaunted cosmopolitanism has no real existence. Its social circle is, only too often, the playground of snobs. Its professed public virtue deceives no one. In Sydney the spectacle of vice undraped is more insistent and more familiar. But in Melbourne there is as much for the Women's Christian Temperance Union to grieve over, though there may be less that meets the casual eye.

When the last word has been said on the subject—when it has been admitted that Melbourne pretends a great deal and poses a great deal, and hides a great deal—it is yet a fact that the city retains among its people much of sterling worth, and many of the elements of greatness. From the army of those who are not what they claim to be, or not what they would have you think them to be, may be picked out a leaven of those who are entitled to respect, and perhaps to something more. Alert, quick-witted, well-read, well-mannered, tolerant, and scrupulously fair—that is the type which may be encountered if the search is keen enough. Hereafter, this type may set the standard. At present, all that can be said of it is that it is there.

The fact must always stand to the credit of Melbourne that it is capable of generous enthusiasms. When it lets itself go, it does so without reserve. Carlyle has remarked that a man who can laugh unrestrainedly, even if he only laughs once, is not wholly bad. A city that can cheer unitedly and unreservedly, whether for a singer, or orator, an actor, or a returned contingent, has at least some prospect of emerging from the wilderness of shams in which it happens to be located. Melbourne rises to greatness the moment it forgets itself.

D

E. J. BANFIELD

EDMUND JAMES BANFIELD, who came in infancy from England to Australia, was sub-editor of the *Townsville Bulletin* when defective eyesight led him to retire in 1897 to Dunk Island, where he wrote of the life about him. The first extract is from *Confessions of a Beachcomber* (1908), the second from *My Tropic Isle* (1911).

IN PRAISE OF THE PAPAW

PROPERTIES varied and approaching the magical have been ascribed to one of the commonest plants of North Queensland; and yet how trivial and prosaic are the honours bestowed upon it. That which makes women beautiful for ever; which renews the strength of man; which is a sweet and excellent food, and which provides medicine for various ills, cannot be said to lack many of the attributes of the elixir of life, and is surely entitled to a special paean in a land languishing for population.

Distinctive and significant as the virtues possessed by the papaw are, yet because of its universality and because it yields its fruits with little labour, it gets but scant courtesy. It is tolerated merely; but if we had it not, if it were as far as that vast shore washed by the farthest sea, men would adventure for such merchandise—and adventure at the bidding of women. How few there are who recognise in the everyday papaw one of the most estimable gifts of kindly Nature.

Some who dwell in temperate climes claim for the apple and the onion superlative qualities. In the papaw the excellences of both are blended and combined. The onion may induce to slumber, but the sleep it produces is it not a trifle too balmy? The moral life and high standard of statesmanship of an American Senator are cited as examples of the refining influence of apples. For every day for thirty years he has, to the exclusion of all other food, lunched on that fruit. Possibly the papaw may be decadent in respect to morals and politics. The grape, lemon, orange, pomelo, and the strawberry, each in the estimation of special enthusiasts, is proclaimed the panacea for many of the ills of life. One writer cites cases in which maniacs have been restored to reason by the exclusive use of cherries. The apple, they say, too, gives to the face of the fair ruddiness, but the tint is it not too bold, compared with maiden blush which bepaints the cheek of the beauty who rightly understands the use of the vital principle of the papaw? Those who have complexions to retain or restore let them understand and be fair.

In North Queensland the plant grows everywhere. In the dry, buoyant climate west of the coast range, and in the steamy coastal tract, on cliff-like hill-sides, on sandy beaches a few feet above high-water mark, among rocks with but a few inches of soil, and where the decayed vegetation of generations has made fat mould many feet deep, the papaw flourishes. It asks foothold, heat, light and moisture, and given these conditions a plant within a few months of its first start in life will begin to provide food—entertaining, refreshing, salubrious—and will continue so to do for years. Its precociousness is so great and its productiveness so lavish, that by the time other trees flaunt their first blossoms, the papaw has worn itself out, and is dying of senile decay, leaving, however, numerous posterity. The fruit is delicate, too, and soon resolves itself into its original elements. Pears and peaches are said by the artistic to enjoy but a brief half hour of absolute perfection. The artist alone knows the interval between immaturity and deterioration. The refined and delicate perception of the exquisite and transient aroma and flavour of fruits deserves to be classed among the fine arts. Some people are endowed with nice discrimination. They are of the order of the genius. The higher the poetic instinct, generally the better qualified the individual to detect and enjoy the fugitive excellences which fruits possess. Can a gourmand ever properly appreciate rare and fragile flavours? Though he may be a great artist in edible discords

—things rank and gross and startling—can he in the quantity of inconvenient food he consumes, be expected to pose as a critic of the most etherealised branch of epicureanism? The true eater of fruit is of a school apart, not to be classed with the individual who, because of the rites and observances of the table, accepts, in no exalted spirit, a portion of fruit at the nether end of a feast. He is one who has attained, or to whom has been vouchsafed, a poignant sense of all that does the least violence to the sense of taste and smell; but, moreover, who is capable of discovering edification in things as diverse as the loud Jack fruit and the subtle mangosteen—who can appreciate each according to its special characteristics, just as a lover of music finds gratification of a varied nature in the grand harmonies of a Gregorian Chant and in the tender cadences of a song of Sullivan's. Are those who have sensitive and correct palates for fruit not to be credited with art and exactitude, as well as critics of music and painting and statuary, and connoisseurs of wine?

As with many other fruits, so with the papaw. Only those who grow it themselves, who learn of the relative merits of the produce of different trees, and who can time their acceptance of it from the tree, so that it shall possess all its fleeting elements in the happy blending of full maturity, can know how good and great a papaw really is. The fruit of some particular tree is of course not to be tolerated save as a vegetable, and then what a desirable vegetable it is. It has a precise and particular flavour, and texture most agreeable. And as a mere fruit there are many more rich and luscious, and highly-flavoured; many that provoke louder and more sincere acclamations of approval. But the papaw, delicate and grateful, is more than a mere fruit. If we give credence to all that scientific research has made known of it, we shall have to concede that the papaw possesses social influences more potent than many of the political devices of this socialistic age.

But there may be some who do not know that the humble papaw belongs to the passion-fruit family (*passiflora*) a technical title bestowed on account of a fancied resemblance in the parts of the flower to the instruments of Christ's sufferings and death. And it is said to have received its generic name on account of its foliage somewhat resembling that of the common fig. A great authority on the botany of India suggested that it was originally introduced from the district of Papaya, in Peru, and that "papaw" is merely a corruption of that name. The tree is, as a rule, unbranched, and somewhat palm-like in form. Its great leaves, often a foot and a half long, borne on smooth, cylindrical stalks, are curiously cut into seven lobes, and the stem is hollow and transversely partitioned with thin membranes.

One of the most remarkable characteristics of the papaw is that it is polygamous—that is to say, there may be male and female and even hermaphrodite flowers on the same plant. Commonly the plants are classed as male and female. The males largely predominate. Many horticulturists have sought by the selection of seeds and by artificial fertilisation to control the sex of the plant so that the fruit-bearing females shall be the more numerous, but in vain. Some, on the theory that the female generally obtains a more vigorous initial start in life, and in very infancy presents a more robust appearance, heroically weed out weak and spindly seedlings with occasionally happy results. The mild Hindoo, however, who has cultivated the papaw (or papai to adopt the Anglo-Indian title) for centuries, and likewise wishes to avoid the cultivation of unprofitable male plants, seeks by ceremonies to counteract the bias of the plant in favour of masculine attributes. Without the instigation or knowledge of man or boy, a maiden, pure and undefiled, takes a ripe fruit from a tree at a certain phase of the moon, and plants the seed in accordance with more or less elaborate ritual. The belief prevails that these observances procure an overwhelming majority of the female element. The problem of sex, which bewilders the faithless European, is solved satisfactorily to the Hindoo by a virgin prayerful and pure.

On plants which have hitherto displayed only masculine characteristics, small, pale yellow, sweetly-scented flowers on long, loosely-branched axillary panicles, may appear partially or fully developed female organs which result in fructification, and such fruit is ostentatiously displayed. The male produces its fruit not as does the female, clinging closely and compact to the stem, but dangling dangerously from the end of the panicles—an example of witless paternal pride. This fruit of monstrous birth does not as a rule develop to average dimensions, and it is generally woodeny of texture and bitter as to flavour, but fully developed as to seeds.

The true fruit is round, or oval, or elongated, sometimes pear-shaped, and with flattened sides, due to mutual lateral pressure. As many as 250 individual fruits have been counted on a single tree at one and the same time. The heaviest fruit within the ken of the writer weighed 8 lb. 11 oz. They hug the stem closely in compact single rows in progressive stages, the lower tier ripe, the next uppermost nearly so, the development decreasing consistently to the rudiments of flower-buds in the crown of the tree. The leaves fall as the fruit grows, but there is always a crown or umbrella to ward off the rays of the sun. When ripe, the most approved variety is yellow. In the case of the female plant growing out of the way of a male, the fruit is smaller in size, and seedless or nearly so.

Another curious, if not unique point about this estimable plant is that sometimes within the cavity of a perfect specimen will be found one or two infant naked fruits, likewise apparently perfect. Occasionally these abnormal productions are crude, unfashioned and deformed.

Ripened in ample light, with abundance of water, and in high temperature, the fruit must not be torn from the tree "with forced fingers rude", lest the abbreviated stalk pull out a jagged plug, leaving a hole for the untimely air to enter. The stalk must be carefully cut, and the spice-exhaling fruit borne reverently and immediately to the table. The rite is to be performed in the cool of the morning, for the papaw is essentially a breakfast fruit, and then when the knife slides into the buff-coloured flesh of a cheesy consistency, minute colourless globules exude from the facets of the slices. These glistening beads are emblems of perfection. Plentiful dark seeds adhere to the anterior surface.

Some take their papaw with the merest sensation of salt, some with sugar and a drop or two of lime or lemon juice; some with a few of the seeds, which have the flavour of nasturtium. The wise eat it with silent praise. In certain obvious respects it has no equal. It is so clean; it conveys a delicate perception of musk—sweet, not florid; soft, soothing and singularly persuasive. It does not cloy the palate, but rather seductively stimulates the appetite. Its effect is immediately comforting, for to the stomach it is pleasant, wholesome, and helpful. When you have eaten of a papaw in its prime, one that has grown without check or hindrance, and has been removed from the tree without bruise or blemish, you have within you pure, good and chaste food, and you should be thankful and of a gladsome mind. Moreover, no untoward effects arise from excess of appetite. If you be of the fair sex your eyes may brighten on such diet, and your complexion become more radiant. If a mere man you will be the manlier.

So much on account of the fruit. Sometimes the seeds are eaten as a relish, or macerated in vinegar as a condiment, when they resemble capers. The pale yellow male flowers, immersed in a solution of common salt, are also used to give zest to the soiled appetite, the combination of flavour being olive-like, piquant and grateful. The seeds used as a thirst-quencher form component parts of a drink welcome to fever patients. The papaw and the banana in conjunction form an absolutely perfect diet. What the one lacks in nutritive or assimilative qualities the other supplies. No other food, it is asserted, is essential to maintain a man in perfect health and vigour. Our fictitious appetites may pine for wheaten bread, oatmeal, flesh, fish, eggs, and all manner of vegetables, but given the papaw and the banana, the rest are superfluous. Where the banana grows the papaw flourishes. Each is singular from the fact that it represents wholesome food long before arrival at maturity.

Then as a medicine plant the papaw is of great renown. The peculiar properties of the milky juice which exudes from every part of the plant were noticed two hundred years ago. The active principle of the juice known as papain, said to be capable of digesting two hundred times its weight of fibrine, is used for many disorders and ailments, from dyspepsia to ringworm and ichthyosis or fish-skin disease.

By common repute the papaw tree has the power of rendering tough meat tender. Some say that it is but necessary to hang an old hen among the broad leaves to restore to it the youth and freshness of a chicken. In some parts of South America papaw juice is rubbed over meat, and is said to change "apparent leather to tender and juicy steak". Other folks envelop the meat in the leaves and obtain a similar effect. Science, to ascertain the verity or otherwise of the popular belief applied certain tests, the results of which demonstrated that all the favourable allegations were founded on truth and fact. A commonplace experiment was tried. A small piece of beef wrapped up in a papaw leaf during twenty-four hours, after a short boiling became perfectly tender; a similar piece wrapped in paper submitted to exactly similar conditions and processes remained hard. Few facts are more firmly established than that the milky juice softens —in other words hastens the decomposition of—flesh. Further, the fruit in some countries is cooked as a vegetable with meat, and in soups; it forms an ingredient in a popular sauce, and is preserved in a variety of ways as a sweetmeat. Syrups and wines and cordials made from the ripe fruit are expectorant, sedative and tonic. Ropes are made from the bark of the tree. By its power of dissolving stains the papaw has acquired the name of the melon bleach; the leaves, and a portion of the fruit are steeped in water, and the treated water is used in washing coloured clothing, especially black, the colours being cleaned and held fast.

In the country in which it is supposed to be endemic it is believed that if male animals graze under the papaw tree they become *blasé*; but science alleges that the roots and extracted juice possess aphrodisiac properties, and who among us would not rather place credence upon this particular fairy tale of science than the fairy tales of swarthy and illiterate and possibly biassed gentlemen.

And as to its beauty-bestowing attributes, an admirer's word might be quoted as a final note of praise—

"The strange and beautiful races of the Antilles astonish the eyes of the traveller who sees them for the first time. It has been said that they have taken their black, brown, and olive and yellow skin-tints from the satiny and brighthued rinds of the fruit which surround them. If they are to be believed, the mystery of their clean, clear complexion and exquisite pulp-like flesh arises from the use of the papaw fruit as a cosmetic. A slice of ripe fruit is rubbed over the skin, and is said to dissolve spare flesh and remove every blemish. It is a toilet requisite in use by the young and old, producing the most beautiful specimens of the human race."

A TROPIC NIGHT

Come and compare
Columns and idol-dwellings, Goth or Greek,
With Nature's realms of worship, earth and air,
Nor fix on fond bodies to circumscribe thy prayer.
—Byron.

For a week the wet monsoon had frolicked insolently along the coast, the intermittent north-east breeze, pert of promise but flabby of performance, giving way to evening calms. Then came slashing south-easters which, having discourteously bundled the cloud banks over the mountains, retired with a spasm upon the reserves of the Pacific.

All day long the sea has been pale blue with changeful silvery lights, and now the moon, half-way down on her westward course, shines over a scene solemn in its stillness—the peace and repose more impressive than all the recent riot and haste.

Here on the verge of the ocean, at the extreme limit of the spit of soft, shell-enamelled sand, where the breakers had roared in angry monotone, the ears thrill with tender sounds. Though all the winds are dead the undertones of the sea linger in lulling harmonies. The tepid tide on the warm sand crisply rustles and hisses as when satin is crumpled and smartly rent. Weird, resonant tappings, moans, and gurgles come from a hollow log drifting with infinite slowness. Broken sighs and gasps tell where the ripples advancing in echelon wander and lose their way among blocks of sandstone. As the tide rose it prattled and gurgled, toying with tinkling shells and clinking coral, each tone separate and distinct, however thin and faint. My solitary watch gives the rare delight of analysing the night thoughts of the ocean, profound in its slumber though dreamily conscious of recent conflict with the winds. All the frail undertones suppressed during the bullying day now have audience. Sounds which crush and crowd have wearied and retired. The timid and shy venture forth to join the quiet revelry of the night.

On its northern aspect the sand spit is the steeper. There the folds of the sea fall in velvety thuds ever so gentle, ever so regular. On the southern slope, where the gradient is easy, the wavelets glide up with heedless hiss and slide back with shuffling whisper, scarce moving the garlands of brown seaweed which a few hours before had been torn from the borders of the coral garden with mischievous recklessness.

The sounds of this most stilly night are almost wholly of the faintly pulsing sea—sibilant and soft. Twice have the big-eyed stone plovers piped demoniacally. Once there were flutterings among the nutmeg pigeons in the star-proof jungle of the crowded islet to the south. A cockatoo has shrieked out in dismay at some grim nightmare of a snake. Two swamp pheasants have assured each other in bell-like cadences that the night is far spent, and all is well.

As the moon sinks a ghostly silence prevails. Even the subdued tones of the sea are hushed. Though I listen with aching intentness no sense of sound comes to my relief. Thus must it be to be bereft of hearing. This death-like pause, this awful blank, this tense, anxious lapse, this pulseless, stifling silence is brief. A frail moan, just audible, comes from the direction of the vanishing moon. There is a scarcely perceptible stir in the warm air—a sensation of coming coolness rather than of motion, and a faint odour of brine. A mile out across the channel a black band has settled on the shining water.

How entrancing these night-tinted sights and soft sounds! While I loll and peer and listen I am alert and still, for the primitive passions of the universe are shyly exercised. To be sensitive to them all the faculties must be acutely strained. With this lisping, coaxing, companionable sea, the serene and sparkling sky, the glow beyond the worlds, the listening isles—demure and dim—the air moist, pacific and fragrant— what concern of mine if the smoky messenger from the stuffy town never comes? This is the quintessence of life. I am alive at last. Such keen tingling, thrilling perceptions were never mine before. Now do I realise the magnificent, the prodigious fact of being. Mine not only a part in the homely world, but a fellowship with the glorious firmament.

It is night—the thoughtful, watchful, wakeful, guardian night, with no cloud to sully its tremulous radiance. How pretty a fable, I reflect, would the ancients have associated with the Southern Cross, shimmering there in the serene sky! Dare I, at this inspiring moment, attempt what they missed, merely because they lacked direct inspiration? Those who once lived in Egypt saw the sumptuous southern jewel, and it may again glitter vainly for the bewilderment of the Sphinx if the lazy world lurches through space long enough. Yes, let me invent a myth—and not tell it, but rather think of the origin of the Milky Way and so convince myself of the futility of modern inventions.

Juno's favourite flowers were, it is written, the dittany (a milk-like plant), the flaunting poppy, and the fragrant lily. Once, as she slept, Jupiter placed the wonderfully begotten Hercules to her alien, repugnant breasts. Some of the milk dripped and as it fell was dissipated in the heavens— and there is the Milky Way. Other drops reached the earth and, falling on the lily, which hitherto had been purple, purified it to whiteness. In similar guise might the legend of the Southern Cross be framed—but who has the audacity to reveal it! And have not the unimaginative blacks antici- pated the stellar romance?

As I gaze into those serene and capricious spaces separating the friendly stars I am relieved of all consciousness of sense of duration. Time was not made for such ecstasies, which are of eternity. The warm sand nurses my body. My other self seeks consolation among the planets.

This huge stage presenteth naught but show,
Whereon the stars in secret influence comment.

A grey mist masks the winding of a mainland river. Isolated blotches indicate lonely lagoons and swamps where slim palms and lank tea-trees stand in crowded, whispering ranks knee-deep in dull brown water. The mist spreads. Black hilltops are as islands jutting out from a grey supermundane sea.

Come! Let me bid defiance to this clumsy dragon of vapour worming its ever-lengthening, ever-winding tail out from the close precincts of a mangrove creek. Shock-headed it rolls and squirms. Soft-headed, too, for the weakest airs knead and mould it into ever-varying shapes. Now it has a lolling, impudent tongue—a truly unruly member, wagging disrespectfully at the decent night. Now a perky top-knot, and presently no head at all. Lumbering, low-lying, cowardly —a plaything, a toy, a mockery, a sport for the wilful zephyrs. Now it lifts a bully head as it creeps unimpeded across the sea and spreads, infinitely soft, all-encompassing. As if by magic the mainland is blotted out. The sea is dark and death-like, the air clammy, turgid, and steamy. Heavy vapour settles upon the hills of the Island, descending slowly and with the passivity of fate, until there is but a thin stratum of clear air between the gloomy levels and the portentous pall.

Lesser islands to the south are merely cloud-capped. This lower level with blurred and misty edges may not be further compressed; but the air is warm, thick, sticky, and so saturated with vegetable odours that even the salt of the sea has lost its savour.

A low, quavering whistle heralds the approach of a nervous curlew, running and pausing, and stamping its script—an erratic scrawl of fleurs-de-lis—on the easy sand. Halting on the verge of the water, it furtively picks up crabs as if it were a trespasser, conscious of a shameful or wicked deed and fearful of detection. It is not night nor yet quite day, but this keen-eyed, suspicious bird knows all the permanent features of the sand-spit. The crouching, unaccustomed shape bewilders it; it pipes inquiringly, stops, starts with quick, agitated steps, snatches a crab—a desperate deed—and flies off with a penetrating cry of warning.

A long-billed shore plover takes up the alarm, and blunderingly races towards instead of from me, whimpering "plin, plin" as it passes and, still curious though alert, steps and bobs and ducks—all its movements and flight impulsive and staccato.

The grey mist whitens. A luminous patch indicates the east. The light increases. The cumbersome vapour is sopped up by the sun, and the coo-hooing of many pigeons makes proclamation of the day. Detached and erratic patches of ripples appear—tiptoe touches of sportful elves tripping from the isles to the continent, whisking merrily, the faintest flicks of dainty toes making the glad sea to smile. Parcelled into shadows, bold, yet retreating, the dimness of the night, purple on the glistening sea, stretches from the isles towards the long, orange-tinted beach.

Let there be no loitering of the shadows. The gloomy isles have changed from black to purple and from purple to blue, and as the imperious sun flashes on the mainland a smudge of brown, blurred and shifting, in the far distance—the only evidence of the existence of human schemes and agitations—the only stain on the celestial purity of the morning—betokens the belated steamer for the coming of which the joy-giving watches of the tropic night have been kept.

C. E. W. BEAN

CHARLES EDWIN WOODROW BEAN, historian and journalist, born at Bathurst, Official Australian War Correspondent 1914-18, and editor of the *Official History of Australia in the War of 1914-18* (12 vols), was on the staff of the *Sydney Morning Herald*, when, in 1909, he was sent to "follow the great industry of Australia down the long track from the farthest fenced areas . . . to the looms in the whirring factories on the coast". His articles were collected in 1910 to form *On the Wool Track*, from which the following extracts are taken.

THE RED COUNTRY

WHEN European writers, and some Australians too, speak of the monotony of the Australian scrub—gum-trees, and gum-trees, and gum-trees still beyond that—they doubtless describe conscientiously enough what they have seen, which is usually a strip of Australia along the coast. But few of them have any right to speak of Australia as a whole; for the greater part of Australia is the part that most of them have not seen, and the chief mark of the scrub which grows in that part is the bewildering variety of trees. Generally, on no two miles, often on no two acres, are the trees the same. The difficulty for a stranger is to know what sort of tree he is for the moment passing: for he may count thirty different sorts in driving through one paddock. Many Australians do not know them by name, much less by sight. But they are the most beautiful trees in Australia.

The most graceful tree in Europe is the silver birch. Householders cram it into their gardens, however small, and artists into their pictures. There's a tree out back which is a close counterpart of the silver birch. One would have thought it would have been transplanted into every suburban front lawn. But few suburban Australians have ever heard of—much less seen—the leopardwood. And at the time of our journey the rabbits were slowly ringbarking it out of the continent.

The truth is that there exists inside coastal Australia a second Australia—the larger of the two—of which most of our people know very little more than do the Londoners. It is the land of those astonishing grasses which spring up, then vanish for twenty years, and then suddenly flush up again to the delight of the oldest inhabitant, who is the only man that can spin a yarn about them. It is the land of the delicate scrub, which is as puzzling as the grass and mostly, as useful; of the mulga, the best of all for stock, and one of the prettiest, with its exquisite black tracework of branches against its "Liberty" grey leaves; of the applebush or rosewood or bluebush, which, when half-dry, is fairly good for stock; of the emu-bush, which droops like the bunch of an emu's tail and is very good fodder—as the rabbits have found; of the native willow, which is good to make yokes of; of the gidgea, which is good for fencing, and which drops beans that are good for sheep, and smells so pestilential after rain that they say at Nyngan they can tell you when it is raining about Bourke, because the nearest gidgea is there; of the leopardwood, which is good feed and bad timber, and crops up again as often as it is cut; of the myall, which is good sheep-feed; of the whitewood, which is fairly good; and the belar, which is very little good; and the wild fuchsia, whose flowers, full of honey, the sheep at any rate think to be good; of the hopbush, which is good for yeast; and the beefwood, which is good for timber; and the deadfinish, which may be good for whip-handles; and the budda, which is good for nothing except to keep the surface on the ground —to stop the wind from blowing the skin of Australia away and leaving her cheek-bones all shiny red and bare and useless.

For out here you have reached the core of Australia, the real red Australia of the ages, which—though the rivers have worn their channels through it, and spewed out their black silt in narrow ribbons across it—still hems in this flat modern river-soil, so that, if you drive only a few miles from the river-bank, you will always come out in the end upon a red land, a slightly higher land, rising sharply from the grey plain; a land which stretches away and away and away across the heart of Australia, with the history of the oldest continent on earth written in interesting little patches—patches of ironstone pebbles, of river-worn quartz, stony deserts, and a thousand other relics of its bygone sufferings—across the whole face of it.

That is the real Australia, and it is as delicate as its own grasses. In parts the sand, which covers it and contains the whole calendar of priceless seeds that have taken a few million years (at a low estimate) to evolve, is not more than one foot thick; so thin and light and delicate a skin that only the delicate Western scrub holds it in place at all.

There, years before "erosion" became a matter of general public concern, a dangerous problem of wind erosion had fully developed. The Western Lands Boards had been studying it and already had taken some wise steps in the effort to check it.

In certain parts, where men had come out on to that country and cut down the scrub recklessly, with rough-shod, ready-made European methods, the surface of the earth had blown clean away. In some places, where all that exquisite, wonderful plant-life had been gradually developing through all the ages, it took just one bad season to destroy it; and instead, we found there great patches of "scalded" clay, as bare as on the day when the last wavelet of some old receding ocean lapped over them and left them to evolve a covering for their nakedness.

How much even some enlightened Australians knew about this greater half of Australia may be judged from a single instance. Not so very many years previously, at a time when that wonderful native scrub was being used as the great reserve of fodder in the West—and being used, if anything, too fast—and when the one useful thing which the Government could have done would have been to pass a law making it criminal to destroy it, it was found that the Lands Department had actually inserted a clause into its Western leases, insisting that lessees must improve the country by clearing

PAPAW GROVE, QUEENSLAND

"Pure, good and chaste food"

DARLING RIVER

"The river opened into a circular basin"

it of scrub. The Western Lands Board had since changed all that, yet the thing that struck a townsman coming out upon it was that the real Australia was, even to most Australians, to all intents and purposes an unknown and unstudied country.

The people out there had come thither of their own choice to make their living in their own way; and though they were doing a great work for their country by experimenting with immeasurably the most difficult part of it, they could not very well expect favours over and above those people who were earning their living elsewhere. But they were justified in expecting that the ministers in the Government, who were their ministers just as much as they were the ministers for Sydney, should be able to look at their questions from their point of view, and they had had some horrible shocks.

Just before one big drought broke, the people of Bourke had received a visit from their Premier. A deputation waited on him there to ask for a few more concessions in railway freights or something. It was hardly necessary to put their case to him, because even people on the other side of the world knew by the cables in the papers what the case along the Darling was just then. The grass had long since disappeared; the face of the country was shifting red and grey sand, blowing about wherever the wind carried it. The fences were covered, dead sheep and fallen trunks had become sand-hills. Millions of trees were killed; the birds had been dropping dead. Except where there were trees, the West was literally not different from the Sahara Desert. Some men's nerves had broken down under the conditions, and they had had to flee from the back-country, in fear for their sanity. The rest of the world had been watching the fight against that calamity as people in war follow the struggle at the front. All the rest of Australia, and even Europe, had given signs of their sympathy. What little comfort the men and women out there had, they drew from this. So there was really no need to put the case to their Premier.

However, just for form's sake, they put to him for about three-quarters of an hour some of the urgencies which had

E

been filling the newspapers for months, and which presumably had been worrying the Government into white hairs. He seemed to be listening. When they had pretty well finished he suddenly looked up.

"What do you do with the country in these parts?" he said, waving his hand towards the window. "What—er—what use d'yer make of it?"

They were a little surprised. They had just been telling him for three-quarters of an hour.

But they said.

"Oh, well, we put sheep on it—that is, when there is any grass on it. . . ."

"D'jever think of dairyin'?" asked the Premier.

Now if he had gone round amongst the men in that room and had hit each one of them hard upon the chest, he would have produced much the same sort of effect as he succeeded in producing when he blurted out that question. They went away almost sick with disillusionment.

That Premier knew something of dairying. Perhaps, after all, he saw as far as most of us do beyond our noses.

PORTS AND FLEETS OF THE DARLING

"Do you catch anything—can you see something white in the trees there?" asked the skipper a little anxiously.

It was on the Darling River, at a point about 180 miles from Bourke by the river, or 60 miles by land—for the river runs about three to one. The nearest city of any real size was Broken Hill, and that was nearly 220 miles away; and Broken Hill itself, when you get there, is a town in a desert —a freak, a modern city in the middle of a basin as bare as the palm of your hand and in colour not unlike it. That was the nearest big town. Stations not very far from where we then were, in seasons when the Darling became too dry to float a steamer, sent their wool to Broken Hill.

So this was a pretty lonely sort of spot. The Darling runs between high banks, as steep as those of a railway-cutting and—in dry times—with about as much grass on them. And, as the river generally flows low between those banks, the view to be obtained from a Darling steamer was much the same as that from a train in a railway cutting.

Many people said that, therefore, the trip down the river by steamer was uninteresting. So it was if a man slept all the time. Because then, naturally, he was not aware of it when the ashen-grey river-banks of modern alluvial soil suddenly gave place to higher banks of red, and you realized that you were running now between river walls made of the ancient red soil which once formed the hills and valleys of all this part of the continent. The grains of the red banks that swam past you were probably—aeons upon aeons ago—the cool red sand to which the olive light just filtered down through fathom on fathom of ocean. Creepy dark things crawled over them, and the deep sea-currents furrowed them. There's not very much of the red soil left along the Upper Darling. But here it still is, in parts, rising so distinctly from the grey that you could probably put one foot on the modern soil and one on the old. Most of the river homesteads are built upon the red, because, of course, it is the land above flood-mark. Every area lower than the floods has been covered with grey alluvium, which has been brought by water from the Queensland hills; and water, in the shape of rain, will always transform that grey soil into a sort of sticky black glue, which even the lightest wheels pick up, until the tyres actually clog against the side. The red soil is the relic of the old soil which still lies beneath the black. It is the same fertile red sand as we had seen cover the fences in the Real Australia, and it grows all fruits well and wheat excellently. The Mildura fruit-farms are built on it, and, when the Darling comes to be dammed, the irrigation settlements will probably be made· on the patches of red soil.

If a man slept all day, he also naturally missed the extraordinary hill which suddenly peeped down at him over the tree-tops at Gundabooka. Its long, flat top possibly marks the actual old surface of that sandy ocean bed, which elsewhere has been worn away. He missed the curious ridges of rock—some of them part of an even more ancient Australia

—which every ten miles or so crop suddenly out of the grey bank on one side, straggle obliquely like some old swimming dragon across the water, and disappear into the grey banks on the other side.

Those rocks entirely bar the river when it is low. As it rises and they begin to be covered, they would still wreck a steamer. And yet when our steamer, the *Jandra*, was drawing 4 feet of water, and there were only 6 feet in the tortuous channel through these rocks, with jagged boulders hidden a foot below the water on either side, we stood beside the skipper and watched him drive his vessel close under one bank, and then shoot suddenly across to the other and back, following a channel of which not a trace could we see. But he knew it by certain ugly oily disturbances here and there in the smooth water. Once, when the river opened into a circular basin—widening for no apparent cause, but really because of the current swirling round a hidden ridge, with an isolated monster called "Big Ben" somewhere under the surface--the skipper stopped the ship dead, put a line ashore, and warped her slowly round the basin close under one bank, as carefully as a battleship is manoeuvred into dock. There was not a sign on the surface to show that you could not have thrashed a battleship fair down mid-stream. But the skipper could read the signs of his navigation. Other skippers watched the clouds, or the season, or the sunset; this skipper knew, by some mark to which the water had risen on some individual snag or rock miles back, that there was not enough water for him over the "Yanda" rocks. Such hidden dangers are the reason why steamers on the Darling did not navigate at night, but tied up to the bank and waited for daylight.

But at the particular point mentioned at the beginning of this chapter the river did not look interesting. It was little different from a railway cutting, unrelieved by rocks or red soil, or even by ducks or pelicans. Only grey bank on one side, grey bank on the other, tops of occasional trees looking over them, and a strip of sky and water between. Nevertheless the skipper was searching for something.

Now, the folk on ships sailing from Chile across the Pacific begin after many days to look anxiously for some sign very, very far away on the horizon ahead—a point or two on one side or other of the bow, it may be. And there turns up at last, perhaps in the early morning, exactly where and when they are looking for it, an intermittent white halo, like the very faintest far-off reflection of a lightning flash. That sign, they know, marks the port of Sydney; and they make for it, and presently lift up a pinpoint flash, which is the South Head light.

This skipper, too, was looking for something.

"Do you catch anything in the trees there?" he said.

Then we too anxiously scanned the bank as tree-top after tree-top wandered past. We could see nothing to cause excitement.

"Ah, there it is!"

The skipper's face was illuminated.

We looked; what was there?

"That sheepskin," he said, "on the lower bough. M'Clochertie said he'd put it there to show where we were to land his groceries."

So here was the sign of a port of call on the Darling. The river is, roughly, 2000 miles long, and looks much the same from end to end. And the captains had to search for—a sheepskin on a lower bough.

That evening we passed another sign. We observed some distance ahead, on our starboard bow, an ancient piece of board—the skipper said it had once been a notice board—nailed across two posts. Beside it was a tree. On the tree was a scar, very old and deep. It was the letter T.

"That's Toorale," said the skipper. "The homestead's eight miles back from that tree—on the Warrego. There's hundreds of thousands of pounds' worth of wool been taken from just here. You can see the mark of it—there."

Down the bank ran a smooth, shallow groove worn in the dry, grey soil by the slipping of thousands of bales. That solitary T was the only evidence of a considerable Darling

River port. In some years its trade must have been not far short of £30,000. There are seaports living on less.

We did not stop at Toorale. Another ship regularly did the trade of that port. We were making for another sign. After panting down river another day, dropping groceries and beer-casks at the port of Louth—taking on fuel by the simple process of tying up, chopping it, and then rolling it down the bank—at last, about nightfall, when the sky ahead was peeping in yellow slashes through the trees, and shining very softly on the dark river below, we turned into a long reach. We had been driving small batches of ducks ahead of us all the afternoon. The crew and the deck passengers were lying in the bows potting at them with a pea-rifle. The captain would not let them shoot pelicans, and the big deck-hand would not let them shoot wood-duck on the bank, because they could not pick them up. So, except for the hawks in the trees, the ducks swimming ahead of us had received the crew's undivided attentions, and were growing pretty shy. Mile after mile they alternately swam and flew in short flights, never leaving the ribbon of river, never letting the steamer get close enough to be dangerous. The assistant deck-hand had just taken the rifle from the fireman for a sporting shot, when the ducks, of course, rose. Only this time, instead of flying on for a hundred yards and then swimming again, they circled wildly to the left, high over the bank, and flashed off like lightning through the trees.

It was another sign for navigators.

"That's how I can always tell when the other steamer's coming," he said—"by the ducks flying back on us, so; or sometimes by the other boat's waves coming up the river ahead of her. And it's the same when we get near a town—it's Dunlop Station this time. The birds won't pass it—they fly back out of the way."

It looked a countrified enough reach in all conscience. We had just passed a sight which one of us, at any rate, had never before seen in Australia—some blue flower, possibly blue-bell, growing as thick between the trees as hyacinths in an English wood, literally a bright-blue carpet of them. During the last day or two we had seen white flowers—both daisy and some sort of peppermint—which you could smell for half a mile, growing equally thick, and a day or so later we found square miles of Dunlop actually carpeted with not only white and blue, but yellow also—one of those extraordinary results which a few days' rain brings from sheer desert in Central Australia. This reach seemed, if anything, further from the world than the sheepskin port. You would not believe it could contain signs of man's presence sufficient to frighten even a duck.

But presently over the edge of the bank there sailed by us the grey roof of a shed. A man passed on the bank carrying a bucket. It was the sign of one of the busiest factories in Australia.

From that day onward for two months the steamer *Jandra* did nothing except make weekly trips to the same quiet reach and thence back to Bourke, getting away as fast as she could load with the cargo from that factory. I happened, weeks later, to be watching the eight-hours' procession of the trades unions in Sydney. On the last wagon, the carters', there came sailing six bales of dumped wool with the brand Dunlop. They had been part of the *Jandra's* cargo.

People did not call these ports "wool factories"—probably because they were out in the fresh country air, where all factories ought to be. But a man who heard on one side the huge shearing-shed buzzing with machinery, and, on the other, the wool-scour pump coughing as it sucked yellow Darling soup far up into the troughs, in another big shed; and who saw the wool fed into the troughs, clawed, clutched, soaped, shaken on iron teeth, finally fed out again and spread on the wool-green to be dried under the sun into a dazzling dead white; who saw it carried into the pressing and dumping shed and pressed into half its size and then dumped with hoop-iron bands into half that size again, and finally carted off to a fourth big shed to wait for the boat—a city man who saw and heard all this for the first time could not help realizing that, whatever it might be in name, it was a factory indeed. There were the usual factory regulations. For instance, the water from the wool-scour must not be returned to the river, so it was pumped out at Dunlop, to irrigate South African Rhodes grass on the plain.

We who for years had watched the railways busily fetching their loads and emptying them into Sydney, had hardly realized that out beyond the furthermost termini there ran another stream of traffic in quite a different direction—up and down, past these wool factories, along one of the longest waterways in the world. This traffic trickled, slowly and fitfully, at right angles to the railways for about 2000 miles —practically from Queensland to the Bight. Up and down the centre of Australia there steamed—even at that time— a quite considerable shipping. For all we heard of it on the sea-coast, it might not have existed. If Parliament could have been transported just for one day, and dumped on the black and white wharves which towered stage on stage thirty or forty feet above the little steamers at Bourke; if the members could have stood on the wharf's edge, by the row of steam-jib cranes, and watched Mildura fruits and Japanese onions lowered ever so far down into the little holds below—then the prospects of the Darling people might have been different. At the time of our visit that river trade was still worth considering. It is true that the railways to Walgett, Brewarrina, Cunnamulla, and elsewhere had cut off great chunks of their hinterland. Before the Brewarrina and Walgett lines were built, 22,058 bales in a year came down the river to Bourke, and 4523 up-river. Since then the whole of that trade from up-river had been diverted to other towns; but when we were there Bourke had fairly recently received by steamer 3000 bales from the down-river stations. There was enough trade left to keep two or three Bourke steamers plying for all they were worth whenever the river was up, and occasionally to draw up-river a larger steamer from the big fleets trading down below.

We had not realized until we were nearly 500 miles from Sydney that this long river was the chief public possession of the people living in about one-half the State of New South

Wales. On the coast people's minds were full of railways and roads, Newcastle coal, Sydney Harbour. But the inhabitants of the far west of New South Wales had one outstanding interest, much more deeply impressed and general than any other—their river.

It was the one great public possession in that half of the State; and yet they hardly possessed it. The people who possessed it were the majority in Parliament, who came mainly from Sydney and the coast, and who thought a great deal of Sydney and the railways leading to Sydney, and did not know or care tuppence about the river.

Of course if Captain Cook had been given a map of Australia before he discovered it, his eye would have caught at once a great basin and waterway, and he would have marked it off as a State by itself—because its people would obviously have one big possession in common, and would want to combine to use it and improve it with their own money in their own way. In that case the Darling would have been carefully nursed, locked, its flood-water stored. And instead of the Sydney railways stopping short of it—in the deadly fear that the river might be of some use in carrying the produce of its own country away cheaply to its own mouth—there might have been a whole system of little railways running down to it on either side to feed it much as the small bones run into a fish's backbone.

But Captain Cook was not given a plan. The Darling, when it was found, was tacked on loosely to Sydney. Sydney pulled a snag or two out of it. The head streams were dammed, and consequently the flood-water reaches the Darling less often than before. When it does reach the river, with the exception of the portion caught by an ill-planned but still useful weir at Bourke, and by the splendid works far down the Murray, it runs into the ocean exactly as if white men had never come to Australia to stop it. We found that no fruit or vegetables or grain worth considering were grown along the Darling. The water would have had to be lifted thirty or forty feet to irrigate them, and it takes a capitalist to do that. Such fruits as we saw often came from Mildura and the chaff from Adelaide. Both are near the river; and the goods come partly by water—but it is generally ocean water. The river water was not there.

In those days, if there was but a chance of a river, the whole country rushed to it. Some years previously wool-teams came from the Paroo to Wilcannia on the chance that a "fresh", recently reported, would give sufficient water to carry their wool. They hurried day after day down the plain, mostly along the part which people who draw maps have marked as the bed of the Paroo River. Geographers in their maps have the grace to indicate the bed of the Paroo River by a dotted line. It is a Central Australian river, and the best way to find its bed is with a spirit-level. The wool-teams had come down it and out on to the red country; and at last through the red and white sandhills into Wilcannia.

When they got to Wilcannia they found the river a thin tawny streak between two dry walls of grey mud as dead as an ash-heap. The river which was expected to rise had not risen. Some rain may have fallen in Queensland and started off for the plains. But it was taken up by dam after dam across the head streams, and had fairly withered and been scorched up under a thousand miles or so of sun and an atmosphere drier than a stale sponge-cake. Anyway, it had expired long before it had got near to Wilcannia.

So the teams turned round and went 120 miles to Broken Hill, then the railhead from South Australia. That is what the river meant to about half of New South Wales.

It seemed to us that for the Western half of New South Wales one thing was bound to be done, sooner or later, because it was the one apparent thing that could be done. If it turned out a failure it would nevertheless have been well worth spending a million on the trial.

The Government of New South Wales, for the price at which it built the Central Railway Station in Sydney, might have changed the map of Australia. Years ago, one of its own Royal Commissions told it that it could put seventeen locks on the Darling for £530,000—and so, possibly, it could have done, in those days. The locking of the river has, indeed, since then been promised, but it is doubtful when it will be carried out. It is really no wonder that we found the people of the Far West a little bitter. It was not that they had any right to look for special favours; although they were out there under immeasurably the hardest conditions, turning to profit the problematical half of New South Wales—and so might well be given every favour by far-seeing Governments—still it was their livelihood; and if they chose to help themselves that way, they could not demand favours on that account. But they could demand that their own Ministers, who were *their* Government as well as the Government for Sydney, should be able to look at *their* questions from *their* point of view.

Yet it did seem impossible for a Government in Sydney, however well it might wish, to stand in the shoes of the Westerner and see things as he saw them. We concluded that the West would get one or another of its needs satisfied just so soon as it could prove that the satisfaction of that particular need was also a benefit to Sydney. Its only other chance seemed to be the slender one that it would some day be permitted to form itself into a separate State, with a capital neither at Sydney nor at Melbourne nor at Adelaide, but in Riverina or the lower Murray, or in some part of those great river-basins whose people have the same wants and the same problems, and could agree to spend their own money on their own projects with an eye to their own benefits, and not to make life easier for the easy livers in a few great cities on the coast.

CHARLES BARRETT

CHARLES LESLIE BARRETT, naturalist and journalist, born at Hawthorn, Victoria, is the author of many books of travel recording his manifold experiences in all parts of the continent. The best of these books are those which contain his fascinating accounts of natural life. "Sea Birds' Haunts" is taken from *In Australian Wilds* (1919).

SEA BIRDS' HAUNTS

PERHAPS it is a relic of boyhood, this keen delight in lonely isles that lures so many landsmen to the sea. Or it may be that sirens send musical messages to win us away. Certain it is that islands, especially such as are inhabited only by wild creatures, possess an elusive charm. Australian seas are rich in isles, many of which are sea birds' nesting haunts.

The islands of Bass Strait have long interested naturalists. Some years ago the Royal Australasian Ornithologists' Union chartered a small steamer for a cruise among the isles, and I was one of her passengers. Later, as a special representative of the Melbourne *Herald*, I enjoyed a cruise on the Federal Fisheries' Investigation vessel, *Endeavour*. These two short voyages enabled me to study "island life" under the most favourable conditions.

King Island, which in recent years has become well populated, lies midway between the south-east of Cape Otway, on the Victorian coast, and the north-west corner of Tasmania. It was frequented only by fishermen and sealers in the early days. Going ashore in November, 1908, at Currie Harbour, we found a thriving township, and stayed at a large and comfortable hotel. Two days were devoted to excursions. The sand-blow, some hundreds of acres in extent, at the south-western end of the island, is a place of bones. Tons of sub-fossil remains are scattered about on the surface, and vast quantities, doubtless, lie hidden beneath the sand. We collected Wombat skulls, portions of the skeletons of "Native Cats" and Wallabies, leg bones of the Emu and fragments of eggshell. Lower jaws of Wallabies were most numerous. Portions of Seal skeletons were observed, and bones of sheep also were scattered over the sand. I had the luck to discover a specially fine Wombat skull, which is now in the National Museum, Melbourne.

A member of our party zealously collected the largest bones he could find and returned to the boat (we had come round the coast in the steamer) laden with the spoils. When he showed them to an expert he was disgusted to learn that nearly all the bones which he had gathered were remains of the common sheep, and cast the "rubbish" into the sea.

Most interesting of the sub-fossil remains from King Island are those of the Emu, a species which has long been extinct. Péron, the French naturalist, saw the great birds alive. At the time of his visit men on the island owned dogs which had been trained to hunt Kangaroos and Emus. The King Island Emu was distinct from the Tasmanian bird (also extinct), and the form that still flourishes in Australia. It is most regrettable that two members of the remarkable family, *Dromaeidae*, should be in the Legion of the Lost. The King Island species was abundant when white men first settled there, and must have been warred against mercilessly. Animals on a small island have no way of escape; hunted from one refuge to another, extermination is their certain fate.

We were puzzled to account for the presence of such vast quantities of sub-fossil remains in a restricted area. One theory advanced was that Bush fires had driven the animals to the place where they perished, and left their bones to astonish naturalists of a future age. Another suggestion was that, feed being particularly abundant in the area now covered by sand, it had become a favourite resort of wild creatures.

Penguin Island, one of the western isles of Bass Strait, is honeycombed with burrows of *Eudyptula minor*. Walking over the rookery, one's feet break through the earth crust and sink into tunnels, so that progress is slow and laborious, unless one is careless of destroying bird homes. Even when caution is exercised, it is impossible to avoid ruining a few burrows. Our party was responsible for the breakage of a score of eggs, but I hope that none of the birds was crushed. We saw little of the Penguins, save when a burrow was explored. Many birds were "at home", but they were unwilling to receive visitors, and more than one naturalist repented of his eagerness to bring a Penguin from its nest. For the brave little birds snapped fiercely at hands which attempted to grasp them. In some cases the burrows were under bushes, and had probably been made originally by Short-tailed Petrels or Mutton-Birds. Cavities at the ends of rock crevices were tenanted. The nest proper, in each instance, was a domed chamber, with a carpet of dry grass or weeds.

The Little Penguin lays two eggs to a clutch. The shell is white and of coarse texture, but slightly glossed. In his charming book *Antarctic Penguins*, Dr G. Murray Levick, R.N., says that the Adélie Penguin, seen for the first time, gives one the impression of a very smart little man in an evening dress suit, an admirable description. The Little Penguin also is "the gentleman". If it were a creature clad in fur, instead of feathers, and could thrive away from the sea, it would become as popular in drawing-rooms as Persian cats and Pomeranians are at present, and children would demand Penguins instead of Teddy Bears. About eighteen inches in length, the Little Penguin wears a light blue coat, while the under part of the body is covered in silvery white feathers. The chicks, clad in dusky down, resemble balls of fluff. They cannot endure strong light, and two that were taken from a burrow on Penguin Island crouched, with closed eyes, against the rock.

Clumsy and slow ashore, in the sea Penguins move swiftly, with ease and grace. They are master mariners. From a cliff at Sandringham, on Port Phillip Bay, I have often watched Penguins chasing fish in the shallows. They dart through the water like torpedoes, propelled chiefly by their paddle-shaped wings. The call note is a curious barking sound, which echoes far over the sea.

On Penguin Island we discovered a small rookery of Pelicans. There were about a dozen nests, each containing two eggs. The birds were extremely wary; they flew out to sea when we were fifty yards from the rookery, and did not return until our boat had left the island shore. The cinematograph operator never had a chance.

From Penguin Island we cruised to Albatross Island, where the big sea birds nest. But waves were spouting high on the granite cliffs, and the skipper refused to risk a boat, though we thought that there was a forlorn hope of landing. We had to be content with a distant view of snowy-plumaged birds, sitting serenely on nests among the heights. Few naturalists have been on Albatross Island, and the birds are fairly safe there, even from plume hunters.

Three Hummock Island, the home of a lonely family and a herd of cattle, was our next call. The islanders were delighted to welcome us, and bestowed generous hospitality. We dined on fried Mutton-Bird eggs, not exactly a dainty dish, but most acceptable when one's appetite had been sharpened by sea air. Close to the cottage, on a slope fronting the sea, was a Mutton-Bird rookery. Borrowing crooks, we explored some burrows, and gathered a score of large white eggs, which were handed over to the cook on the steamer.

The eastern islands of Bass Strait are in some respects more interesting than those of the west. Cape Barren Island, visited in the course of our ornithological cruise, is the home of a remarkable people. Truganina, the last of the Tasmanian race, died in May, 1876, at the age, it is believed, of seventy-three. The tribes of Tasmania were terribly persecuted, and their story is one of the saddest in Australian history. Those who wish to read it can do so in Bonwick's pages. In the early days many of the native women, chiefly Tasmanians, became wives of white sealers and sailors, who made homes among the islands. Some of their descendants live at Cape Barren. There is more than one type; some of the

natives possess woolly locks, and others long, lank hair.
Many of the children are handsome. One boy especially
caught our fancy. He had abundance of curly hair, a finely
moulded face, and large, intelligent eyes. The skin colouration
of the Islanders varies considerably. Some of them are nearly
white, some pale-brown, and others so dark-skinned that they
would pass for pure-blooded blacks. A few white people live
on Cape Barren Island. There is also a school, and the young
Islanders are educated. Many of them read and write well.
They can sketch, too, on slates, and a boy showed me a
spirited drawing of a Mutton-Bird. The drum and fife band
is a popular institution. One need not be dull at Cape Barren.

The Islanders live in small huts clustered around the
harbour. The men are boat-builders and navigators, and make
voyages in small craft across the stormy Strait to the Mutton-
Bird islands. Their principal industry is gathering nestlings
of the Short-tailed Petrel, which form their staple food during the greater part of the year. A little sealing is done, but
it is upon Mutton-Birds that the Islanders depend for sustenance and trading. On Babel and other islands, where large
rookeries exist, they have built rude huts, which are inhabited
during the periods of harvesting chicks. An exodus from Cape
Barren to the bird-isles takes place when the time for "business" arrives. Young birds are killed by dislocation of the
neck, the bodies are plucked and scalded, and the feet removed. Subsequently, when they have been decapitated and
cleaned, the birds are pickled in barrels. Birds preserved in
this manner are marketable.

Though the Islanders have been engaged in the Mutton-
Bird industry for many years, the rookeries still give abundant yields. It is impossible to estimate the number of these
Petrels that nest on Bass Strait islands. In summer they appear in great flocks, which darken the sky or extend for miles
over the sea, forming a dusky carpet, that rises and falls with
the ocean swell. Matthew Flinders records having seen a
flight of Mutton-Birds in the Straits in December, 1798. On
the lowest computation, he thought, the number of "Sooty
Petrels" could not have been less than one hundred millions.

Above: BASS STRAIT GULLS *"These scavenger birds are beautiful"*

Below: PENGUIN ROOKERY *"A very smart little man in an evening dress suit"*

Above: NORTHERN TERRITORY CROCODILE *"Old-man Ghingi the Dog-chewer"*

Below: BULL BUFFALO ON THE RUN *"A bad-tempered, red-eyed, russet-hided cleanskin"*

In the vicinity of Cape Woolamai I have seen flocks composed, certainly, of more than a million birds.

Cat Island is the nesting place of thousands of Gannets and the rookery presents a wonderful sight in the breeding season. Nests are so numerous that, walking among them, one is within reach of sharp beaks all the time. The birds are rarely disturbed, and, consequently, are unafraid of man. When we visited Cat Island most of the Gannets were brooding. A dozen members of our party invaded the rookery, and only a few birds took wing. The report of a gun served to scare some hundreds more. We had come not to kill, but to study, and the object of the shot was to enable a cinematograph operator to take a flight picture. He had great expectations, which were not fully realised, for the seabirds declined to rise in a body. The air, however, was crowded with flying forms, mostly Gannets returned from fishing. Every minute some descended while others rose from the rookery, here and there. The moving picture man exposed a long film, and became more cheerful.

The Gannet lays only one egg to a clutch. The nest, composed of soil, debris and guano, is mound-shaped, and concave at the top. It may measure five feet or more in circumference, and from four to six inches in height. The Cat Island rookery resembles a little city, in which all the houses are alike. The nests are built at nearly an equal distance apart, in rows, and the rookery shows more evidence of design than do many Eastern villages. It would repay continuous study in nesting time. Naturalists have made only flying visits to Gannetopolis, whereas a month would not be too long a period to spend there.

Dispositions differ, even on Cat Island. Some of the birds are peaceful, others are inclined to quarrel. If a homing bird alights too near its neighbour's nest, it may be greeted by a peck, though serious disturbances are rare. But there are enemies within the gates, Pacific Gulls and Silver Gulls, which nest among the tussocky grass around the rookery, and prey upon the eggs of their big neighbours. If a Gannet leaves its nest unprotected for a few minutes a Gull is sure

F

to seize the opportunity—and the egg. The Gannets, however, are wary, and such chances rarely occur. Gulls do not disdain to feed upon the "crumbs" left over from Gannet meals; they patrol the rookery and pick up bits of fish. These scavenger birds are beautiful, and it seems a pity that their habits should be so depraved. The Pacific Gull, much the larger of the two species, possesses a raucous voice, while the Silver Gull's notes are rather pleasing, at least to a bird lover. Whenever I hear Gulls calling along the coast near my home I long to be among the isles again.

Before leaving Melbourne we were advised to "look out for snakes" on Cat Island. It was stated that venomous species swarmed among the grass tussocks, which must be traversed to reach the rookery. On landing, we remembered the warning and walked warily. Some of us wore leather leggings, others had puttees, and one of the sailors went barefooted. Snakes may abound on Cat Island, but they were not much in evidence on this occasion, for only two were reported. Apart from the main rookery, we discovered a small colony of birds, the aristocracy of Gannetopolis, no doubt. I spent some time there and obtained a fine series of photographs, as the birds were quiet and posed beautifully.

Close to Cat Island lies Storehouse Island, where several Cormorant rookeries exist. Landing on the wave-swept granite rocks was difficult, and one member of our party met with disaster. He leaped too late as the boat was falling back, and splashed into the sea. Fortunately, he managed to reach a rock and scrambled ashore, drenched. Then he emptied his coat pockets, displaying a mess of broken eggs, studded with coins and miscellaneous objects. This mishap was retribution for robbing nests in the Gannet rookery. Our comrade was unprovided with collecting tins, and had slipped two or three eggs into his pocket. He was philosophical, and laughed with us, as he stood shivering on the rocks.

The Cormorants were nesting close to the landing place, a company of solemn-looking birds, with white breasts and greenish-black plumage on the upper part of the body. Some were standing, with wings outspread, others sat on the nests.

As we drew near the birds became suspicious, and presently all were gazing in our direction. Cameras were used quickly, and, foot by foot, we crept forward, till a dozen birds took wing; a minute later the others rose and circled in the air. The nests, composed of seaweed, mingled with evil-smelling guano, were built in terraces on the bare rock; some were on ledges only a few feet above the sea. Both eggs and nestlings were observed. The latter were ugly objects covered in dusky-brown or blackish down. The odour arising from the rookery was so strong that we did not linger there. Death had been busy among the nests, and decayed bodies of many chicks were festering in the sun. Some of the innocents had been trampled flat. One nest contained three chicks, two dead and the other alive. Decomposed pieces of fish were scattered among the nests. No sanitary inspectors here, to insist upon cleanliness. Farther along the coast a second rookery was discovered. There were over one hundred nests, nearly all containing eggs.

Fishermen regard Cormorants as their worst enemies. They assert that the birds take heavy toll of edible fishes, and urge that the race should be exterminated. It cannot be gainsaid that Cormorants are fish-eaters, with hearty appetites; but fishes are so abundant in the Straits that the birds should not be grudged a share in the harvest.

Cat, Storehouse and Babel Islands lie to the east of Flinders Island, the giant of Furneaux Group. We arrived off Cat Island in fine weather. But the captain had warned us that, if the wind changed, he would have to clear out, sharp. The wind did change. We naturalists were all ashore when the steamer's siren rang shrilly over the sea, twice, impatiently the second time. We hastened to the boats, but one man who had wandered far around the coast on Storehouse Island caused delay. He was missed when the roll was called. The sea was rising and the wind began to blow fiercely. Even the short passage to the steamer was rather dangerous. Immediately all were safe aboard, the vessel made for the open sea. She had to win through a narrow channel, and all the time the wind was pressing her towards the rock-bound shore of Cat Island. Beyond the entrance to the channel we saw surf flying over a reef. It was a passage perilous, or seemed so to landsmen, and none of us was sorry when the steamer reached shelter under Babel Island, where she rode out a stormy night.

Flinders Island, like its western sister, King Island, is becoming civilised. But at the time of our visit there were few inhabitants. We put in to Killiecrankie Bay, where several half-castes were living in little log huts. A ramble along the beach to Killiecrankie was full of interest. Some of us climbed high among the boulders, while others enjoyed a swim. Black Oyster-catchers were parading the beach, uttering their mournful notes. A downy chick was captured near a rock, and photographed. It did not offer any objection, in fact, became rather friendly.

In *The Lost Tasmanian Race* Bonwick relates that Walter, the son of "King George", a Tasmanian native, presented to him "some pebbles in a bit of rag". These were Killiecrankie "diamonds", gathered on Flinders Island; they were the poor man's treasure and Bonwick cherished them as a memento of his "friend Walter". Among the shingle at the foot of Mount Killiecrankie, there were quantities of these crystal-like pebbles, and we filled our pockets with them. Some were large as marbles, others the size of a pea; they varied greatly in shape, the majority being very "rough diamonds". Real treasure trove was obtained at one of the huts. An object of the call at Killiecrankie was to obtain information regarding the Wombat, and, if possible, collect specimens. The half-caste men were familiar with the "Badger" as they called it. A naturalist's roving eyes discovered in a deserted hut two skins of the much-desired marsupial. These were secured, and arrangements made for the natives to obtain living "Badgers" and send them to Melbourne.

The Bass Strait species of Wombat was long believed to be extinct, though some naturalists thought that it survived on Flinders Island. Mr J. A. Kershaw, F.E.S., Curator of the National Museum, Melbourne, was a member of the

Ornithologists' party that visited the island in 1908. He obtained the skins, as described, and gathered other evidence to justify the belief that the species was not extinct. The skins which he secured had evidently been used as mats in the old hut; now they are treasured in a great Museum. Subsequently, living Wombats were sent from Flinders Island to Melbourne. I saw one of these at the Museum. It was a friendly animal, and allowed its head to be stroked—indeed, seemed to enjoy the caress.

When at Endeavour Bay in 1909, I went ashore for an hour, and strolling along the beach, found a Wombat's home, a low cave in soft rock some thirty feet above high tide mark. There were fresh footprints on the sand at the mouth of the cave, whose dimensions, however, were too small to permit of exploration.

On the voyage back to Melbourne the steamer called in at Kent Group, some fifty miles south-east of Wilson's Promontory. Five islands compose the group, Deal being the largest and most picturesque. Erith and Dover Islands, linked by a narrow isthmus, are opposite Deal Island, and the intervening seaway is known as Murray Pass; it is about one mile across, and a strong current flows through. Rowers need muscular arms to pull a boat from Deal to Dover. The remaining islets are named South-West and North-East respectively. The former is a bleak rock, and the latter, on which Mutton-Birds nest, has an area of about five acres.

On Deal Island there is a lighthouse, 900 feet above sea level. We naturalists received a warm welcome from the lightkeeper and his family, and a day was spent, pleasantly enough, rambling over the island. One of the keeper's daughters owned a delightful garden, sheltered from the winds by a brushwood fence. It was not large, but when the young gardener flung open the gate and invited us to enter, our eyes were dazzled by glowing colours. Here were old-fashioned plants blooming on a lonely island; the sight was refreshing, and the perfume sweet. Around the fence grew giant mallows, with crimson flowers; here was a bed of mignonette, there a cluster of larkspurs, purple, pink and

Kingfisher blue. There were daisies and marigolds for borders, a plot of roses, and shrubs and creepers. We were presented with buttonhole posies, and carried from the island-garden some seeds which germinated in ground hundreds of miles away.

A pet Opossum was proudly displayed by the young gardener. We made overtures which were not kindly received; the marsupial clung to its mistress, and, when she put it down, scrambled over the fence and disappeared. The Short-eared Phalanger is found both in Tasmania and on the mainland, as well as on islands in Bass Strait. On Deal Island, it is stated, these animals rarely leave the ground, and instead of eating Eucalypt leaves, feed upon succulent plants. Fossil remains of a Kangaroo have been recorded from Deal Island.

On the way from Kent Group to Port Phillip, our steamer was caught in a gale off Wilson's Promontory. She rolled to an alarming angle sometimes, and could scarce make steering-way for a while. But it ended all right. For the most part, the weather had treated us kindly, and the gale was only a boisterous farewell from wind and wave.

JACK McLAREN

JACK McLAREN, novelist, short story writer and journalist, born
in Melbourne, travelled widely in the South Seas and Eastern Australia. His eight years' experience on a coco-nut plantation on Cape
York Peninsula provided the material for *My Crowded Solitude*
(1926). The following extract takes up the narrative at the point
where his natives leave to go on a walkabout.

IN THE ABSENCE OF HUMANS

IT took three and a half months to sate the natives of
their other haunt and bring them back gladly to labour-
ing and consequent enjoying of white men's foods and
goods, and for the whole of that time I was completely alone
—save only for the companionship of Togo, my dog—seeing
not one human being and having no communication whatever with the outside world.

I set out upon that period with a great fear in me. I guessed
I would see no man, for I had obtained my quarterly supply
of stores only a little while before, and there was no reason
why another vessel should call. I was afraid of that great
loneliness. I saw it as a long, long line of succeeding samenesses, broken nowhere by anything new or strange. I recalled that it was a well-observed fact that without the new
and the strange the minds of men died. I recalled the parallel
fact that Man was essentially gregarious. Solitude made men
mad. In my roamings I had seen many cases of it, and heard
of many others—of men whom need for companionship had
driven to holding long and involved dialogue with themselves, with their dogs, with the stumps of trees; of men who,
conversely, had lost almost entirely their power of speech;
of men who fled from approach of other men, as from something fearsome; of men who mingled actuality with queer
imaginings and knew not how to separate them, or even that
there was need to separate them. The fear in me that I might
become as they was so strong that the first few nights I

could scarcely sleep for thought of it, and often during the day I sought to catch myself in the act of soliloquy.

Maybe the surroundings of those other isolated men were peculiarly empty of interesting things. Maybe these surroundings of mine were peculiarly full. Maybe my gregarious instinct was only partially developed. I don't know. All I know is that I found there was no long, long line of succeeding samenesses at all. I found that all about me were things so intriguing of my attention as to compensate very considerably for lack of human association. As during those weeks I was alone on Turtlehead Island I discovered that everywhere was engaging variety, so did I discover that everywhere here was engaging variety also. My solitude was filled with tragedies and comedies and dramas, with wise deeds and foolish ones, with beauties and uglinesses—just as the haunts of men were filled with them. It was a crowded solitude.

There was, for instance, the engrossing behaviour of the birds. There was one group which inhabited a tree close to the house, and which I christened "The School Kids". A dozen or more there were of them, little grey creatures, smooth of feather and a little shiny; and soon after dawn each day they would come forth and perch in a row on a conveniently horizontal limb—the largest at one end, the next largest at the other end, and the rest graded according to size—and make such an uproar of quarrelling as to awaken me and send me forth to look; and at my presence, as though in deference to it, they would at once become silent, each looking straight before it and never moving. But after a while one of the little ones would begin to fidget, moving from one leg to the other, or maybe turn and face the other way; whereupon the large one at the one end would mutter disapprovingly, and the next largest at the other end vent a shrill rebuke—to both of which the rebellious one would chirp back cheekily. Then others in the row would begin to fidget and turn the other way and preen their small wings and whisper noisily one to another; and the head teacher's muttering would become an angry shouting, and the lady assistant's shrill rebuking rise to a loud thin screech; and soon the whole class would be in a frenzy of screaming revolt, with much changing of places and fluttering of wings and cries of indignation, and perhaps a giggle or two. Then, after the using by the teachers of a multitude of harsh, commanding words, the disorder would die down, and the class return to its quiet and decorous demeanour—till such time as another young imp disturbed it all by fidgeting.

There were birds to whom life seemed mostly one long joke—laughing jackasses—in other parts of Australia drab things of grey and white, but here gay riots of twinkling hues—which came with the rising of the sun, singly, in pairs, in scores, in any old number at all, flying from out of the jungle with a great free flapping of wings and throwing laughter as they flew—laughter wholly uncontrollable, cackling, giggling, chuckling, schoolgirl laughter, all the different kinds of laughter, obese Bacchanalian laughter, laughter that made great high crescendos, obscene laughter, choking, hissing, bursting laughter, laughter that set me laughing also, laughter that greets a smoke-room story, guttural, gurgling haw! haw! laughter—filling all the sky with it, flinging it out across the sea, making the dour jungle echo it, flooding all the world with ribaldry.

They had their quarrels, though, did those gay laughers. One morning I saw one of them, hunting alone, catch with its beak a small green snake and, laughing uproariously, carry it high up a tree, from where, according to custom, he repeatedly dropped it and caught it again before it reached the ground. Presently some of his fellows came and joined in the game, taking it in turns to drop and catch the snake, and enjoying themselves thoroughly the while. Then one made off with the snake, instead of returning it to the tree-top. The others for a moment were silent, as with astonishment; then came from them an outburst of indignation, and they went after the thief and, cornering him, denounced him—harshly, threateningly, accusingly, telling him he was a traitor to his tribe, one who could not be trusted, that he was no sport—and then, suddenly, one of the crowd boldly snatched away the snake and, with the others in pursuit, fled as the first thief had fled. And for the rest of the day the silence of the bush was so repeatedly fractured, in a different place each time, by an outbreak of that harsh and threatening denunciation that it seemed to me as though every one of those feathered reprobates had a turn at embezzling the snake, and that the matter remained unsettled so long as the reptile withstood the strain.

There were birds which neither quarrelled nor laughed, indeed made scarcely any sound at all, but seemed content with a quiet revealing of a beauty and a daintiness and a grace which was theirs. Among them was a kind so small that I could have concealed one completely within my hand; yet their colours were expansive, complete, ranging from subtle greens and subtler blues to the red of oranges and to blacks with hints of fire in them, with all in between half-tones and shades of half-tones and shades of those again, and the whole so perfectly blended and matched that never was there a touch of conflict or harshness. And, as though they knew that their beauty showed not to the full in the shade, they flew mostly in the sun; and the twinkling of their wings was as in sweet rhythm to the twinkling of their hues; and when they rested among the flowering shrubs of my hedge, as often they did, they looked like flowers themselves. I called them the Birds of the Sun.

Another decorative bird was one called the Rifle Bird, a true Bird of Paradise, and the only one of the very few known to have a habitat outside New Guinea. In the vicinity of the plantation there were not many of them, but most of what there were lived in trees near the house; and early of a morning they would call one to another with a soft and rounded whistling; and presently one or more would come forth and perch so that the sun shone full upon them and gave life and sparkle to the great blue spread of their breasts—a blue like the blue of an old church window, but brighter—and touched with flitting red the collars of gold about their necks, and lent to the blackness of their bodies a sheen as of new coal. And there they would stay, an hour, or more perhaps, admiring themselves and one another, turning this way and that so that the light would be upon them at varying angles, holding themselves vainly, giving to each movement a deliberate grace. And I, entranced, would watch them all the while, but always from between the canes of my veranda's lattice, for despite their vanity they were keenly shy of man.

There was a bird which defied all precedent and cast tradition to the dogs. A cuckoo it was—a true cuckoo, though large as a barnyard fowl—and its revolt against things as they were was contained in the fact that, instead of, in the manner of its kind, depositing its eggs in some other bird's nest for hatching, it built a nest of its own and did all its hatching itself. It was the most independent bird of my acquaintance.

There were certain little friendly birds, cheery, cheeky, cadging birds, which took possession of a clear space of ground before the house, and which became so used to my giving them scraps of food that whenever I appeared they would flutter about me expectantly, and whenever I was absent go up the steps, along the veranda, into the kitchen and steal. I came to know those birds so intimately that I gave them individual names; and they came so to regard the space before the house as their own that if a stranger appeared among them, he was immediately driven away.

And there were flocks of birds which came from distant lands—from Java, from Japan, from islands away to the eastward—for this was a great resting-place for birds in migratory flight: strange birds, some of them, birds obviously ill at ease in these, to them, foreign surroundings, and not a little afraid; birds that scarcely knew where to search for their own particular food; and birds that, because of many previous flights knew the place so well that they stayed here quite a while.

Once I saw two of these stranger-birds come in from across the sea—a queer pair, for one was of one species, and one of another, one being grey of feather and thick of bill, and the other blue and brown of feather and long of bill; and for a time I wondered why two such probable enemies should fly in company. Then it came to me that, stragglers from their respective flocks, they had met in their solitary flight, and determined to sink their antipathies in the need to protect themselves and one another till they came to land once more. Their arrival was the end of an epic of sorts, of dangers endured and survived; and when they dropped exhausted in the grass above the beach, I watched to see what would happen. And the only thing that happened was when they were rested a bit, first one rose, and then the other, and as casually as may be, went off in different ways in search of their long-lost flocks. A common danger had made of these two enemies friends, and now that the danger had passed their intimacy was done.

But while I derived great interest from romantic imaginings such as these, there was always before me the plantation and the jungle's attacking growths. Those growths were a hard actuality, though by now the rains were nearly done and the attack was considerably less insistent and vicious. Sometimes I took a tool and slashed at the growths myself; but one man could do nothing against such a multitude of hostile vegetations. I consoled myself with the thought that the natives when they returned would be fresh from their long resting and be able to give to the task of clearing the palms a vigour they had not given it before.

At times, too, there came to me desire to see a human being—not an overwhelming desire; more a liking than a desire, but sufficiently strong to make me think of various populous places in which I had been, of men in thousands, and tens of thousands, of the crowds I had passed in streets, sat with in trains, in buses, in tramcars, and to whom I had never addressed a word. Here I would have talked for hours to any one of them. It seemed to me that in my time I had wasted a distressing number of opportunities of companionship—and conversation.

As for Togo, my dog, he was very distinctly lonely. He didn't find interest all about him, as I did; the new and strange in his surroundings he had exhausted long before. He seemed to long for the company of other dogs—even the natives' dogs, which, though he had treated them more or less disdainfully, were at least companions of a sort, with whom if need be he could have quarrelled or fought. Now, all he could do was growl at the little friendly birds and, with a great display of ferocity, drive them away, after which he would come to me with on his face an expression which seemed clearly to ask what the deuce had happened to the world that a dog of his breeding and attainments was reduced to the frightening of small and harmless birds. I had never seen a dog so bored as he was.

I wrote much in my diary during that period of solitude, and also read a great deal—I had a plentiful supply of books —always for many hours at night, and often for most of a day. But my primary interest was the interest in the things outdoors. A book was, after all, merely a record of life, and often much of the record was blatantly untrue; outdoors was life itself, and all of it was vividly true.

Even the insects had intriguing aspects. In the dry sand of the upper part of the beach, between the high-tide mark and where the vegetation began, was a kind of earth-fly which lived precariously by trapping ants. The trap was a hole shaped like a wide-mouthed funnel, six or more inches across the top and only half as deep, and at first seeming was merely an accidental depression in the sand. But when it was entered by an ant, the fly, from a place of concealment at the bottom, threw up immediately a puff of sand in such manner that it fell on the ant directly from above; then it sent up other and other puffs, and flurries of puffs, and columns that went up and descended like fountains; and with all this sand falling on him the ant would be forced down and down the slope of the hole, swept off his feet, sent rolling, tumbling, staggering, battered and weak and entirely helpless to where the ingenious engineer of the contrivance awaited him. But that subterranean fly must have often gone hungry, for though the trap lay directly in the midst of thick ant traffic, only rarely did one enter it. Perhaps a word of warning had gone round among the ants.

In a clear space near the back of the house lived a ground-spider whose home was a tube-like hole fitted with a door on a hinge—the door being composed of grass cut into diamond-shaped fragments and bound with an intricacy of silver web. He was a little, grey person, that spider, with small eyes wrinkled like those of a querulous old man; and often did I watch him come home from his hunting of leaf-insects and the like, lift the door and close it after him, exactly as a man lifts and closes the door of a cellar. And as often I would tap the door with a tiny stick, get back out of sight and watch; whereupon the door would open a bit and the little grey person put out his head, turn his wrinkled eyes in all directions, as though wonderingly, and then, apparently concluding he had been mistaken about hearing a knock, go indoors again. After which I would give a further knock, and this time the little grey person would come right out and make an exhaustive investigation of the neighbourhood, going even to the grass edging of his cleared space and looking behind the tufts, moving quickly, jerkily, like a man exasperated and exceedingly annoyed, the while seeming vehemently to exclaim: "Drat those boys!" and when at last he returned to his home it was as though he had determined not to be fooled again, for no amount of knocking would bring him forth once more.

There was a lizard with whom I became quite intimate, even to the extent of naming him George. He was a grey-brown slip of a thing, four or less inches in length, delicately graceful of body and movement both; and each morning, as I breakfasted on the veranda, he would climb the leg of the table and perch at the edge of the cloth, his head high and arched and his tongue showing from between his lips like a triangle of thin pink paper; and there he would remain without stirring—taking no heed of the various noises and movements I made—till the meal was done and I had pushed back my chair. Then he would immediately set to work cleaning up the crumbs, with almost incredible swiftness darting over the plates and between them, circling the saucer and the cup, making diagonal traverses of the table's whole width, flashing this way and that, his slim body twisting and curving and doubling, and the pink triangle of his tongue a dancing spot of colour—and never once pausing a moment, but taking the food in his stride. George's exhibition of nimbleness put me always in good humour for the day, and when at last some accident befell him and he came again no more, I missed him as I would have missed any highly entertaining friend.

I became intimate with the habits and manners of many such creatures as these—creatures which hitherto I had scarcely thought of as possessing habits and manners at all. They became to me companions almost as satisfying as many humans could have been. It was not that I was interested only in the spectacular and peculiar. Others of these companions of mine led lives as dull and drab as the lives of men can be dull and drab—small animals which went about their daily food-hunting quietly and without display; birds which sat unobtrusively among the trees and picked humbly at whatever fruits and berries they could find; insects which performed their common-place tasks in a common-place kind of way. Nor was it of any great importance to me that it was only by the exercise of the imagination that the doings of the others were as the doings of humans—that the little ground-spider was not really annoyed, that the "School Kids" were not really at school, as they sat in a row on their limb. It was merely that I was viewing Life in another—and maybe truer—perspective, understanding and sympathising where hitherto I had not thought there was need to understand and sympathise at all. If only I could have attained the perspective in which the birds and insects and things saw Man, my vision of Things As They Are would have been complete.

But there were creatures with which I had no sympathy at all—snakes. At any time snakes were sufficiently numerous to make journeying through the bush a matter for carrying a stout and springy stick and keeping a wary eye. They were of all kinds and lengths. There were carpet snakes—so called because of their skin having carpet-like patterns—a dozen or more feet long and as thick as the leg of a man, which held no poison in their fangs, but bit as a dog might bite, and as severely, and destroyed their prey by constricting it, afterwards sliming it with saliva and swallowing it whole. In the interior of one I once shot I found the complete body of a kangaroo as large almost as a man. There were brown snakes. also of considerable length, whose bite could have fatal results within four hours; beautiful and glossy they were, and more noiseless of movement than any reptile in my experience. There were black snakes, slim and of the evenness of a piece of rope, some of them having a length of eight or nine feet, but most of them very much shorter; and tiger snakes, striped black on a red-brown background; and yellow snakes splotched with black; and several others of many colours and patterns, lengths and thicknesses, and all of them exceedingly venomous.

But though snakes were so numerous, in all the years I was there cases of people being bitten were extremely rare, the reason for this being that the snakes were timid things, which, despite their venomousness, avoided so far as they could all contacts with men. "Plenty snake look you and me when we walk about, but they run 'way quick feller," a native explained to me once. " 'Cause man all-time fight them, they fright' longa man. S'pose plenty man live this place, then no more snake." He said this, incidentally, in the tone of one who considered that the disappearance of the snakes would be something he would not care to see happen, for to the tribe snake was an article of diet, and the disappearance of an article of diet was distinctly a serious misfortune.

As evidence of this timidity, the snakes when the natives were about kept so almost entirely to the bush that the finding of one in the neighbourhood of the camp or the house was a matter which called from the people cries of astonishment mingled with expressions of belief that some evil-minded spirit had sent it. Now, with the camp deserted, I saw them often about the huts, and their tracks in the sand were numerous. Also, for the reason that there was now but one man present, and no comings and goings of many men, they came frequently to the cleared space about the house—came boldly, insolently, scarcely stirring out of my way when I went forth. In the third month of my solitude I shot eleven of them. But this did not deter them greatly. Indeed, some of them became bolder, coming right up to the front of the veranda and basking as casually as though contemptuous of my gun. I began to think that snakes were not so timid after all. One night one entered the house itself.

That snake provided me with one of the most dreadful experiences of my life, and with certainly the most outstanding event in my period of solitude. It was a little after midnight when it came—a dark night, it was, so close and hot that for an hour or more I had lain restlessly on my bed in the little room, naked save for a Malayan sarong, and so still was it that the lapping of the tide on the beach made a clear and rounded tinkling, and the breathing of Togo, my dog, as he lay asleep on the floor in the other, and larger room, was as a sad sighing, and all other sounds came to me isolated one from another and distinct. Suddenly I heard a slight rustling on the Papuan mats on the floor of the other room. I threw up the mosquito-net, rose, took my gun, lit the gas and stepped to the open doorway, guessing the while what had caused the rustling.

I had only a glimpse of the other room, for the gasometer was empty, and there was only a breath of gas in the pipes, but the flicker of light was sufficient to show me, in the middle of the floor, making straight for the sleeping dog, a carpet snake a full two fathoms long. I shouted, and Togo awoke at once into barking and snapping and snarling activity and much rushing hither and thither; then the gas gave its final flicker and went out, but not before I saw the snake make for the wall and up towards the roof. Evidently it considered that while a dog asleep was one thing, a dog very much awake and filled with active antagonism was another thing altogether.

I made a bonfire of matches on the table which occupied the centre of the room. To have recharged the gasometer would have taken such a time that the snake would probably have disappeared before I finished. The bonfire of matches

G

discovered for me the snake lying along the ridge-pole of the house, and when with a spear that hung on the wall I had poked it till its head was in such position as to allow me to get at it, I shot it—both barrels of a 12-bore shot-gun. And with that the snake's great long length came down and down, till it hung straight over the table and the flaring of the matches like a mighty rope. And then it stopped. Despite the fact that its head was shot almost completely away, it was still filled with life and vigour, and with the end of its tail had taken a good, strong grip of the ridge-pole.

Togo sprang up on the table and sunk his teeth in it. I beat at it with the gun. I jabbed the spear into it. I was more than a little unstrung. Those long weeks of solitude had affected my nerves. That horrible, slightly-swaying rope was something from a place of slimy demons. In the now flickering light its diamond patternings shone like dreadful eyes; when a match exploded they gave quick and vicious gleamings. I could have screamed. I think I did scream. Blood from its shot head dripped on to the bonfire, spluttering. Snake's blood! Frenzied, I beat at its thick, long length, then I dropped both gun and spear and grasped it with my hands and pulled.

Then suddenly the thing released its grip of the ridge and came tumbling down in a mighty monstrous mass that blotted out the bonfire and splashed my face with blood; and the next moment I was hanging on to the doorpost as I had never hung on to anything before, for in falling the Thing had taken around my arm a full round turn, covering it from elbow to shoulder, and with its tail got a grip of the further side of the table in order to give it "purchase"—and was constricting with all its strength. I know I screamed now. I remember screaming, distinctly. The great coil about my arm was hard as iron, and as cold. It was a little slimy. I felt the muscles tauten against mine. The power was terrific. My arm was paralysed. My reason was paralysed. I tried to bite that awful coil. It was like biting steel. With my bare foot I tried to kick at where it stretched to the table. I tried to wrench my arm sidewise and free. I knew these efforts were futile. Still, I tried them. And all the while that cold, hard grip became harder, and seemingly colder. The pain must have been very great, but I was not aware of it. Mental shock had rendered physical shock subservient.

The Thing's half-head hung down from my arm a little way. The blood from it dripped on my foot. My sarong came off, fell on my foot and caught the blood instead. I was thankful for that. Togo was snapping at the head, now and then gripping it and pulling. Sometimes he brushed my naked leg; and the warmth of his body felt gratifying after the coldness of the coil about my arm. I shouted words of encouragement and praise to him, though why I should have shouted them I did not know, for, willing though he was, he could do nothing.

Then, when it seemed to me I had clung to the doorpost for hours—though it was really only a few minutes, as I saw afterwards by my watch—and when my arm was near the breaking, the coil began to slacken. With the pull of the snake upon it, the table was turning over. The snake was losing its "purchase". A moment later the table crashed over, the coil slackened completely, dropped heavily to the floor, and my arm was free. I sprang into my bedroom, found some matches and struck one. The Thing was making slowly out of the main doorway, on to the veranda, Togo still hanging at its head. By the time it had reached the ground where I could see it more or less plainly in the clear darkness, I was ready and waiting for it, and with charges of buckshot blew it to pieces. Then I recharged the gasometer, and lay in the brightness of the light till daylight, trembling as from fever or from cold, afraid to shut my eyes for fear I should see again that monstrous, gleaming rope. And for many nights afterwards I lay fitfully awake because of thoughts of it; while as for Togo, I am sure he knew full well that he himself had been the object of the snake's intrusion of the house, for often he would awaken with a short and sudden yelp and spring up bristling, exactly as though he, too, had imagined a quiet rustling on the Papuan mats of the floor.

That experience disrupted my interest in the life about me. I felt I was a fool to live here like this. My crowded solitude was too crowded altogether. I came to hating it, and so to ache for the presence of humans that for hours at a time I would sit on the beach and stare far down-coast at occasional smokes from the natives' fires and try to persuade myself they were a little nearer than when I saw them last; and whenever the sail of a vessel showed on the shining field of the sea, I would speculate eagerly as to whether it were coming my way. But the smokes stayed always so distant that they were as hints of cloud, and the sails passed steadily on; and I would think again of the men with whom I had sat dumbly in trains and buses and trams, and call myself a fool once more.

And then, early in the fourth month, I had an experience which made on me an impression quite as enduring as the episode of the snake, and rather more eerie besides—an experience which finally determined me never again to live an extended time far from haunts of men. It came about through the attack of my old enemy, New Guinea fever—an attack which for days I fought with quinine and other febrifuges, but which at last so overcame me as to compel me to take to bed.

It was morning when I thus gave in, and hour after hour I lay there, with the fever mounting and mounting and setting fire to my blood, and the quinine giving to my head a mighty throbbing ache, and at sundown came a merciful coma; and when I came out of it the grey of dawn was in the room, and, despite the fact that I was feeble as a month-old child, the fever was utterly gone, and, though I was more than a little awed by the thought that for twelve full hours I had lain there in my solitude as a dead man might have lain there, I was exceedingly thankful for this safe ending of a rather distressing experience.

But there was more to it than that. Some weeks later, the captain of the quarterly store-ship, sitting with me on the veranda, made passing reference to the day of the week as being Thursday. I corrected him—it was Wednesday, I said;

and on his repeating it was Thursday and declaring I must have made a mistake, I brought out my diary and showed him each day and the events of each day carefully entered. That diary was my only means of keeping positive record of the passing of the days, and I was proud of the meticulousness with which I kept it entered up. I almost felt slighted that this man should doubt it. I could have sworn he was wrong.

But he persisted, and in proof that he was right brought forth documentary evidence the truth of which there was no denying, and as further proof called up members of his crew and bade them tell him the name of the day of the week, and at last I knew there was no doubt about my diary being wrong. It *was* Thursday. From my carefully kept record a day was missing. But how that omission had come about I did not guess till some time later, when I realised that instead of awakening from the coma in the dawn of the day following the evening I became unconscious, *it was in the dawn of the day after that.* Instead of lying there like a dead man for twelve hours, I had lain there thirty-six. I had lost a day out of my life, and but for the diary would never have known it. There's something creepy in being in such circumstances that one could lose a day from one's life and never know it.

A. M. DUNCAN-KEMP

THE daughter of a grazier in south-western Queensland, Mrs Duncan-Kemp, in her picture of nature and man in that area, *Our Sandhill Country* (1935), draws upon her experience of the life she knew in childhood as well as in maturity. It is an intimate and faithful record by one whose respect for native customs enabled her to win from the blacks secrets withheld from the women of their own blood.

WHERE THE PELICAN BUILDS

IN some parts of inland Australia the country at first glance resembles a desert, particularly far inland, round Boulia, Bedourie, and towards the centre of Australia. True, the country is very arid, but it is not barren. Give it moisture, and the whole region is transformed. The desert of yesterday blossoms as a flower garden to-day. Red and white sandhills are strewn with vivid bouquets; orange-yellow, rose-red, imperceptibly blend with palest lavender, pink, and buttercup; patches of Wild Almond bushes rub shoulders with acres and acres of blue flax-plant flowers and Wild Turpentine, whose bell-shaped blossoms change from white to lavender as they grow upon the thick-set shrub. The landscape is one riot of colour; the air heavy with scent and vocal with the droning of bees and other insects.

It is difficult to realize that from the first meagre forms of land plant-life Mother Nature evolved all the wonderful varieties that exist to-day. There is no desert so barren that some form of plan or animal life cannot adapt itself and not only survive but flourish under trying conditions.

The Cotton-bush, Bluebush, and other saltbushes have evolved a series of cambium or soft cell tissue which lies beneath the dead bark, dormant, despite years of drought. With the flurry of rains the earth stirs to the throb of pre-natal life, anxious to be up and glimpse the sunshine. Sleeping cells awaken down below the surface of the ground, and these plants grow restless with sap, throwing up new shoots from dead sticks.

South of Bedourie, a small township in south-western Queensland, where the limestone knolls known as the Solitaries rear their bald heads above the Georgina timber, large waterholes are to be found, some fifteen miles long; these holes have never been known to be dry, not even during the biggest droughts.

Strange and interesting is the aquatic life to be found in these stagnant waterholes; myriads of crawling, swimming life abound in all stages of development. Some are not really aquatic, but the larvae of colourful dragonflies, mosquitoes, and numerous other insects.

The surface of the water is the towri of water-striders, pond-measurers, and whirligig beetles. Below the surface lurk little beasts of prey: the water-stick, aquatic bugs, vegetarian water-moths. Sometimes the little water-flea (a transparent mite) can be seen by a patient observer; this minute morsel of marine life is a true crustacean, a diminutive relative of the yabbie and lobster.

Some of the water inhabitants have wings, and at night fly round the lamps in the huts, or about the swagman's head as he reads by a lantern's light. Boatmen and water-scorpions are here, sometimes miles from any waterholes. Lying in the sandy beds of the creeks is the freshwater mollusc or mussel with its ovate grey-white clam shell. The blacks like this mussel; to European palates its pallid flesh is tasteless.

Where the tree-trunks or boughs hang over and on to the water, periwinkles or *accishans*, as the blacks call them, are to be found clinging to the submerged portion of a log or bough. These snail-like creatures are a source of amusement to white children and blacks; they carry their houses on their backs, but unlike the snail they have a hard reddish flap over the front of the shell where their eyes and horns ought to be.

Here are two edible frogs, large, flat, slow creatures which live for years deep down in the mud of dry creeks. They have little storage tanks in their abdomens; by this means they conserve sufficient water or moisture to satisfy their moderate needs until rains fill the holes.

Sometimes, in one spot, rain does not fall for five years. But the blacks, digging down in the beds for soaks, reach the blue-black mud, four or five feet from the sandy surface, and find there the frogs aestivating—the large grey-green one and the minute red-capped singing frog, as well as some species of fish. When lifted out to the light these mud-dwellers are very lethargic. The spawn or slimy eggs of the frogs, shrimps and fishes seem to live indefinitely in the mud of creeks and claypans, patiently waiting their opportunity to hatch when rains fall upon the sun-baked creek-beds.

Here, too, the wild life of the bush abounds, here are the homes of the spoonbills, ibises, cranes, and numberless other waterfowl. Here the black cockatoo builds its home in the hollow limbs of the lofty river gums or coolabahs that fringe the rivers' banks. Three or four white eggs are laid among a mass of leaves that form the nest.

There are two kinds of black cockatoos, the yellow-tailed and the flame-spotted variety. They both have very powerful beaks and can strip the thickest and hardest of bark off any kind of tree. They are slow, heavy fliers with a water-logged flight action, and slow clumsy seed-eaters; the tongue is hardly more than a dry stump. They fly five to ten miles from water and alight for hours upon feeding-grounds, dropping grass seeds everywhere.

The blacks hold them sacred, and touch neither birds nor young. Each season, when the pretty yellow or flame-spotted tail-feathers drop out, the blacks gather them carefully and use them in the sacred corroborees, especially in their elaborate water-totem ceremonies.

Not for nothing do the blacks worship these birds; they are harbingers of water in desert regions. Many birds, and animals, too, head towards water perhaps miles distant. Budgerigars (Grass Parrots) fly twenty or thirty miles for a drink. Not so the black cockatoo; ten miles is as far as he cares to fly. Cattlemen and blacks shun any route or track where there are none of these birds. "No black cockies, no water." And in one memorable instance a cattleman and his blackboy were correct. Six hundred travelling cattle had to face a sixty-mile dry stage in a lively sand-storm.

And in this district the old-time mystery of where the pelican builds her nest is solved. During the nesting-season the hillocks or islands in the lakes and swamps are almost smothered with nurseries of pelicans and wild black swans, as well as thousands of other waterfowl. Acres and acres of eggs are spread over the ashy soil interspersed with grey brushwood or lignum and water. By and by the acres of eggs become masses of downy chicks, squirming and chirping incessantly. It is a miracle how the birds know their own particular nest and young. The air is thick with screaming, fluttering birds. A wonderful sight, which once seen is never forgotten.

It seems strange that wild creatures should breed and flourish in such a barren-looking land; the plains, except where rains fall, are more or less bare of grass-seeds and insects that form the birds' staple diet. Although the holes never dry, they become low and smelly with leaves and droppings of birds and animals. After a year or two without flushing, the holes about the saltbush and saltpan country become brackish, with a strong mineral taste.

Anyone camped on these holes may chance to hear at night sounds of plop, plop, blue brackish mud oozing out from the lower portions of the steep banks and falling into the clear greeny waters. Under ordinary circumstances the water would become muddy and bad—unfit for use. It is the salt ooze minerals, and fallen eucalyptus leaves that help to keep these big permanent holes comparatively healthy.

Another strange fact: on the saltpans or lakes, here, hundreds of miles from the sea, may be found in the nesting-seasons, seafowl—gulls, gannets, and other sea birds. Here, too, are the age-old camping-grounds of the aborigines, who, in the rainy season of the year, when the marshes and swamps were veritable floating birds' nests, came many miles to feast upon the mighty harvest that the gods had sent them on

the bosom of the flood-waters. The harvest still comes every
flood-time, but the blacks no longer gather or feast. Most
of them have long since been gathered to their forefathers;
the region is now peopled mainly by their ghosts.

Scattered over the river-flats and high lands may be seen
the remains of humpies, circular impressions where a one-
time humpy stood with earth scooped out and piled round
the back and sides to form a moat or drain for rain waters;
yerndoos, or cracking stones, where they cracked their shell
food before or after cooking; *jara-jaras*, or large sandstone
grinding-slabs, some with elaborate hieroglyphics and
carvings upon them; stone chisels and bluestone tomahawks;
burnt-out clay ovens; charcoal ridges in the soil that denote
middens and the dead ashes of many camp-fires; a few battered wooden or flint weapons; old wooden coolamons and
smaller pitchis corroded by age and sands; mounds of red
and yellow ochre, in chalky slices or lumps mixed ready for
some long-forgotten corroboree; glittering mounds of crab
and mussel shells bleached white by sun and winds—are all
that remain to record the passing of the original owners of
this bushland. To anyone who troubles to read them, these
mute records unfold a poignant story.

Where the Georgina flows south-westwards after passing
Lake Machattie, the sea of stunted Bluebush and lignum
that marks its channels gives way to a low plateau, where
limestone knolls and wide ashy plains take the place of the
sandhills. A monotonous, lonely country, you may think.
Perhaps, for those who haven't the eye to see. But for those
who have, the country is alive and pulsating with beauty
even during a drought. Every channel, creek, or claypan has
a quaint aboriginal name applicable to itself, every cold camp-
fire or deserted cattle-camp a friendly story to tell.

Ka-ku-ri is one of the native names of this big white
plain; *Toora-kun-gu-ru* is the aboriginal name of Roseberth,
and also of one of the Georgina creeks; *Cuttaburra* is the
old-time name for Glengyle and its creek; *Cutiteera* the
black stockman's name for Annandale station.

Ka-ku-ri means "dry", Toora-kun-gu-ru, "the plain of

Kangaroos", and Tool-koo-roo, the "big red-gravel plains country". There are hosts of others, half forgotten now except by a few old hands. What a wealth of poetry lies hidden in these names! But it takes the caressing tones of a Myall to bring out their rhythm.

To reach the Diamantina from Ka-ku-ri means a rough ride of over seventy miles across a rugged limestone stretch, practically waterless except for the blacks' secret wells, many of which are known only to the *nulunjera* or medicine-man.

The Georgina and the Diamantina are to the back country and its inhabitants what the Nile is to Egypt and the Egyptians. The blacks waited for, and depended largely on, the waters of these two streams for their good seasons and festivals. No rains, no river-floods, no glad festivals; only solemn dour food-ceremonies and frenzied heart-breaking corroborees, enacted by starving drought-weary blacks to propitiate Kun-ma-re, the Rain God.

Before traversing the Diamantina country, let us explore a little farther the green riband of timber that marks the south-west and westward course of the very interesting Georgina. Let us wend our way through the stunted scrubby growth, past clumps of sparkling evergreen saltbush, over patches of flat, pink swamp flowers to the plateau and gaze, as the blacks did long ago, over the waste of plains that are one of the most striking features of the lower Georgina country. Plains everywhere clothed in Bluebush and drab grey-green lignum with occasional clumps of saltbush round their edges. Lines of stunted gidgees mark small gil-gils and anabranches of the larger Georgina creeks.

Curling gossamer threads rise from the far horizon; wreaths of wind-blown smoke coil themselves into hoops or writhe in long spirals or short as black messengers transmit their "talk" in smoke telegraphy from tribe to tribe up and down the rivers. Outer tribes relay to still farther back tribes the news of the moment. Only when they meet a hostile tribe are the messages held up.

The air is filled with the screams and flutterings of myriads of swamp birds, roused from their love-making and domesticities by the sound of hooves and the jingle of bells and hobbles as our pack splashes through the water and up on to the low plateau.

A few hundred yards to the left the Georgina's course is swallowed for a space by a white glistening plain, stretching into the distance until lost in dancing blue waves of mirage. Here lies that home of countless wild fowl, Lake Machattie, so named after Machattie, of Baird, Machattie and Strachan, pioneers of the early eighties. It has an area of a hundred and twenty square miles, and lies some thirty miles south-west of Cluny head station.

We skirted the lake, it being a good thirty-mile ride round it; little water lay about its centre. When full, its depth is anything from two to eight feet, perhaps more. Having no banks, the various winds whip the wavelets from side to side, thus irrigating dry land on either side for half a mile or more; it all depends on the force of the wind and volume of water, which is brackish at first and very salty when at its lowest ebb.

On some of these salt lakes, in the dry seasons, are to be found mound springs and seepages of fresh water. The subsiding flood or surface waters cause mineral deposits and the result is a mound, measuring eight inches to two or three feet in height, with a crater or cup-like depression containing sweet water at its summit; the craters measure, roughly, from two to eight feet across and ten to eighteen inches deep.

These saltpans (or lakes) are usually cracked and scaly, especially so after a long drought. The glistening salt has a pinkish tinge, which blacks call *poora-unna*; the uneven surface of the pan throws into mirage, as if mocking the weary brain, lakes of cool blue water bound by umbriferous scrub, like some glorious oasis in an apparently dead land.

At these springs bird and animal life foregather at early morning and evening to drink, gambol, or preen themselves.

As we rode by Machattie we passed a handful of Short-horn cattle recovering from the effects of a long drought; with soft eyes, wistful, they gazed and sniffed at the green and gold of grass and shrubs as if doubting their reality.

A few station horses fed about or stood in the sun, head to tail, switching at the myriads of flies that hovered round. A drover's pony ambled past with quiet assurance and sipped the water, snorting at its own shadow, ears flattened, pink-rimmed eyes cast back expectantly as if watching an unseen foe.

A whinny, loud and imperious, broke the silence of lignum and saltbush flats; a brumby stallion appeared and trotted along a well-worn pad straight for the water, his harem of sleek matrons behind him. A lovely picture of beauty and unleashed power! Slender tapering ears set on a broad, refined head; long, silky mane and tail fluttering in the breeze, his sleek coat gleaming like mirror velvet; rounded supple limbs with flinty cup-shaped hooves; noble eyes flashing, as ready for a fight as for a drink.

When the chestnut saw our party he stopped abruptly, and with a whistling snort wheeled, as if on a threepenny piece, and galloped off round the lake, disturbing thousands of crested brown pigeons which flashed by to settle amid acres of creamy grass clumps, their black-tufted heads bobbing up and down as they industriously picked the wind-blown seed.

In this limestone and desert country are to be found *nurrawadgerees*, small *gnammas*, and native wells. The latter are narrow holes three to forty feet deep, known only to blacks within the towri and a few bushmen, who, through kindness, have gained the confidence of the natives in that particular territory.

Nurrawadgerees are wells or springs through which moisture seeps at night only; the seepage begins about seven o'clock in the evening, reaching its zenith between eleven and midnight. After that hour the seepage recedes, until by midday the top soil is comparatively dry. Unless initiated into the valuable secret, no one would suspect the presence of water in any shape or form. Some of these night wells secrete sufficient water for man and horse. *Gnammas* are rock holes in the limestone country. Like *nurrawadgerees*, they are rare and jealously guarded by their owners. Several of these watering-places are on sacred ground. The blacks cover them carefully with flat stones to keep out marsupials, emus, and other birds who drink there and make a foot-bath, polluting the clear water.

Blacks gathered their salt supplies from these saltpans, and ate any edible roots or grubs found in the vicinity. No doubt the saline properties of the water and edibles enabled the blacks to travel long distances and go practically all day in blistering heat with hardly a pint of water—features particularly noticeable among blacks and stock who live in saltbush and saltpan country.

Another attraction, one of the principal ones for the blacks, was the pituri plant, which grew upon the banks of various Georgina creeks. A narcotic shrub of the *Duboisia Hopwoodii* order, it was much sought after by all tribes who used it in their harsher tribal initiations to deaden pain and fear, and to chew on long marches, for, when taken in small quantities, pituri has a decidedly stimulating effect.

Plenty of good grazing land lies round the Machattie region. Most of it is only suitable for cattle culture and must be held in large areas. The greatest difficulty is the absence of regular rainfall; another trouble is the lack of evenly distributed water for stock. There are the permanent creeks and river channels, but, unfortunately, they are all in one place. It seems a pity that nature was not more considerate and generous in her distribution of waterholes. A thousand pities, too, that there is no method, as yet, of conserving the hundreds of millions of gallons of precious water that rush foaming down these sun-baked channels every flood-time—only to be wasted. Water in these regions is often more important than grass. Many runs have abundance of dry feed but no water, unless the owners go to the considerable expense of a deep bore. Sometimes the water is there, but on the wrong end of the run, twenty or thirty miles away.

Both the Georgina and Diamantina have subterranean waters. In dry seasons large soaks (*mickeries*) capable of watering numerous stock, can be obtained by digging down into the sandy channel beds.

The Georgina is the more favoured in this respect; its channels are more sandy and with better holding clay at their bases than the Diamantina's. Still, there are no complaints about that river.

The age-old channels of the Georgina, their cracked banks resembling brick-kilns, twist and turn in their gnarled courses, receive the Mulligan above Kalidgaworra station, take a sharp turn south past Cutiteera and, finally, cross the South Australian border to be lost, except in exceptionally rainy seasons, in the loose, ever-shifting sands—the fate of many useful rivers and creeks.

FRANCIS BIRTLES

FRANCIS BIRTLES, author and explorer, was born in Melbourne.
He played an important part in opening up new territory in the Australian inland. His *Battle Fronts of Outback* (1935), mainly a record
of some of his work in South Africa and Australia, contains in addition
the story of his pioneer motor drive from England to Australia.

IN ARNHEM LAND

I was on my way to Arnhem Land, to see new country
and to have a few months with my old friends the
blacks.

Kangaroos were lolling about beneath shady trees. A big
old-man 'roo rose from his noonday camp, where he had
been having a nap. He wiped his eyes with the backs of his
paws and stood erect, throwing his chest out and his head
back, and looking proudly defiant at the throbbing machine
as I brought it to a halt. He was showing off before his
harem of several wives.

Quietly I gave the word to my dog, who slipped overboard, sneaked quickly and unseen through the grass from
behind, grabbed the buck's tail and upended him. Grabbing
my camera I ran over to the mix-up, but the 'roo broke away
and departed rapidly, following in the direction that his
wives had already taken.

I camped on a waterhole, and a brownbacked, grey-
breasted bower-bird came hopping around, looking at the
bright parts of the car. Taking fright, it flitted into a nearby
bush. From the bush there came the sound of a frog screeching in agony. Then a distant kite-hawk spluttered and
whistled. A young crow was heard practising its notes. I
heard the rustle of dry boughs in the wind. The bower-bird
was the cause of it all, giving a marvellous imitation of these
sounds.

I pushed on, the nose of my car headed for the tropics.
Little ghost sprites of dust sprang up and danced across the

shimmering plain. Blasts of heated air came from the stony ridges and patches of scalded earth. The steady hum of the engine caused me to doze over the wheel once or twice. Toward noon I halted in the shade of a gum-tree with about six leaves on it, boiled the billy, and ate a meal. All signs of life had disappeared, even the flies. I was drawing on my emergency water, as the car was using it at the rate of about a gallon to ten miles. The lime, soda, and alkali sedimentary deposits created great heat.

Cloud-flecked was the blue sky, giving a promise of rain. The car was delving into brown, powdery dust, which the front axle would scoop up in a blinding swirl, right over the top of the hood. In this shadeless land lean cows were standing to create a shadow where their young calves might rest.

In low gear I forced the car along over the devil-devil lumps and the big cracks in the ground. The tracks led on through a large pool of water on a claypan. Dinkum anxiously started to look and sniff. For a few minutes I was, myself, deceived. It was a mirage. Half an hour later we halted on the steep, clay banks of a waterhole. There was no shade thrown except from the leafless limbs of a cockatoo-eaten tree. Out into the yellow muddy water I swam. It was lukewarm but I swirled up some that was icy-cold, and then I filled the water-bag and canteen.

With my rifle I shot some ducks. The entrails I put into an empty benzine-tin and lowered it into the water. In a few minutes I hauled it out again quickly. Several shrimps were inside. With these I baited and threw out some fishing lines. Yellow-belly, or golden-perch, up to a few pounds in weight, bit readily. As I angled, V-shaped flying squadrons of pelicans winged their way northward toward the Gulf of Carpentaria. The plaintive cry of black cockatoos also interested me. They did not, as a rule, inhabit the regions I was traversing. There must have been a big drought in the unexplored land.

That afternoon I rescued a calf that was being attacked by a mob of dingoes. Something attracted my attention when passing by the scraggy trees surrounding a water-hole. I

H

alighted and, stalking between the trunks, got within fifty
yards of the disturbance. There were fourteen wild dogs, some
white and others yellow. The mother cow would charge into
the mob. They would open out and stand back a few yards.
Some would stretch out on the ground and yawn. The calf
would stand up, shivering with fright and pain, in front of
its protector, only to be knocked down again by the cow
as she charged a dingo that gambolled in front of her. Then
the dogs would close in again. To watch them it seemed as
if they were playing a casual game. It was a real battle, and
it was being fought in deadly silence. There was no snarling,
bleating, or bellowing.

With my .44 I blazed into the pack. Dingoes bolted in
all directions. Some, not seeing me in my hiding-place behind
a tree-trunk, came leaping my way, and, seeing Dinkum
moving toward them, halted to give fight. He would have
been badly mauled. Yelling, I ran at them, firing as I went.
My dog grabbed one by the throat, but could not get a firm
hold. He came back to me and spat out a mouthful of hair.
The dingoes scattered, and the cow and the calf trotted away
up a gully.

Sweeping torrents of dust enveloped the car as we ran
before the wind. Kangaroos, in little groups, were camped,
stooping, with their backs to the gale. It was interesting to
see the young ones sheltering under the lee of the mothers,
who crouched over them. They all ignored the car. Rain
started to spatter down, and the dust disappeared. Soon,
clods of sticky soil were being hurled up by the wheels.
Lumps like bricks were landing on top of the hood. At sundown I came out on to dry land.

On the McArthur I pitched my camp and arranged with
a mob of natives to go down the river in canoes, as it was
impossible, at this point, to proceed right down the coast by
car, for the native wells were all dry. Some hundreds of
coastal natives were scattered along the river, hunting and
fishing. They had walked scores of miles to come in before
the wet seasons for the annual young-man-making ceremon-

ies. In connection with these a fight was being enacted down the river.

Out on a grassy plain I sighted them, scattered groups of wildly excited beings. A few spears were whizzing and boomerangs were hurtling. Angry and voluble were the arguments; impolite, forcible, and uncomplimentary were the actions and the language. The women were taking part in it, making vicious swings at each other with fighting-sticks, screeching, scolding, and leaping. Children were crying and dogs were howling. Painted men neatly dodged missiles of war thrown by others who jumped up out of natural hollows in the ground, and disappeared.

Several sad-looking young men were sitting in the shade of a big tree. They had not eaten food for days. They were to be the chief figures in the evening's ceremony. They had to go through these rites before they could gain the women of their parents' choice. One, a Boorooloola boy, confided to me, "Too much marry no good. Too much stop in one place."

The young men were being subjected to endurance tests to prove their fitness or otherwise for the status of manhood, among which was starvation. They had been required to spend a day and a night, without protection, in a mosquito-infested swamp, leaving it at moonrise in the evening; they had been forced to lie all day, naked, in the blazing sun. To increase their torment their heads had been swaddled in soft paper-bark. While they lay there, coolamons of stinging insects had been poured on their sweating bodies. They were forbidden to cry out or exhibit any sign of suffering. The weaker ones sometimes died as a result of the hardships of these ceremonies. If one of the older men had reason to be jealous of one of the young men being initiated—perhaps wanting his girl—he would not be above increasing the young man's torture in the hope that it would kill him.

While the young men were going through these ceremonies—which lasted about a fortnight—the old men of the tribe instructed them in the ancient tribal laws. They were told of the laws governing women, marriage, hunting, and food.

There was the law of the four blood-groups, the Fish, the Reptile, the Bird, and the Animal, which of these might mate and which might not. This was knowledge that had come down by word of mouth from the dim past. It was regarded as being of greater importance than all the other laws; and over the finer distinctions involved many arguments had occurred among the elders. While the young men were enduring the pangs of hunger and thirst the corroboree-singer came and sang to them the Song of the Barramundi. It was a lengthy song, rendered in an expressive tenor voice. It depicted the barramundi gliding through the cool waters; obtaining his food; swimming leisurely in the shade of the river-bank trees; darting hungrily upon his prey; and, at last, gliding from sight into the depths of the stream.

While the ceremonies were going forward I decided to go down-river. Early one morning we were afloat, navigating a cockle-shell of a dinghy with a tarpaulin as sail. Two dug-out canoes accompanied us. They were loaded with an assortment of yabbering, singing natives, whining dogs, cooked reptiles and fish. Each put up a sail made out of an old Government blanket. They rippled along, one on each side of the stream.

Sometimes the sun would reflect on a shining lump floating on the water. This would slowly sink out of sight—it was a wet crocodile watching the proceedings. A white blob on the water ahead kept bobbing up and down, travelling sea-wards. With difficulty we over-hauled it, and it proved to be a white goat carcass being towed along by a crocodile. The blacks kept away from it for fear of the crocodile showing fight and upsetting the canoes. They came paddling toward us, a curve of water under their bows showing the power behind the hefty paddlemen's stroke. The canoes were balanced on the gyroscopic principle of "keep moving along". A line of bubbles showed where the crocodile was crawling along the mud-silted bottom. From the banks of the river, as we drifted along, sounded nature's alarm. From woodland creature to flying bird the approach of man was heralded. That curse of the stalking hunter, the ever-watchful

and squawking white cockatoo, was spying on us from
overhead. Then the animal warning. In the scrubs we could
hear the thud of wallabies making away along their pads.

Splotches of yellow sand, stirred up from below on
a three feet deep sand-bank, meant sport. The aboriginal
never tires of his spear. It was a stingaree digging in, in an
effort to evade the notice of a hungry shark that was lurking
at a little distance. Quivering with eagerness the spearman
peered into the murkiness below. Savagely he drove a spear
downwards. A fleeting shadow below the surface darted into
shallower water. Streaking along the top like a periscope was
the spear-shaft. It came to rest again.

Leaping overboard, with spears quivering ready to strike,
three natives waded after it. The shark was still hovering
about. The periscope streaked toward a native, then a big
floppy mass volplaned along the surface. Yelling, scattering,
and scared of the stabbing barb with which the stingaree was
equipped, the natives hurled spears into it. Flopping feebly,
its blood tinging the waters, it sank to the bottom. From there
it was hauled ashore. The barb was at once broken off, to be
used later for a spear-head.

On landing I shot a wallaby. The natives cooked it by
putting red-hot stones inside it and burying it in the hot
sand. As a delicacy they made a haggis of various parts.

A glorious sight to be seen in the Gulf country at the
monsoon changes, and known as the "Evening Glory", appeared in the sky. Swiftly moving gloomy clouds, golden-
edged from the setting sun, rolled up from seaward. Arched
across this was a rainbow. The spectacle had a strange effect
on the natives. The rainbow was their traditional omen of
danger. All yabber and chatter ceased around the camp-
fires. Their smiling faces became downcast, their eyes held
a look of furtiveness and uneasiness, their nerves were on
edge. They remained like this until the sky cleared—then all
was well.

During the next few days I tramped about the surrounding
country. It was almost all open forest with small grassy
plains. Fine shady trees were everywhere. Numerous smoke-

signals were to be seen. Distant tribes were coming in, hunting as they marched, to the man-making ceremonies, enacted just before the wet season commences. Some of these young men were with my party. They anxiously watched all the native tracks for the footprints of both friend and foe. By the tracks they could name every aboriginal who had passed. One pair of small footprints, pigeon-toed, with two toes missing from the left foot—probably burnt off while the owner had been sleeping too near his camp-fire—was a cause of speculation and concern. They were the tracks of an old reprobate who acted as medicine man, astrologer, doctor, wizard, rain-maker, hauler out of devils from the body, etc., at the forth-coming rituals. Having not yet reached manhood the young men were privileged to show fear. Incidentally, these young men are often the best to take on a long journey. Married men are liable to disappear without notice. They all suspect their wives and the other fellow.

All day long food-supplies were brought in. These were roughly sorted out and cooked by the men and women who were considered too old to go hunting and digging. The amount of food brought in would determine the duration of the ceremonies. Mysterious little groups were scattered about down in quiet gullies, busily painting themselves and their boomerangs.

As the sunset glow faded away behind scraggy overhanging pandanus palms, there arose the sound of tapping boomerangs, the booboo of didjeridoos, the odour of baking meats and the subdued hum of many voices. The orchestra was tuning up, or rather, warming up for the opening scenes. The flickering of the firestick torches from various directions moved toward the reflection of a big bonfire, against which were outlined moving nude shapes and grotesque phantoms.

From out of the dark scrubs came a shouting challenge. Into the circle of firelight came a branch-waving, white-painted group of aboriginals, spears at the ready, the barbed points quivering as they danced toward a common centre. Knees knocking together, toes turned in, bodies wriggling, they gave a quaint exhibition of the very latest in dingo trots.

Loud boomed the didjeridoos, emphasizing the downward stamp of feet. Clackety-clack tapped the boomerangs, giving the time to the dancers' bodily movements. A monotonous clop-clop came from the many hands of the audience.

High above the babel of sound came a quivering falsetto voice—wailing of the trees of the dead men. From the outside darkness a blunt pointed spear whizzed into the group, slid snakily and fast along the ground, leaving a streak of dust behind. It was smartly dodged. The master of ceremonies promptly stepped forward, spear at the ready, peering toward and cursing at him who had thrown the spear and who represented the hidden enemy. This ended the first part of the ceremony. The dancers took their places among the audience. The meat was brought, and feasting commenced with much laughter and shouting.

After supper the greater part of the audience dispersed. This was in accordance with tribal law. The women and children went first, weeping and wailing, then the younger men. At last only the young men who were to be initiated and the old men were left. Their ceremony, which was a secret one, lasted until dawn.

The sun rose that morning upon weary groups of overfed, underslept, bleary-eyed natives. They gossiped in undertones. In the white ashes of the burnt-out camp-fires a conglomeration of women, children, and dogs slept. Remnants of meat and half-picked bones strewed the camp. Swarms of flies seethed everywhere. In the tree-tops hungry crows cawed and croaked; and a hot tropical sun shone over all.

I left the camp that day and, with the two boys, I sailed back up the river. Reaching the motor-camp I spent a few days overhauling and repacking for the journey around the coast to Arnhem Land.

The car, in low gear, was slowly pushing a way through fifteen feet high grass. The heavy log bumper-bar, swinging from the front dumbirons, forced the growth downwards in long graceful swaths. It passed beneath the chassis with a peculiar hissing sound. The revolving drive-shaft was packed tightly all round and looked like a huge cotton-reel.

To front and sides the extent of vision was limited to the wall of grass, but looking backwards, there could be seen the lane along which we had come. Some natives were following us, for heads and shoulders, bobbing up and down, could be seen. The heat of the tropic noon, inside that forest of grass, was intense. The grass-dust was stifling, and the glare from the wall of stalks made our eyes smart and become inflamed.

There was danger of fire from the red-hot exhaust-pipe. Several times small fires started among the rubbish that lay a foot deep inside the car. Each time I doused them with water from the water-bag. We had a hundred and twenty gallons of petrol aboard, several gallons of oil, a case of cartridges, and thousands of feet of cinematograph-film.

The grass plain gradually became rougher and rougher, and developed into that curse of the overlander known as devil-devil country. At the bases of the tall grasses were eighteen inches high tussocks. These caused the car to swerve and buck, making driving both difficult and tiring. Prickly-grass seed-heads came zipping over the radiator like millions of small arrows. They pierced the clothing and penetrated the flesh with their minute but thickly barbed ends.

The long grasses began, almost imperceptibly at first, to change colour and character. They became greener and ranker. My two aboriginal boys got out and made their way ahead, stabbing sticks into the ground in order to test for underlying bog, and I followed slowly with the car. We halted. There was a two hundred yards wide bog. It could not be avoided as there were big swamps at each end of it, at a distance of a mile or so. We had a special method of crossing these belts of bog. The aboriginals who had been following us now came limping up. They had been forcing their way through these lands for some days. The long grasses dragging between their skinny legs had made the inside parts raw. They were bleeding and full of prickles. In their usual hunting walkabouts these places would have been avoided until dry enough to burn off thoroughly.

They got to work on the long bamboo-like growths in

the channel. The bog was bottomless and the car would sink out of sight if it once got off the track we were about to make. The grass was smashed and trodden down systematically. The lower layer was put down fore and aft of the way the car was to go, and to the full width of the wheel track. The adjoining reeds were then bent over and stamped crossways over the first layer. In a couple of hours we built a very effective semi-floating bridge to the firm land on the other side.

We off-loaded and carried the kit across, then partly deflated the tyres and put chains on. Gently I drove the twenty-three hundred-weight mass on to the partly floating reeds. The bridge sank down until the muddy soakage was up to the axles. The top layer of cross reeds started to float, and the bumper-bar scooped these along until they bunched three feet high. To overcome this, the natives stood on the reeds, yard by yard, as the car moved along at a snail's pace. Then, for the last few yards, I fastened the crocodile-trapping flexible wire rope to the car and the natives hauled steadily as I let the clutch in.

The car was sinking right down, as the reeds were quickly losing the air that was enclosed in them. I took a chance and stepped on the accelerator. The car made a dive at the natives as it came safely out.

Ahead of me was a wonderful sight. Whirling clouds of woolly white smoke were going up thousands of feet into the air, a winding white column against the blue. Below the white smoke were majestic rolling banks of black smoke, hundreds of feet high and miles long. Beneath all was a lurid red glow. Among the swaying trees of a tea-tree forest, flames were leaping, crackling, and thundering. Across the plain the fire was making a clean sweep of the long grass at a rate of about ten miles an hour. It might travel hundreds of miles, right across the big buffalo plains for which we were bound. So I sat and watched for a couple of hours in order to let the stifling smoke clear away.

Far away to the south was a line of blue hills. Long columns of smoke were rising, one by one, and coming toward us.

The "Stone Men of the Hills" were replying to us. They, too, were coming down to the coastal plains to eat of fish and of buffalo meat. "Mulga wires" had told them of the arrival of "Motocar Frank" and plenty of tobacco. I always encouraged them to visit me. I was fond of fishing and shooting, and with plenty of blacks to eat the spoils of the chase I could pursue my hobby untroubled by the dislike of needless waste and killing. It also gave me a chance to study and photograph them.

That afternoon the country changed to tea-tree flats and open forest. The ground surface was of a heavy, sandy loam. Everything was black from the bushfire. Soot, ashes, and smoke came swirling along in suffocating eddies. My two blackfellows were blacker than ever. I, too, was quite black, and a powdering of charcoal covered the kit in the car.

On low gear, nearly axle-deep in sand, the car boiled along. Sometimes it was necessary to charge across acres of those infernal burrows of sand goannas. The axle would strike and scoop up blinding, choking showers of ashes and hot cinders. Once a back wheel stuck deep in a hole right alongside a hollow tree that was blazing inside like a furnace. The limbs overhead were ablaze, and at any moment one of them might have fallen on top of the car.

When once more moving onwards, the fiery branches of the burning trees that we passed were a danger, and the two natives, seated on top of the baggage, kept a sharp look out. When we came to a safe spot I gave the over-heated engine a rest, while the aboriginals got down and hunted for snakes, goannas, and bandicoots that had taken refuge in hollow logs and ground holes. All this tuckout was put on top of the rear luggage. One item of their collection, a big rainbow snake, came to life again! We were driving along. The first hint I got of the snake's return from the shades was when the two blacks tumbled over backwards and fell off the bouncing car. I had no shirt on. The reptile slithered across my spine, went downwards among the cargo and stowed away there.

I pulled up, but found that the aboriginals' interest had

become centred on some tracks on the ground—they forgot
the snake. They pointed to the spoor of a big bull-buffalo.
We decided to follow it up. They trotted in front while I
came close behind with the car. We were still two days'
journey from the real buffalo-hunting ground.

Suddenly there were yells and a stampeding crash: a big
bull rushed out from among the bamboos, halted for a
moment, swung round at sight of the car, and then leapt
over the edge of a ten feet deep breakaway. He stumbled on
to his knees, got up, and rushed away up the other side of
the creek. We were beef-meat hungry! The creek was un-
crossable here, so I abandoned the car and all hands got on to
the bull's tracks. The aboriginals, as they walked rapidly along,
kept stooping over, picking up dust and rubbing it under
their armpits. They said it was "to kill smell alonga black-
fellah."

Now, a wounded bull-buffalo is one of the most dangerous
of big game. He is cunning and will lie down, or wait behind
a tree, until the pursuing hunter has gone past. He will then
charge—and he is a devil of wickedness. His victim, once
down, is trampled and smashed to pieces. His senses of hearing and smell are very acute.

One man tracked while the other black and I kept a sharp
look out. Presently a medley of mongrel yelps told us that
a mob of natives must have discovered the old bull. The
sound came from a spot half a mile ahead of us. Arrived at
the place where the blacks and dogs were gathered, we found
the bull at bay in a pool. He had his stern up against a clay
bank that was overhung by a bushy tree. Now and then
he would charge out at the dogs that were tormenting him,
and strike at them with his front hooves. The aboriginals
were holding off as they did not want to smash up their
spears on the tough hide.

As I came panting up, the bull came out on to the bank
of the pool. He was covered with mud. Water streamed off
him. His little tail kept twitching, and his eyes were red and
bleary. The natives had not waited for his near approach.
They were swinging from branches or scrambling up tree-

trunks. He backed into the water again and would not come out. I did not want to kill him there. The position was badly placed for skinning—and I would have to drink that water at night. But there seemed to be nothing else for it. One of the swimming dogs got within range of him and he butted it, smashing it to pulp against the clay bank by using his bony forehead in a series of short jabbing stabs.

While he was prodding I fired and the bullet struck him at the base of the big horns, and he dropped. The natives rushed in and hauled the carcass to shallower water. It took them some time to do this as it was then dusk. To enable them to see to carve up the beef a big fire was lit and kept blazing. The night wind was chilly, and the shivering, naked natives hacked off lumps of meat which they warmed at the fire and devoured while it was still quivering.

The following day we went on our way, and two days later reached the real buffalo country.

We had not far to seek for game. Just as we were ready to start, we saw, away in the distance, what appeared to be dots of light moving slowly through the timber. These were buffalo coming out of the jungle, with their dew-wet backs reflecting the slanting light of the sun. We mounted and set out. Stiffy—I had nicknames for the boys—was in the mechanic's seat as tracker and pilot. Moses was jammed into a cubbyhole in the back of the car as observer.

I took the car out on to the plains and began to circle the mob of quietly feeding buffalo. As we got closer the cows with calves became restless. They trotted out toward the car and then bolted back again. Then the mob started to ring. They opened out, cantered, and then broke into a lumbering gallop.

Selecting a big fat cow I opened up the throttle. Clouds of dust rose from the flying herd. Bumping and heaving over tussocks at twenty-five miles per hour, the car, with difficulty, got in amongst them. With a burst of speed I drove the car up to the animal I had chosen and ranged alongside. I was steering with one hand, and with the other I gripped my shortened .303 carbine. Watching a chance, and almost touching the ribs, I fired. Down fell the beast. Out of the dusty mist the dim forms of buffaloes were racing along, the roar of the open exhaust subduing the thunder of their hooves.

I was fearful lest we should strike the timbered edge of the plain—in the dust there was no seeing where we were going. Then just as a bull was about to gore the racing car, I dodged abruptly. We very nearly capsized. For a moment the bull was thus going in the opposite direction to us. He swerved and followed at a great pace. We struck a flat claypan, where I was able to speed up to forty miles per hour. A belt of thick timber lay ahead. The buffalo had fallen astern, but he was going—or rather—coming strong. I pulled up suddenly and the boys made a beeline for a nearby tree. The enraged bull stopped a hundred yards away. He shook his massive head. His attention was diverted from the car to the two blacks, both trying to climb the young tree at the same time. He started to trot, swinging his head down between his forelegs and then bringing it up again with a long powerful sweep of his horns. He broke into a gallop, heading for the slim tree on which the thoroughly scared boys were perched. All this happened while I was reloading the rifle-magazine.

The first shot made him slew round and come straight for the car. As his head threw upward at thirty yards I fired for the throat. He stumbled, but came on. I made a frantic, running jump to get on to the other side of the car. Dinkum scrambled to meet the buffalo and, dodging the beast's fore-end, expertly grabbed him by a hind leg. The bull swerved to meet this new opponent. I got a side-on shot at the shoulder-blade. He went down, with Dinkum still hanging on.

We flayed the bull and, after removing the best cuts from the carcass, returned to where the cow had been shot. Our activities had attracted the attention of local blacks. While we were skinning the cow they came streaking toward us across the plain to make friends and to share in the supply of "strong fellah beef". Very seldom would they themselves

attack a buffalo; not only because of the breaking of spears
into the making of which much time and labour had gone,
but because of the days that would often have to be spent
in tracking down the dangerous, wounded beast until it became too exhausted to move. It was not long before I had a
camp-following of bucks, lubras and piccaninnies sufficient
in number to consume gratefully all that my rifle would
provide.

The next day I encountered a cow-buffalo and two calves
coming down toward the water. It would have been useless
slaughter to have used the rifle—the blacks were miles away
—so I lay watching them. A few minutes later another cow and
a big bull came trotting playfully down. On the edge of the
pool they drank deeply and then waded out into deep water,
eating the tops off the water-lilies and softly squawking to
each other. The very young buffalo has a call like a child's
trumpet being blown, but the mature beasts are almost voice-
less; the best they can manage is a frog-like croak.

A hundred yards away from where the buffaloes were
feeding two pairs of bubbles appeared on the surface of the
water. They were the eyes of two crocodiles looking greedily,
I have no doubt, but fearfully, I think, at this supply of
succulent beef. The old bull must have seen them. He began
to blow nervously, then the small herd started to heave and
splash toward the opposite shore. The wind changed, and
they caught a sniff of my camp, which they had not, up till
then, noticed. Clattering away over a rocky bar, they trotted
into the gloomy depths of the jungle.

Next morning, and I was once more on my way. Out on
the plains hundreds of beasts were peacefully feeding on
the short sweet grass. The number of these creatures—
Asiatic water-buffalo really—in the north is astonishing. They
were originally imported from the Orient for the use of the
pioneers at the long since abandoned settlement at Port
Essington. Going bush, they multiplied until thousands of
their descendants roam over the ten thousand square miles
of the Territory coastal lands. They never wander inland,
but keep to country adjacent to the Arafura Sea. They are

gregarious when on the open plains, grazing hundreds in a mob. When not feeding they go in little parties to their mud wallows and haunts in the tidal mangroves, river, and bamboo-swamps. They are of enormous strength, being bigger than any domesticated cattle, and are courageous and keen-witted in an emergency.

I intended rejoining the blacks, as they would be looking to me for further supplies of "strong fellah beef". The buffaloes took very little notice of my passing across the plain. Here and there one would arise from under a shady tree or from a wallow in a swampy pool and gaze at the growling car, but that was all.

Two young bulls attracted my attention. Their antics were so strange that I stopped the car and started to stalk them with my camera. One was amusing himself by driving his powerful horns into a big ant-bed, and, with an upward swing, throwing the earth all over himself. Near him two birds of the plover variety were skipping about picking up the swarms of white ants rendered shelterless by him. Near by a cheeky brolga was waiting to get a chance at all this wriggling tucker. The buffalo, sighting this long-legged bird, charged. There was a dead even sprint for about fifty yards. then the brolga flew, the buffalo passing just beneath it. The other buffalo was resting on the shady side of an ant-bed, head down, half asleep, stern against the mound. The beast that was in playful mood turned from his pursuit of the brolga, lowered his head and charged the ant-bed, striking it full tilt. It tipped over—it must have weighed half a ton—on top of the beast that was dozing. He lunged to his feet in a cloud of dust, then they both made off in opposite directions. This alarmed the whole mob. They gathered, and with a thunderous sound of hooves and a crashing of vegetation tore into a bamboo thicket.

Ahead of me smoke-signals were rising. I walked over to where some giant paper-barks were growing in a swamp and at the base of one put a firestick. In a few minutes the tree was blazing from top to bottom, sooty black smoke curling upwards into the air. Then I followed along the tracks of the retreating buffalo. In the jungle, at a little distance, I heard yodelling "Yak-khis" called to me from various quarters. Then, laughing and calling out, a group of aboriginals greeted me. The hurtling mob of buffalo had scattered them in all directions—mostly into tree-branches.

Looking down into a ravine I heard yells coming from its depths, so I left the car and followed the natives cautiously. Moses had met a wild bull, not a buffalo, but a bad-tempered, red-eyed, russet-hided cleanskin. It had taken a dislike to the native's red loin-cloth and had charged. He had, with the speed of a scared goanna, climbed up the first escape available—a looping, prickly jungle vine—and was now clinging to this. Every time he tried to climb up a little higher the vine disobligingly slipped down a little. Below was the bull, rampant, slobbering froth, pawing at Moses's hat, which had fallen to the ground, and now and then gazing up at the boy.

Dinkum went to Moses's rescue in true cattle-dog style, attacking from the rear. The boy took quick advantage of the distraction. He dropped to the ground and, like a flash, scrambled up the steep banks of the ravine. The aboriginals wanted me to shoot the bull, but I had no liking for a rough and tumble scrimmage with a possibly wounded and savage bull among the hooked and clinging lawyer-vines.

We left him and soon afterwards the boys got on to the tracks of some of the buffaloes. They picked out the tracks of a fairly large beast and followed it briskly, while I followed behind in the car. The nature of the country, plain and jungle, forced me to make short detours. I was returning toward the blacks when I saw from their behaviour that something was happening. They were snapping their fingers excitedly. Hearing them, I stopped the car and ran forward. In and out among the timber and the ant-beds, a buffalo calf that had lost its mother in the stampede was struggling with two dingoes. One had a grip of its throat and the other was hanging on to its belly-flank. It had its four legs outstretched, trying to stop the calf from running. I shot one dingo. Dinkum and a black-fellow's dog tackled the other. There was a

HERON ISLAND; CAPRICORN GROUP

"Winter or summer"

INLAND PLAINS

"A wonderful awakening"

glorious scrimmage that ended only when the dingo was cleverly speared by one of the blacks.

Moses grabbed the calf by the tail—on seeing us it had, with misplaced faith, come trumpeting toward us. The blacks wanted the calf for tuckout, so they killed it. Camp was made at a muddy buffalo wallow. No stones being available for cooking purposes the boys obtained clay and, after rolling it into balls, placed them on top of the camp-fire to dry and become red hot. These were placed on top of the buffalo veal, after it had been put in a shallow hole and covered with water-soaked tea-tree leaves.

While the meat slowly roasted, the natives made long rolls of grass. Using these as drags they netted the wallow and brought out scores of small fish and yabbies. These were cooked on the coals of the camp-fire and eaten straightway, just as an appetizer for the forthcoming feast.

At night I lay for a little while, identifying the noises. An owl, alighting on the car, softly called "Whuk-wuk! Whuk-wuk!" For a while there was silence. I heard the scuffle of his wings as he flew away. Not long after, frantic guttural noises were intermingled with hisses. The owl had met a native wild cat and a fight to the death was taking place. Amongst the long grasses a frog screamed; rapidly its cry came closer and closer. Then I felt it bury itself in the folds of my net. There was a slithering sound and then quietness. I switched on my hand-torch and, without moving my body or raising my head, put the beam where the frog was hiding. A snake was prodding its head in and out of the folds of my net. The light disturbed it and it slipped away into the darkness.

As a lurid morning sun peeped over the dense mangroves the tide was nearly at the full. Wanting bait, I walked over to a deep rocky pool in a nearby creek. This was teeming with pilchards, so I tied three hooks together in grapnel shape. fastened on a line, threw out, and then hauled in rapidly. This acted as a jag on which several fishes were impaled. I got some crickets, too, in case the fish would not take the

I

pilchards. These were got simply by shovelling the loamy sand into the water and catching them as they swam ashore.

I was after the fifty-pound barramundi, which I could hear rumbling and turning over the stones in deep water at the foot of a small red bluff. They were hunting out small red crabs.

Now and then one would come swirling up in pursuit of its prey. Sometimes this would be a flying fish, and there would follow an exciting race along the surface of the water. It was comic to watch this, as invariably there would come tearing along the fin of a shark, and Mr. Barramundi would leap upwards, an affrighted, gleaming streak of silver against the blue sky. Sometimes, in his fright, a barramundi would became stranded in a maze of ever-shallowing channels.

Old-man crocodile soon became aware of this. He sneaked cautiously along the bottom. There would be a terrific bang of his powerful tail and a stunned barramundi would fall back to be grabbed in his grim jaws. The saurian would then waddle out on to the sand-bank and, like a dog chewing a bone, dine slowly but heartily.

There were watchful eyes other than mine. Even as the fish's head fell from the crocodile's munching mouth there was a swoop of white wings. Swinging talons seized the tit-bit, and a fish eagle zoomed upward, circled, and made away to a six feet wide nest in the head of a cypress pine.

The tide waters were now dead calm, but the under-current had set in. From out at sea there came faintly the voices of blackfellows chanting in a canoe. Old man "Wire-whiskers" had harpooned a big fat dugong. He had dived overboard, stuffed its nostrils with soft paper-bark, and now, astride its slippery back, in a high-pitched tenor voice was singing it dead-fellah, bone-fellah, dead-fellah, fat-fellah.

We left camp at sundown and sailed for a while. The moon rose later, and shone brightly. The natives, singing softly, paddled quietly along the deeps, or poled cautiously through the shallows. All kinds of queer things lurked in the mysterious depths. Once a crocodile slithered in close by, and another took a flying leap into the water from a high bank. He looked, as he jumped, like a giant frog. The backwash, following his impact with the surface, made our frail craft rock dangerously. He was a particularly cheeky saurian and soon came barging along to inspect us. Head and shoulders high up above the water as he surged along, he looked like a small motor boat. Evidently, on closer view, he decided that we would be too dangerous for him to attack. In the bottom of the canoe a small fire was burning on a flat stone. Strips of paper-bark were lighted and, whilst still flaring, were flung overboard. The crocodile promptly disappeared.

Toward midnight we came to a long stretch of shallows. Sometimes a crocodile would grunt in the mangrove-forest, or a sea-curlew shriek overhead. To lighten the canoe and to decrease the draught, most of the natives waded alongside with spears in their hands. All the dogs, too, had to get out. They followed astern, swimming, and whimpering with cold and fear. The musk reek of crocodile hung heavy above the waters. I was wading with a heavy calibre repeating rifle in my hands.

We made camp close to the water's edge—of necessity, as swamps began a few yards back from the bank. The crocodiles, if they were very hungry, might come out and make a rush at the dogs. In case this should happen I had two of the blacks' mongrels close to my net. Dinkum I had inside with me, and my loaded rifle was close at hand.

Before turning in I served out tobacco. This was my currency and it was in great demand. As I lay in my bunk I could hear some of the natives hard at work. They were chopping branches of trees and pulling up grass: getting ready for the next high tide, which would fill all the smaller creeks.

At dawn the tide changed. The flow from the ocean had commenced. The formerly placid waters were in a turmoil —banging, swirling, and jumping. They seethed with fishes. The natives were waiting at a creek channel that branched from the main stream. It was thirty feet wide and about five miles long. Its incoming waters were flowing strongly but silently.

The natives, having been taught to be cautious, were peering from behind trees, and talking to each other excitedly—not by word of mouth, but silently, by animated interchange of hand-sign language. A big "run" of fishes was going upstream. The smaller ones crowded past first, and then, as the waters ever deepened, came the bigger varieties. A big bull crocodile drifted and paddled by with only his watchful eyes and keen nose above the water. Then the waters stilled to a high slack tide, and there was for a few minutes a scene of intense activity.

Poles were hastily driven down into the six feet deep water; bushes were interlaced with them and grass packed against them right across the stream. The natives swam and dived, making all secure. Their nerves were on edge, but their work was all done methodically, quietly and quickly.

The barricade was finished. In the water, on the up-stream side, expert spearmen stood with their weapons at the ready.

Without warning, the bough-barricade shuddered under the impact of some hidden power beneath the muddy waters. A continued movement of the poles indicated that it was seeking a way through. In silence the natives waited. A floppy fin arose above the surface and a big black body rolled over exposing the yellow-white under parts of a five-hundred-pound groper. It was a menace to our structure, and we would perhaps lose all the fishes. A heavy spear was jabbed into it. In pain and fright it swung around, and, with the spear bolt upright, swam back up-stream and disappeared behind a mudbank.

I followed it with the rifle, and could see the quivering spear-shaft apparently lying on the mud. Half sliding down the slippery bank, I tied a stout fishing-line to it and began to heave slowly. The aboriginals were driving spears into the bigger fishes and dragging them out. No time was wasted because old-man Ghingi the Dog-chewer was close by and as the tide got lower and lower he would be sure to come our way.

About three tons of big fish were now flopping and gasping on the banks. The waters were reduced to eighteen-inch pools filled with quietly moving masses of salmon, mullet, bream, perch, and crabs. We went away up-stream, searching every section of mudbank and sand-flat for the crocodiles. We found the groper stranded, and a Johnstone River crocodile camped alongside it. He had been tearing lumps of flesh off the big fish. He was cheeky, and greeted us by standing stiffly on all four legs, blowing his body up and gurgling. He was hit a resounding whack on the nose with a lump of wood, collapsed and shut his mouth. His "long fellah" nose was promptly tied up.

A call came echoing from the mangroves. The old-man crocodile's tracks had been found. They were winding in and out, between and under the maze of tangled mangrove roots. It was impossible to follow them directly through the sombre shades. We had to balance and crawl, four feet above the slimy ground, over those slippery, shell-encrusted, flesh-cutting roots. We could hear a monotonous, dribbly sound. Then we found him lying low in a mud puddle along-side a mangrove log. With yells of fiendish delight the savages greeted their enemy. They knew him. He was a sixteen-foot black crocodile with one forefoot missing—it had probably been bitten off in an encounter with a shark.

He gave a few subdued bellows and then squirted two jets of water through his nostrils. He opened his mouth, gaping until I could see the barbed spikes of a catfish which had become embedded in his palate. These open jaws were the danger signal, but swing his tail he couldn't, as the mangrove log and the roots near it prevented him.

There was a scene of exultant carnage. The eyes were prodded out with spears. Into the mouth was thrown a rotten hunk of wood on which the ferocious teeth closed and became embedded. The natives spat on him, belted him on the nostrils, then cut off his tail with blows from a tomahawk. He was carved up while still alive and carried away in quivering sections.

THOMAS WOOD

THOMAS WOOD, Mus. Doc., visited Australia on a commission from the University of Oxford in 1930-2. His popular *Cobbers* (1935) is the personal record of his wandering in Australia.

PLACES

Brisbane

WE rounded another bend in the river, going dead slow. There were palms along the spit. Behind them, set in terraced gardens and grown over with sprays of crimson blossom, stood white houses perched on stilts. A woman waved to us from a veranda. Two bare-legged laughing boys scrambled away from our bow-wash as it swept the shore. We were nearly close enough in to shake hands with them. The Captain leaned over the bridge and beckoned to me. "Here's the place," he said; and grinned. I grinned back.

He had told me the story the night before, when I went to his cabin, as usual, for coffee. The voyage from Melbourne had made us very good friends, and I never got away before midnight. It was easy to believe that the Captain's father had been a Dean. Eloquence evidently ran in the family; though I doubt if the father's sermons could have been as good as the son's tales. The talk, by some odd chance, had turned to the value of reticence in art. I quoted Lessing on the Laocoön statue, and the silence that follows the trumpet-call in *Fidelio*. The Captain smiled his slow wise smile.

"And only the true artist knows the moment when reticence is wanted," he said. "I've told you about old Mac, who had this ship before me?"

"The man that used to swear so?"

"The man that used to swear so. And he *could* swear. Remember that. In his own way he was an artist. You were saying yesterday that few people swear with any imagination. Quite true; but you've never heard old Mac. And he looked so convincing! He was a little peppery chap with red hair and the temper that goes with it—kept handy. Well, he was going up the Brisbane River once, where we'll be early to-morrow. Lovely day, bright sun, blue sky, no wind, everything just right; and old Mac on the bridge in his slippers, drinking his early morning tea. It's a fine river, as you'll see, but full of bends; and just round the twistiest of all the bends was a boat right across the fairway, and a fellow in it, fast asleep. He'd been fishing. I'll show you the place to-morrow. Well! It was a case. Not time to do much and not much room to do it in. If you starboard you're ashore; if you port you're aground. The hands on the fo'c'sle yelled, and the pilot hung on to the whistle lanyard, and old Mac skipped up and down like a cat in a beehive, cursing brimstone and fireworks. They *just* squeezed by; and as the boat came abeam of the bridge old Mac leaned outboard and emptied his teapot, full of hot tea, on the man's head, and got him—plonk! That woke him. Swear! It was a revelation, the pilot told me. Mac, at his best, absolutely outclassed. All the paint came off the ship; all the leaves fell off the trees; all the river began to smoke; and there was old Mac hanging his face over the dodger, wreathed in smiles, drinking in every word. He wasn't competing with *that*! And when he could hear no more he turned round to the pilot and said, '*What* a rude man!' "

I grinned again, and entered Brisbane as it ought to be entered—in high spirits. This city is the gateway to Queensland as well as its capital; in Queensland anything may happen and most things do. A happy State. I loved it. Brisbane itself is more like Perth, W. A., than any other of the Australian capitals—not in appearance, but in spirit. Both cities are bound up with the country behind them and are not ashamed of the fact. Both cities are full of men and women who have travelled. You fall at once into their habit of treating distance with contempt. You are going to Cairns, up North? Well, it's only a thousand odd miles. The first dozen men I met in Brisbane had been much farther in their own State

alone. Three of them had ridden over more country than
I went through later, by train; and knew it as only horsemen can. They talked about their stations up North or out
West as other people talk about the allotment across the
road. I began to feel that New Guinea was only round the
corner.

Brisbane has been kept so busy getting rid of the wool
and beef and hides that these wanderers send in that it has
never had time to do more than experiment with architectural styles. None has been settled on yet. There are some
fine buildings here and there—the State Insurance Office is
one—but they are individuals, too few in number to give
character to the city. It is the river which does that. Never
were such serpentine curves. I lived in Brisbane many happy
weeks, but I failed to master the windings of that river. It lay
in wait to surprise me. I would forget it; forget everything
except that I was walking through bare sun-dried streets:
that the roofs were tin, painted red, and that the hoardings
were tin, striped yellow; and then—there it was, another
reach, blue and cool and sparkling, a delight. I liked this
river's sly jokes much better than the show-places Brisbane is
so proud of—the new City Hall, and the view from Mount
Coot-tha, which (like every other view in Queensland) is
the finest view in the State. On the other hand, I am in complete agreement with Brisbane about the beauty of the poinsettia. It may be an immigrant, but it has made itself wonderfully at home. This is not surprising when it finds a soil rich
enough to let any one grow a banana tree in his back garden:
rich enough for arum lilies to be looked upon as weeds. The
crotons and the jacaranda, the bougainvillaea and the poin-
ceana have all stolen their colours from tropical sunsets, but
none has thieved so successfully as the poinsettia. Its flaming
scarlet splendour makes England seem far away. The ban-
yans and the bamboo groves and the custard apples bring
England no nearer. You are at the threshold of the tropics,
in Brisbane, and a little of the tropics comes over the threshold
to meet you. None of the teeming pulsing life of the East,

not all its colour and smells; but the heat and the fruits and the flowers, the velvety nights, the stars like lamps in the sky. You sleep under a mosquito net; drink orange juice when you wake; start breakfast with paw-paw and a slice of lime. You have a shower-bath whenever you can get one, and find that the unceasing hum of refrigerators is tolerable since their produce is so welcome. Winter and summer, wet and fine, you can wear your thinnest clothes. They suit all weathers except the rains. Then you want a diving suit.

I feel I am giving you a romanticized picture of Brisbane —letting you believe that this city knows nothing of wharves and trams and markets. It does; but I escaped from them so readily that in retrospect I forget they were there. I lived in the Queensland Club, which is comparable with the clubs at Singapore and Colombo. I need say no more. My bedroom opened on to a wide balcony, cool and airy and shady with palms. At night the only sounds were the rustle of their fronds and the chorus of crickets, softened by distance, which never stopped. I could imagine myself miles away from any city. By day I could keep up the illusion, for I had only to go into the gardens across the road and I saw cassowaries, and pelicans, and native companions—strange white stalky birds on stilts whose courtship dance is a marvel—and wallabies and emus. Instead of paying calls in Toowong and Indooroopilly, I spent my afternoons watching wallabies hurdling, and the emu practising the hundred yards. He would run as fast as the wind, his long ramrod legs working like pistons; then he would stop dead, stride back, and fix me with a wonderfully steely eye. A disconcerting habit. I thought of the man I had met in one of Brisbane's many inviting bars who told me that he had paced an emu once, west of Charleville, and that the speedometer registered thirty-eight miles an hour. Later in the evening that emu was doing forty-five. Was this emu, emissary of a vanishing race, trying to tell me—as the fish do—that men are such liars? Or did he want to say that if those railings weren't there he could do sixty?

The emu was not the only mystery I left unsolved in Brisbane. It was pointed out to me that the streets in the city are named after the kings and queens of England; the kings running NW.-SE., in line, the queens NE.-SW. In theory you have only to gabble through the list you learned at school when you come to any corner, and you can find your way to any other corner. In practice this plan breaks down. The queens are not in chronological order and there are not enough kings. I found only three: George, Albert (who was a Prince Consort, anyway), and Edward. Then I came to Creek Street. Who was King Creek? He was new to me. Was this an obscure reference to Canute, whose courtiers vowed he could rebuke the waves? No one could say.

And no one I met could throw any light on the biggest mystery of all. Brisbane has many places of refreshment. Some of them aim only at feeding the passer-by. Far more are ready to quench his thirst. This is to be expected when the climate even in winter is genial, and in summer can be oppressively hot. "It's this humidity in the atmosphere that gets you down," says Brisbane gloomily. "Have another drink?" I had many drinks, chiefly soft ones, sipping them, English fashion, while my hosts poured theirs down, Australian fashion, in one; but not a word did I hear about the place which, to judge by its name, ought to have offered me the softest drinks of all. I made the discovery on my own one Sunday afternoon, a hot and dusty day. I wandered through streets that looked as parched and grubby as I was. No one was in sight. Every door seemed shut. I found warehouses and a row of shuttered shops, and then a strangely forlorn notice over one of them, in tired white letters—*The League of Nations Restaurant*. I could not get in. No one could tell me anything about it, or explain why a proprietor who made such a gesture, as the politicians say, to the brotherhood of man should meet with no better support. Any city should be proud of a League of Nations Restaurant. But I must class it, here, with the emu and His Majesty King Creek: Brisbane's mysteries.

Adelaide

THE pleasant thing about Adelaide is the fact that if you get lost among its stiff straight streets, people will direct you by the hotels. This discovery cheered me up enormously, for never has a city been worse treated by its friends—its literary friends, at least. Their descriptions purge it of every comforting human foible. Do they mention the friendly bars of Adelaide? Hush, Hush!

They write about the Athens of the South; calm, cultured, cloister-like, serene. This is depressing, but the ink is only lavender yet; wait for the purple. The City Beautiful, they say, where, in the atmosphere of the quadrangle, the student, the poet, and the recluse can draw their inspiration from the steadfast and enduring hills . . . They then add three dots, to let your imagination rove; after passages in royal purple, five.

If a city can look you in the eye after all this it deserves any man's respect. Adelaide had mine, for it can.

Two men planned Adelaide, a soldier and a Quaker. An unusual combination. They had ideas that were unusual in the eighteen-thirties. The first said there must be no slums. The second said there must be no straggling. A Garden City was what they were after, which was a bold bid a century ago. They had brains and money and goodwill to back them; hills and plain, river and sea for a setting; hard grey stone and monumental trees to build with; plenty of water and a sky as blue as Italy's. So they built them a Garden City. They might have built the Model City, but one tragic accident ruined the whole scheme.

The soldier lost his compasses.

I can explain these acres of straight lines in no other way. Colonel William Light, this soldier, had a Service career which even in those spacious days was remarkable for its vigour and variety. He served with success in the Royal Navy, the 4th Dragoons, the 3rd Foot—the Buffs—and the Spanish Constitutional Army, besides being A.D.C. to the Duke. It was the very life for a schooling in discipline, but not one to make a man think about graceful curves. And in all his forty-three Peninsular engagements not one musket ball gave him a first-hand impression of what roundness is. When he was working at those new plans in Adelaide he would take off his tunic, naturally, in the heat, so that he got no hint from its buttons, and the sun was too bright to look at. Therefore, when his compasses disappeared, all hope of crescents and circuses went with them. A heavy loss.

I have tramped the Adelaide streets for miles, marvelling that the right angle should have so vast a shrine; utterly depressed to find that when I had reached one corner, going north or south, I had only to count one hundred and sixty paces and I was bound to come to another. I felt that if Adelaide belonged to me, I would willingly have swopped all the statues in North Terrace—except the War Memorial—for half a dozen curly streets with kinks in them, or one really good maze. Knowing when the next corner will come is all very well for tram-drivers, but it kills drama. Mr. Winkle's adventure with the sedan chair could never have been staged in Adelaide; Mr. Dowler would have caught him round the first block. Colonel Light did his job with soldierly precision; but John Wood, who built Bath, was kinder to Winkles.

On hot, still afternoons I would walk along North Terrace, skirt the hospital, turn into the Botanical Gardens (do not fail to notice the lily-pond when you go yourself), and cross a knobbly wooden bridge to a small island in the lake. It is a peaceful place, soothed with the rustle of leaves and the chuckle of water-fowl. There I would smoke a pipe and brood over this Adelaide mystery. The regularity of its criss-cross streets worried me; cloister-like I never felt it to be, in spite of its two small neat cathedrals; the air of the quadrangle is more easily breathed—and smelt—in the Turl than in this sun-trap. And yet I liked the place. Why? (I never once had to ask myself why I liked the people. The answer was too easy.)

I could not tell; until one day the ever-courteous official at the Tourist Bureau gave me a folding street-map. Then I saw at a glance. Adelaide was the work of a soldier and is

a soldier's dream of what a city should be. I like soldiers;
therefore I liked Adelaide.

Every detail on the plan bore out this reasoning. The city
is a battalion drawn up in mass: head-quarters in the middle
—Victoria Square; the four company head-quarters spaced
round it equidistantly—four other squares; shops dressing by
the right; trees falling in two deep; transport—the railway
station—in the rear; cantonments—North Adelaide—farther
back still. There is a military neatness even in the placing of
the race-course and the cemetery, those homes for the quick
and the dead. They balance each other, an oval on either side
of the main body; and soldierly forethought has made the
first twice as big as the second.

The solving of this puzzle delighted me. I closed my eyes,
as the new biographers must do, and saw the scene a century
ago when Colonel Light planned the park-lands of Adelaide,
that enviable green belt which goes right round the city.

"Next item?" asked the Colonel.

"Lands, park: people for the use of," said the Adjutant,
wiping his forehead.

"Well, how many acres shall we allot?" asked the Colonel.
"A thousand? We must leave plenty of room for games, and
playing-fields for the children."

"No children born yet, sir," replied the Adjutant.

"There will be, in this climate," said the Colonel, con-
fidently. "Plenty. We mustn't stint them for room. Double
the acreage."

"Very good, sir," said the Adjutant, picking up his quill.

"Read when you're ready," said the Colonel, leaning back
in his chair.

The Adjutant cleared his throat, brushing away a fly at
the same time.

"Lands, park: people *and* unborn children for the use of
—two thousand acres."

"Good," said the Colonel.

And it is so.

In one of the company head-quarters, Light Square, stands
a column bearing the Colonel's name. With the greatest

respect for him and it, I suggest that no conventional stone is needed to keep his memory alive. A finer tribute is paid to him every night in the year. You can see it best from the top of Mount Lofty, which stands behind the city. All you have to do is climb up and up in some friend's car—Adelaide is so open-hearted that you can dispense with one of your own—through the orchards and the pines, the almonds and the laurels until you come to a cleared space, which looks straight down on the plain as a cliff looks down on the sea. Then you wait, while the little wattle-birds say good-night and go to bed, one by one, and the sun draws his curtains and goes to bed too. This is the moment for the Light Memorial. Hundreds of tiny bright points spring up in the dusk below, as though some ghostly R.S.M. had shouted, "Fall in, the Markers!" As you watch, long lines of lights ripple across the plain, steady themselves and stand, rank after rank, filling the blackness at your feet with a regiment of lamps drawn up in perfect alignment. People tell me some place in the States can match this sight, but I know nothing so good of its kind in England or Australia. It is unconscious homage: torches held up to honour a great man, Colonel William Light, who built the Soldier's City, and would have built the Perfect City—among the moderns—if only he had remembered the regimental drum.

Broome

THE place where the pearls come from. The port which the luggers make, laden with shell. The home for a floating population of Japanese, Chinese, Malays, Koepangers, binghis, half-castes, and whites; who try for a living, and hope for wealth, among reefs and shoals, heat and sand-flies; working hard, dying quick, and buried before night in a graveyard that divides them, even in death, into Anglicans, Methodists, Catholics, Mohammedans, Buddhists, Jews, and Doubtful.

Broome is not Juan Fernandez, or Nombre de Dios, or Tidore, or the Galapagos—magical names from a world which seems as remote as it did in Drake's time; but it has something in common with them. You can say this now that you are home again, for they are hard-headed men in Broome; and any mention of magic or romance—if you so far forgot yourself—would make them stare, and say, kindly, that the sun was a cow till you got used to it, and what about another spot? The implication is that you are free to keep your illusions; theirs they have lost, as men will who stay too long anywhere. The end of the rainbow is always over the hill.

But I am glad I went to look for it in Broome. Even when you have reached Australia, making a conventional landfall, the place is so far away, so legendary, that you are tempted to think it is nothing more than a name on the chart and a home for tall yarns. But be patient. Last week it was the next port of call. Yesterday the Malays got cargo on deck ready for landing—boring plant and a dynamo, and a dozen barrels of beer. Last night the Captain said we ought to be alongside at six, if there's enough water at the jetty. And this morning came a thump on the cabin door and the Purser's hearty voice, "Rise and shine, Doc.! Here's Broome."

The sea was green, like palest jade, and the sky was lavender. A lugger drifted by. Every rope, every stay, every seam in her deck was vivid in that radiant sunshine. Her people stood like statues and watched us, shading their eyes. Black statues, with crispy wool for hair. One man had a red scarf round his head. Inshore was a cluster of small craft and a schooner at anchor; behind her, a beach and sandstone rocks, copper against the polished glass of the sea. There was a tree or two; some roofs, achingly white; a jetty dotted with wagons; some men sitting on sacks. We leaned over the rail and stared and stared. So this was Broome.

An engine, and a truck whose bleached unpainted timbers looked like salvage from a galleon, steered along the jetty, crossed the foreshore, and after a mile of indecision stopped for good alongside a shed. Nothing else was in sight but sand and tussocky grass. Friendly souls explained that she was only doing the short trip to-day, being Sunday, but the town wasn't more than half a mile off. Straight on up the street. And the Pearling Inspector lived in the house with the hedge. I couldn't miss it.

I had heard this encouragement before and knew its value, but for once it did not let me down. Here was the hedge. Hibiscus? Too hot to make sure. I thumped on a table in the veranda, hopefully. I thumped again, and sat down. At least there was shade, though the air was heavy and damp. And still, wonderfully still. The palm by the steps might have been cast in bronze. Over the hedge I could see the street they had talked about. It was a stretch of rough grass as wide as a cricket field, with a path and a railway track in the middle and some houses on the far side, harshly white in this straight hard glare. A beetle sailed in through the jalousies and buzzed. He was the only person with energy enough to break the silence, except me, and my time was more precious than his. I thumped again.

The Pearling Inspector appeared in pyjamas, apologizing, his chin covered in lather. But why not pyjamas? I asked, on a Sunday morning; and such elegant pyjamas too! Their owner read my credentials, smiling through his soap. I wanted to see luggers, shell, pearls? Give him ten minutes and his time was mine. The flourish of his razor as he skipped through the door intimated that all Broome would be thrown at my feet.

We began, naturally, at the "Roebuck". I say naturally because life in the outposts centres round an hotel. That does not mean that men in the outposts do nothing but drink. Some do; and the sun kills them. Others ride in for an occasional burst, throw a cheque across the counter saying "Wake me up when that's done," and proceed to drown all memory of how they earned it in one gloriously comprehensive non-stop binge. They stagger away, broke; but who is to judge them? Not suburbia. And such whole-heartedness is rare. Most men prefer to keep alive and solvent. They want to see their friends, and hear the news over a drink or two, in the cool. The natural meeting-place is the hotel.

The men at the "Roebuck", sitting on the steps in their shirt-sleeves, bade us good-day with the unfailing courtesy of the North, and asked what we were having. The East went by while we had it—Malays in groups and a Japanese

Above: A NORTHERN TERRITORY RIVER *"In the shade of the river-bank trees"*

Below: NORTH AUSTRALIAN ABORIGINES *"Bodies daubed over with coloured ochre ... a truly wild company"*

Above: ADELAIDE FROM COLONEL LIGHT STATUE *"Unconscious homage"*

Below: PEARLING FLEET, BROOME *"Every rope, every stay . . . vivid in that radiant sunshine"*

or two; and across the way was a Chinaman's shop with the owner at the door, bland and ready for business. But Australia came back on the foreshore, the Australia of the pioneer: rusty tins and a railway line. This was where that train came then, when she was doing the long trip, all the way from the big ships' jetty to the luggers' beach. A good two miles. Even on week-days she could get no farther, for the line died by the pearling sheds, untidily, old rope and sea-weed piled on its grave. The tombstone was an anchor.

The luggers' beach had a jetty of its own, and at the seaward end of it a long way off a black boy was waiting in a dinghy to row us out to the fleet. I am calling it a jetty now, because Broome does; what I called it when I was going out to the dinghy surprised me at the time. I did not know I had such powers of imagery. A jetty should be firm, safe, solid. This derelict put me in mind of that classic definition of a net—a lot of holes tied up with string. Say laths for string and you have it; use the imagination I wished I had not got just then and you can see it—slips of matchwood, bleached and split, whose silvery frailty said the end was near. Below them, green chasms. Don't look down. Never mind the sweat trickling into your eyes. Keep your mind off the sharks. Think of that anchor, the symbol of hope. Once aboard the lugger. . . .

The dinghy was solid, at any rate. We sat in her broad and comfortable stern-sheets, where the wood was hot to the touch, and stretched out our legs luxuriously. The black boy grunted at his oars, sweat hopping off the end of his nose. But he grinned; so I was content to watch it hop. The sea was asleep. We rose and fell with the quiet of its breathing.

You can board a lugger by standing on the thwarts of a dinghy; and once you are on her deck nothing in the world will prevent a sea from sweeping you off it except your sense of balance or a grab at a stay. And there is room for everything but the crew. Forrard is a fo'c'sle for five men, packed tight. Aft is a cockpit as big as a tea chest. This is a fair comparison, not a picturesque phrase; for the occupant

K

is a Japanese, who squats, with no need for head-room. He lives alone as a skipper should, and spartanly. To comfort him through a three months' voyage he has a mat on the floor and a picture on the bulkhead—cherry-blossom time, or maidens crossing a bridge—and for self-expression he has a writing brush and a penny bottle of ink.

Amidships is a well. It houses a pump for giving the diver air, his tow-line, boots, and rubber suit, and a goggle-eyed helmet that took me back in a jump to Portsmouth and the salvage men. For some years every lugger carried a pumping-engine, which enabled divers to work in pairs. Now the engines are gone. They saved wages and they saved sweat, but they killed prices. Broome solved its own problem of over-production by going back to hand-pumps—one lugger, one diver. Upon the skill and judgement of this one man the success of a cruise depends.

They lower him down to the bottom of the sea and drag him along it, the lugger just under way. When he sees an oyster he twitches his line, signalling to heave-to while he puts it in a bag slung round his neck. The pearl oyster has little in common with Colchester natives. He is as big as a football, grows a long trailing beard, and shuns society. A diver may be dragged many a weary mile before he finds a single one of these hermits. And picture the hunt—a man in the gloom, fathoms down: air and light and help as high above him—at times—as the top of Tom Tower from the quad; searching among ooze and rock and razor coral; breathing through a tube which any prowling shark may snap in two. He himself is safe from sharks unless blood is about, because the bubbles streaming from the helmet scare them away; but gropers, sting-rays, and giant clams are just as hungry and not so nervous. A diver earns his pay.

It is high enough to tempt him from Japan, bind himself by a contract, and work day and night at the bottom of the sea. If his luck is out he dies—gropers or paralysis. If his luck is in he goes home rich. If he serves in a lugger at Thursday Island, in the Torres Strait (where I was a year later), he may have a bag of pearls to pack up with his money.

The diver keeps what he finds in the Strait. Pearls are smaller up there and sell for less. At Broome a "shell-opener", who is an Australian, goes out with each lugger, and in theory extracts every pearl. In practice no one is sure. You hear tales of oysters which have been opened by a pan of hot water, closed by a dip in the sea. Who gets the pearls then? In any case it is the shell that is the stand-by; mother-of-pearl, commerce calls it. Once it fetched four hundred pounds a ton. When I was in Broome it fetched a hundred and eighty, no more. If a lugger brings home six tons in the season the owner calls himself a lucky man.

I did not want to leave the fleet. My lugger was neat and trim and well-found; and her crew, grinning, fell over one another in their zeal to show new things to the stranger. The water lapped her sides silkily. The sunlight splashed over her deck and gear, and spilled into the dinghy bobbing under the counter. She was inviting enough to tempt me away pearling; enticing enough for my chancing the stink of drying oyster gristle* and the size of the cockpit. But my ship had to catch the tide. If there ever comes a day when I need not catch my ship, I shall seek out my host in Broome and go off with him in his schooner, collecting shell from the fleet. But I have no stomach for fifteen-fathom diving. If I want a pearl I shall bargain for it like the experts.

Even in open-hearted Broome you cannot expect pearls to be given away, but you can buy them. Dealers from Paris make the round once a year—Broome, Thursday Island, Singapore, and home again. They want pearls, good ones, and they know what to pay for them. In spite of artificial pearls, and cultural pearls, and synthetic pearls, the oyster pearl still gets its price. I saw four, taken out of a safe, with care, and slid from an envelope into my hand. I held the worth of a lugger, or a semi-detached villa, or a Daimler saloon—say sixteen hundred pounds. Three white filmy spheres and one golden one. Strange progeny of irritation!

I left them in the safe; for should I have made myself any

---

* The crew is given the inside of the oysters, which are dried for curry. No one grudges them this delicacy. A stomach which could face its musky rankness would never be found ashore.

happier by taking the lot? I doubt it. And my Letter of Credit was not intended for such heroics. The shells I brought from Broome have given me more pleasure than those pearls ever would. They are four disks as big as cheese plates, gleaming, and iridescent and lovely, scattered about with "blisters". They came from a shed where a wizened old Malay worked, in the dark, piling the luggers' cargoes shoulder-high like crockery in a warehouse.

I had nothing to give in return for them but my good wishes and the material for a toast, which we drank at the "Governor Broome"—

"Here's to the price of shell."

MYRTLE ROSE WHITE

MRS WHITE, wife of a station manager in the Lake Frome country, tells in *No Roads Go By* (1932) the story of seven years' residence on the cattle station of "Noonameena".

WOMAN IN THE INLAND

WHILE living at the depot, I found a second lonely little homestead tucked away on the edge of the downs unfolding to the south-east of us. It was hidden away behind the last belt of mulga scrub and had no near neighbours, at least none nearer than seven miles.

It was evening when I first drove up to it. A smiling-faced woman came across the downs to meet us with her two little girls trailing behind her, their hands filled with ham-and-egg daisies which they had been gathering from the acre-wide patches growing within easy reach of the house. She greeted us as old friends, and the best she had was ours, poured out in largess that overwhelmed. Such hospitality would have been embarrassing given other than as a true bush woman gives it.

She was a young woman with a large family, a mother born. Serene, sunny-natured, even-tempered, she remained so in the face of all demands made upon her. Sudden illness, rising temperatures, damaged limbs, she met them all with an unruffled demeanour; taking them more or less as a matter of course. She doctored and nursed, never doubting that all would be well.

Since then she has reared a family of nine of the finest children imaginable. Cooked and cleaned, nursed and educated the children, sending several of the older ones to finish at Boarding School—a no mean achievement for a struggling household. She did this so that none would be educationally handicapped when eventually they left her to face the battle of life in the outside world.

She had never seen the sea, but how wise she was in bush-lore! Like many another bushwoman, she sets out at night to see the world when seated in a comfortable chair at her own fireside. All is well then, she has the knowledge that her work for the day is done, unless there is bread to set. Her children are washed and fed, and the smaller ones in bed and asleep. An hour at the mending basket, and then the treat she knows that she has earned—an hour or two with her books and papers, roaming out in the wide, wide world, meeting other people, seeing other sights, learning of other customs. Sharing with another woman her love story, rejoicing with her in her joys, as she reads, sorrowing with her in her sorrows, and hoping, oh so earnestly, that all will come right in the end.

Ah, what joys a parcel of books brings to a bush home! What secret thrills they give! What dreams they foster! What food they are for the hungry mind!

It was arranged that the two mothers were to visit me in turn, and as the Little Mother had already paid her visit I seized on the Boss's second trip in that way to go for the Mother of Nine. Four camels in the wagonette, the wagonette fitted with seats, and a mattress or two on the floor for the use of the little tots, and away we went.

On the return trip we camped for the night at the Twenty Mile swamp, making our beds under the wide canopy of the purple night sky. We gathered endless armfuls of soft greeny-grey saltbush, thickly padded with creamy-yellow seed-pods, round and delicate as fairy playthings, and spread our blankets over these fragrant mattresses.

The campfire painted queer pictures on the tree-trunks and tinted the under branches with a rosy glow; the still swamp water was dark and dank under the trees, but in open patches it was jewelled with reflected stars.

As we sat the Little'un pointed out the Duck lying on his back pricked out in gold on the eastern sky. Later on in the small hours of the morning I saw him low in the west, on his feet this time.

Gums were laden with fragrant honey-scented blossom,

laden too, with flowers that bloomed only for the night. Brilliant parakeets, pink-and-grey galahs, cockatoos of purest white, and gay little blue-bonnets rested among the flowers.

The sound of children's voices, and the glare of the campfire disturbed the birds' dreams, and much sleepy protest was indulged in, with a private quarrel of a more serious nature now and again.

The billy was put on for tea, steak was grilled on the coals, potatoes baked in their skins in the ashes, bacon grilled on the end of a forked stick, and bread toasted in the same way. These, with biscuits and cakes to fill in loose packing, made our evening meal.

What fun it was! How those little ones revelled in the novelty of it all! And how everyone talked!

I heard the Boss telling of how he and Billy Newland lost their pack-camels one night and had to camp without even a drink. Their camels had got away from them in the dark and as they were not belled, and as the sand deadened all sound, they had perforce to turn their riding camels loose, too, and camp on the bare sand till it was light enough to go and look for them. And even as they talked I saw how one by one the children dropped off to sleep, too tired, for once, to kick the covering from their limbs.

The men's voices sank lower. Then matches ceased to flare and the aroma of fine Capstan to drift on the waves of the night. A sleepy good-night kiss; a quiet jest across the fire, and the women were left to talk themselves out.

Midnight came and went, and still we talked on in muted tones; voicing at last the pent-up thoughts of years—thoughts that women can voice only one to the other, and then only when they know where wait understanding and sympathy, and love.

A boobook owl slowly drifted from tree to tree along the dark padding of timber in the centre of the swamp, calling with an eeriness that made us draw closer together: *Mopoke!* *Mopoke!* It kept it up for hours, growing faint with distance, then gradually louder as again it drifted back over its course. A curlew added to the uncanniness of the quiet solitude as its wail swept across the night, until one looked at the swamp that was still and dark, and thought that it must surely be goblin-haunted when the world slept. Why are the calls of our night-birds so weird and disquieting?

There came a wonderful awakening in the morning. The bird-music of thousands of feathered songsters was something to remember. No more beautiful welcome was ever sung to a coming day than we heard then.

Towards midday it warmed up unpleasantly, and on reaching Starvation Lake we found the depression under its farthest rim hidden beneath a ghost-grey pall. Strange, but this seemed always to lie in that one particular spot! As we advanced it retreated. It was the mirage, slipping from closer contact like a prowling thing creeping back to its lair.

Herbage grew thickly where the basin of the lake curved upward, and emus, kangaroos, and rabbits were so plentiful there that it looked like a game reserve.

The land rose in a long slant from the flat grey bed of the lake. The going was very dead over the grey sand. The wheels cut deeply, leaving a double weal across its uncovered expanse. There had been no water in this lake for twenty years and over, and since the country is continually changing its formation owing to the unbridled winds silting up old channels and cutting new ones, or blowing away one dune and building up two, it is probable it will be another twenty years before it holds water again. It is well called Starvation Lake.

As we climbed from the bed of the depression we found growing under its western rim wild fuchsia with its flame flowers, native tecoma, beating the air with yellow flower-clusters, and yellow-cupped, heavenly-scented boronia. This beautiful shrub has many species, and at its naming tragedy presided. For it is said that it is named in honour of a young Italian, Francis Borone, who, when studying flowers in Western Australia, attempted to gather a fine specimen of the shrub, and losing his balance, fell over a precipice to his death.

After climbing over the lake's rim we were faced with the flat sandy country again—the red heart of Australia! The timber on these flats was still quite untouched, so that it stretched away, and away, and away. The vista down the long space between the sandhills was blue-grey with densely packed mulga, the tree with the black tracery of branches spined with long narrow leaves; there were also splashes of vivid green where grew a bullock bush, and two-toned grey where the slender mottled trunk of a leopardwood grew straightly to branches holding foliage as exquisite as rare old lace. Beneath the trees, tangled in their shadows, was the rich emerald of the round buck-bush, which, when dry, rolls over and over ahead of the wind-storms, until anchorage is found against some tree or shrub; and with it was the close-knit spread of greeny-grey annual saltbush, which, in exposed positions, was rosy with ripening seed-pods.

Red, green and blue-grey! They were the predominating colours of this corner of probably the oldest continent on earth. A corner that still held the quiet of the beginning, the solitude of the ages.

We came to a big open claypan; sun-scalded ground from which the delicate skin had been torn away. The sun shone on it, throwing back a brilliant reflected glare. Why had the sand shifted from these patches leaving them bare, and baked, and polished? Obviously because there had been no growth to hold it. Here these places were spread everywhere through the open country. One found them where never a hoof had trod, and that seemed to give the lie to the general belief that the sheep were largely responsible. For many believe that the sheep, pattering in hundreds of thousands over the country, have loosened the surface soil and beaten it to a fine powder for the winds to blow away and leave the naked underclay.

As we travelled the little folk did not take kindly to the dip-and-come-again motion of the camels and wagonette crossing the sandhills, and much delay was caused by having to drop and take on again the human load.

On reaching the top of one sandhill we came upon several

half-grown emus passing with "staid demeanour" down the open narrow flat. The children were greatly entertained—so, too, were the emus! They lined up, watching with bright, inquisitive eyes the strange new creature invading their territory.

We climbed the sandhills till nightfall. The sun departed, leaving the soothing fingers of the darkness to freshen up the herbage and cool down the hot sands, then against the distant red a white blur showed up. It was the homestead at last!

"How dreadfully lonely you must be!" exclaimed the Mother of Nine when first she glimpsed the place; "I don't think I like it. It is too far out!" And then she smiled a jolly smile, and added, a large tenderness in her eyes, "We must not waste a minute of the next fortnight! Have you anything for hoarseness in case I talk my throat sore?"

DARLING SHOWER

On the day that I came into the world myself, one of the worst dust-storms known in the history of the Barrier was blowing. But that fact did not endow me with a love for dust, which, in view of the many pecks I found I was to swallow in later life, was something of a pity.

The dust-storms of the West Darling are something extra special of their kind, but those of the "open country"—well, you, who know the Darling Showers, can picture just how much worse they would be, released in a country where there is no tree-growth worth mentioning, and only sand, sand, and again sand. The blinding, stinging, infinitesimal specks sear the flesh with a million hot pin-points; a thick yellow fog completely obscures the world. Day after day, night after night, it blows, and blows—north, south, east, and west. From all points of the compass it comes; and oh! the horror of living through it.

Food is prepared with dust sifting down from every crack and crevice; food is cooked with dust pouring down the chimney into the pots and pans; food is left waiting until there is a sufficient lifting of the reddish-yellow blanket in which to serve it. Dishes freshly washed are filmed with dust and grit as they are laid on the table; follows a meal with grit the one and only flavouring from start to finish.

Quite often the lamps are lit at two o'clock, although the sun does not set until seven and after, but as an illumination a lamp would be only a farce. In a dark room, there is a lighting towards the centre, a nimbus of fog around the flame.

The thought comes that the crust over Hades has broken, and that the orange-red, sulphur-yellow fumes have drifted through. At times when the wind drops, an uncanny silence grips the dust-choked world. For a fleeting moment, sheds, harness-room, meat-house, and kitchen are seen, unfamiliar and indistinct shapes through the gloomy pall. Then with terrible venom the wind sweeps down the depressions between the sandhills. Such ungovernable fury is released as will surely brush one from the face of the earth. Timber creaks and strains, roof-iron begins to lift and flap, and window-sashes rattle and shake as if in the grip of ghostly hands. A noise of rending wood, a strange boom, boom, boom, and a new ten thousand gallon rain-water tank is rolling ahead of the storm to be crumpled up like tinfoil before it reaches the second sandhill. Satisfied with the destruction of its plaything, the wind again drops, this time to a thin haunting whine; all the lost and lonely souls in the world send their plaint on that lowering note. First it is under this corner of the roof, then under that; the saddest, weirdest, soul-shaking whisper that ever was. Meanwhile, the dust thickens and deepens to a dull dead black and closes in, closer, closer, and closer, until one stifles and feels that all hope is lost.

A week of this and one emerges fit for a full course of the latest nerve treatment. Nature knows that and provides her own cure. If you can take it with a Christian spirit, thankfully, uncomplainingly, you are the salt of the earth. Personally I never could.

Picture a house camouflaged from floor to ceiling with red sand; your curtains, that you stencilled with such pride, deep red with sand; the soft moss-green carpet that rests your tired eyes when there is no living green for miles and miles, buried under barrow-loads of sand; sheets, pillow-cases, quilts, blankets, crockery, and walls all covered with sand; the corrugations in the iron roofs running sand; the six-foot iron fence that borders the garden enclosure, buried, absolutely buried, beneath the sand. There is no longer need to open a gate, a nice sloping bank leads to the top of the fence, a nice sloping bank leads down the other side. If you can put in a week wielding a broom, and battling with a wheelbarrow which pours hour-glass sand from six or seven holes and as many cracks, while hot suds gradually bring back a semblance of your old home—if you can do that and come up smiling—well, then, it's hats off all round. You are something more than human, you are divine.

C. PRICE CONIGRAVE

CHARLES PRICE CONIGRAVE, explorer and author, editor of
the Journal of the Royal Australian Historical Society, spent fifteen
years in the administrative service of the Northern Territory. His
North Australia (1936) is a vivid picture of the area he came to
know so well during those years.

ACROSS BATHURST ISLAND

FIFTY miles to the north of Darwin lie, like sleeping
sentinels, Melville and Bathurst Islands, the former
having an area of 2,240 square miles, whilst the latter
is half as large. They are separated by Apsley Strait, which
is fifty miles through from south to north, and about a mile
wide. As one goes along the muddy fast-flowing waterway
towards the north, the wooded hills, dense patches of vivid-
coloured jungle, and open, swampy plains of Melville Island
lie to east, whilst to west are the thickly-timbered heights of
Bathurst Island, with dense mangroves giving contrast in a
deeper green at the water's edge on either side.

On many occasions I visited the islands, my first trip there
in 1914 being aboard Joe Cooper's lugger, the *Buffalo*.
Cooper* is one of the few living survivors of the very early
days of the Territory. Going there as a young man from
South Australia, he is now in the sunset of life and he looks
back on a very adventurous career, of which encounters with
blacks and shipwrecks have been but minor, every-day
incidents. In his prime Cooper was the great buffalo shooter
of the North, and in addition for many years he lived among
Melville Island tribes, learned their dialects, and became
thoroughly acquainted with their inmost rites and customs.
No less an authority than the late Professor Sir Baldwin
Spencer paid glowing tributes to Cooper's influence among
these once wild native peoples. He first took up residence
on Melville Island when merely to land there was to take

* Since dead.

one's life in one's hand. But he did not escape scatheless, for he carries an awful, cup-shaped scar on his shoulder, where he was speared by a native who was hiding behind a big tree trunk. It was in the neighbourhood of Fort Dundas, the old ruined military settlement. Cooper was making his way through the dense forest thereabouts, when he was felled by a spear thrust from behind. A large, javelin-like, terribly-barbed spear had entered the flesh over his shoulder. He was left for dead by his assailant who went bush. Cooper was young and virile then, and he survived the attack, and as time passed, the blacks came to know and appreciate him as a fair and a just "white". It is no exaggeration to say that it was largely due to his influence among the once wild aboriginals that it became possible, twenty-four years ago, for a Mission Station to be established by the Roman Catholic authorities on the south-eastern end of Bathurst Island. This was shortly before I first went to the islands, and when we anchored off Cooper's camp on Melville Island, the new station was seen peeping from amid heavy timber on the other side of the swirling strait.

It was November of the year, and being just prior to the breaking of the wet season, the weather was uncomfortably hot and humid. Cooper's lugger lay at anchor off Fort Hill, Darwin, and his blackboys were taking off stores and gear to her in a very leaky dinghy. Bags of flour, sugar, ammunition, and all sorts of odds and ends lay about ready to be taken off to the lugger.

"Which way, Joe?" I asked a fuzzy-headed island lad in the dinghy.

"Him go aboard stow'em cargo," he replied. "Jokuppa bin talk-talk you bin come."

As we went off to the lugger there was an uncanny stillness in the air which betokened a storm in the offing. The heavy foliage along the cliffs, below the town, loomed black, whilst the L-shaped jetty that fronts Darwin was outlined by a row of twinkling lights. It is only when a ship is due from South or overseas that Darwin troubles about lighting its jetty. At other times the jetty that cost South Australia in days gone by £100,000 is practically deserted except by lovers and those who would try conclusions with the fish which swarm in the harbour.

This night, it was dead low tide, and the high, stilt-like, iron jetty looked terribly top-heavy, minus twenty-nine feet of water, and reflection of jetty and lights streaked across calm water and oozy mudbank to where, to the accompaniment of gurgle-gurgle-gurgle against the prow and creaking of rowlock, we were rowed off to the *Buffalo*.

"Hullo, there," called Cooper to Gerald Hill, Government Entomologist, and myself as we came alongside his white, trim lugger, and then, in native lingo, he grumbled at the boy's carelessness in bumping the counter with the dinghy. Joe, though he was always ready to have a laugh and a joke with his native crew, was ever the skipper and all hands knew it. To ease the tension, another boy apologetically explained to us, "Him big-fellah growl. Him clumsy fellah, him knockem off new-fellah paint."

To west the sky blazed with colour whilst in the southeast, away across Channel Island, heavy black clouds piled up ominously. Stars played hide and seek in the scud, vivid lightning streaked the horizon low down, and "the deep thunder peal on peal afar" rolled across the fifteen-mile wide harbour of Port Darwin.

Urged on by Cooper's "murka murka" (quick fellah), the boys hauled up the anchor to the accompaniment of much singing and laughter. They were a happy-hearted lot, those lads from Melville Island. One of them, a lanky fellow of about fourteen years of age, had been to Darwin for the first time. Until then his mental horizon had been limited to "my country close-up along Jokuppa", and I noticed that even when he gave a hand with the rattling, rusty old anchor chain he divided his attention with the lights of Darwin that shone here and there amid the tropical vegetation on the plateau top. They signified the opening of a wider world for him. For good or ill civilization had commenced to affect his life, though, poor chap, he perhaps did not realize the fact.

As we dropped down the harbour, making for the open
sea, to right, in a break in the line of cliffs, we picked out
the friendly lights of the hospital, an oasis of comfort for
many a Territorian who had been brought there through
the years, down with fever or some other ill that flesh is
heir to. Then there was the flash of Emery Point lighthouse,
and sixteen miles to the west it was answered by the stronger,
more important light of Point Charles. On the edge of the
red sector from the latter, which signified the limit of marine
safety, our lugger poked her nose to sea. We hoped to pick
up the islands towards dawn.

Aboard the lugger one does not get much comfort. Down
aft is a small cabin, fitted as a rule with two bunks, but only
as a last resource does one turn in there, preferring to roll
down on the deck in the pure, fresh air. Every northern
lugger is alive with cockroaches, the craft reeking with their
pungent, unpleasant smell. They are beastly things, and they
have been known to make inroads into the toenails of a hard-
sleeping blackfellow before he became conscious, wondering
what was tickling his feet. So with the stench down below
and the cockroaches, we threw our swags on the deck and
turned in. Joe was at the tiller, and as the craft lifted to the
growing swell a wake of fire ran astern, for tropical seas are
very phosphorescent. Once, like a torpedo of living light,
a large shark shot by us a fathom or two beneath the surface.

My last conscious thoughts were of "Jokuppa"—a solitary
figure astern, silhouetted against the lightning, and of some
of his remarkable experiences here and there in the Territory.
Towards midnight, however, we were awakened by Joe's
"Get up, boys, there's a puff coming". Rolling up our
blankets quickly, we tossed them down below and awaited
events.

We did not have to wait long. First came the wind in
fitful, angry gusts, each more spiteful than the last. Mast
stays strained and creaked as the lugger heeled, rail-under.
Everything aboard was rattling and groaning, whilst the
white-topped combers gave the plunging lugger a race northwards into the wild darkness. There is something majestic

in the onslaught of a North Australian storm, especially if one
be offshore in the night watches. The whole heavens to south
and east, within the space of a few minutes, blacked over,
except down towards the horizon, where the almost continual lightning illumined the lower edge of an angry
cloud, whose swirling mass billowed along as if insistent on
following our small craft to the open, heaving depths. Sail
was shortened down, big rollers pounded aboard, and with
a terrific burst, the storm broke. It was a wild scene as the
lugger wallowed in the trough of the white-topped seas,
and vicious rain squalls, with anger and menace, whipped
our faces, and every time that the bow dipped to lift half
a ton of water inboard there were make-believe, agonizing
cries from the blackboys huddled together in the chain locker.
As each succeeding squall heeled us over, one of the boys,
with a high-pitched voice, yelled out, "Jokuppa, big-fellah
wind, my word, big-fellah wind."

Whilst the blow lasted there was plenty of excitement.
Water and spray were over everybody and everything, and
to landsmen it seemed that the lugger was more under water
than afloat. However, to the imperturbable Joe it was nothing more than a very ordinary occurrence.

"She'll ease directly," Joe yelled to us above the howling
wind, and sure enough within an hour the "bust" had passed
over, the sky had cleared, and the stars shone, as is invariably
the case when such disturbance comes and goes with much
spume and smother of foam.

"Ulintera, that way," was a boy's call from the bow just
at dawn.

"Ulintera, what name that one?" asked Hill.

"Side Bathurst Island close-up along sunset," explained the
native. In other words, we learned that he could see the
western shoreline of the island, and when the haze cleared
a bit we could pick out the littoral, with high casuarina trees
waving in the breeze.

Soon after sunrise we were offshore at the southern entrance
to Apsley Strait. Astern lay the low-lying Buchanan Islets,
covered with dense mangroves, and we were told, "Turtles,

L

full up there". A large dug-out canoe, containing four big bearded natives, came off to meet us. Each muscular fellow was quite naked, was daubed over with red ochre, and had white ochre on his beard. As they swung a broad-bladed paddle apiece, the canoe came ahead at no mean pace, and there was much talk between our crew and these people when they got close to the lugger, which was leading in with a fine breeze filling her sails. The natives of both Bathurst and Melville Islands are splendid watermen. They use dug-out canoes and also other smaller craft made neatly from bark, but it is only in the former that they go much to sea. Felled in the jungle, the "dug-outs" are worked up boat-shape from the logs, and in such a craft the natives go long distances along the island shores or even over to the mainland, the nearest point of which in Clarence Strait approaches within twenty miles.

We dropped anchor off Joe Cooper's well-established camp on Melville Island, right at the entrance to the strait, and after cargo had been landed, we were taken across to the Mission Station on the opposite side of the strait, where we were welcomed genially by the Father Superior, Father Gsell, who, having come from Alsace-Lorraine when a young man, has been engaged for many years past in mission work among the natives of Papua and North Australia. Through the Father's kindness we secured the services of about forty natives to accompany us as carry-boys on our proposed tramp across Bathurst Island. Our swags, cameras, food, scientific gear and all other impedimenta were carried by these natives, who were young and old, stout and thin. The loads were lashed to shoulder-sticks, and then, two and two, in Indian file, we moved off with our black entourage. One little chap, who insisted on carrying a big camera tripod and a canvas water-bag almost as large as himself, we dubbed "Gunga Din", and a tall, exceedingly thin fellow, Pindan by name, who with his 6 feet 4 inches towered over us all, went by the soubriquet of Long'un. Mariano, a big, muscular man, who spoke a little English, elected himself chief boy, and we were amused at the authoritative manner in which he ordered about those who were old enough to be his father, and generally, how he acted as if he had the full force of "white fellah gub'ment" to support his every order. Mariano was the only one of our dark company who wore anything in the way of white man's clothes, his confrères all being naked. Fully-dressed with an exceedingly short coat and a wide leather belt, Mariano strutted along at the head of the cavalcade in the best style of an irascible sergeant-major on parade. And it was woe to any native who dared to express an opinion in opposition to that voiced by this black martinet. Anyway, my memory is grateful to him, for he saved us infinite trouble, both when we were on the march and when in camp. He was no mean naturalist, either, for he knew all the ways of beast and bird. Sometimes he would tell us that "old man kangaroo sit down here las' day", or, noticing some parrakeet on the wing, he would advise that "that one pretty fellah he bin hav'em little fellah baby along tree inside", which being interpreted meant that the nesting-place was within a hollow tree branch. When Mariano found that we were anxious to secure specimens of small marsupials he soon explained in his native tongue to his "brigade" what the white men wished, and thence on we had plenty to do in camp with skinning all sorts of interesting creatures that were brought to us. And if, perchance, some particular species gave us special interest, as being very rare, its native captor was not slow in asking for a double issue of "bacca". The black man is an adept at picking up the sophistication of the white and in getting to know the relative value of things.

The island blacks, in many respects, differ greatly from the mainland tribes. They are a particularly hirsute race, for on attaining maturity the men grow long beards, some of these being of quite patriarchial proportions. During certain of their tribal ceremonies the beards are pulled out, hair by hair, which painful procceding they treat with utter disdain, certainly with less fuss and facial distortion than the average white man makes when having his morning shave. The upper lip is kept bare, also, which practice seems but to emphasize the magnificence of the beard. Shocks of hair, sometimes standing six inches high, also add to the handsome appearance of the men, and I often thought as we strode along behind these muscular fellows, when we were on the day's march, what living examples they were of the natural, open-air existence. With perspiration streaming down over their bodies, and with every muscle rippling and playing in motion, they looked the very acme of physical development. One has to be in good fettle in order to keep walking with them, for an average pace of four miles an hour, and sometimes more, will be kept up during the march. It is not a mincing walk either, for with big feet, and with legs swinging clear and clean from the hip at each stride it is surprising how the miles of country are covered in comparatively short time.

An amusing lot these natives were, also, for like all aboriginals, they had a keen sense of fun and humour. Only my companion or myself had to slip on wet ground, or to catch one's foot in a tree root, as sometimes happened, with the result that one had an undignified fall, and very quickly the ludicrousness of the situation would appeal to the imitative faculty of one of our coloured company and he would go through a similar performance with variations, for the benefit of his confrères. Natives take their pleasures and joys simply and innocently like so many children. It is only when civilization has blighted them, when they have picked up the customs and vices of the white man, and when they have viewed American cowboy pictures with plenty of revolver play therein, that their mental outlook changes, to their detriment for the most part.

Mention has been made of the differences that exist between these islanders and the natives of the mainland tribes. This is evidenced further by the fact that the rite of circumcision is unknown among the former, in which regard and in other respects such as language, origin of descent, burial rites and so on they constitute an interesting study for anthropologists. Baldwin Spencer termed these people "the finest natives I have met", and for their own sakes, as well as on the grounds of the value of scientific research, it is to be hoped that for

long years they will be untouched by the results of the onward march of settlement. In this connexion the fact that
miles of ocean separate them from the mainland, with its
disintegrating influences, is all so much to the good.

In the midst of well-wooded country we came to several
burial places and saw a number of queerly-carved ironwood
posts, which had been up-ended in the ground round the
last resting-place of natives who had "shuffled off this mortal
coil". These posts, some eight feet in height, had been carved
in varying patterns and had been painted in very decorative
designs with red, yellow and white ochre, with charcoal giving sharp but artistic contrast. The number of posts varies on
different graves, but personally I have never seen or heard
of the number, recorded by Baldwin Spencer, thirteen, having
been exceeded.

The departed native, having been interred in a grave about
four feet deep, large slabs of bark are placed over the mound;
but, in most cases, many months elapse before any posts
are placed, stilt-like, in position round the grave. The actual
planting of posts follows the ceremony of painting them,
in which latter operation men, women and piccaninnies all
take part. The painting is anything but a sombre, doleful
proceeding; much to the contrary in fact, for there is
abundant laughter and general skylarking on the part of
young and old. Neither are the artists hidebound by the
conventions of any particular school of design. There is a
glorious irresponsibility about the designing and painting. If
a pattern, somewhat novel perhaps, is evolved, there is much
praise or ridicule, as the fit takes the onlookers. And, as
sometimes happens in "white" artistic circles, the cocksure
critics, who sometimes are so cynical or satirical in their
comments, could not, if their lives depended upon it, do
so well themselves as the particular artist whose handiwork
is passing under review.

Following on the completion of the post painting, a dance
takes place at the grave, and usually the mother of the
deceased is prominent in this ceremony. Painted from head

to foot with red ochre, the mourning parent has a most grotesque appearance.

In due course, sometimes months later again, a weird burial corroboree is held, and we had the good fortune to witness such a performance. It took place in a wooded dell round which great blackbutt gums stood guard. Near by was a patch of vividly-tinted jungle where snowy-white Torres Strait pigeons fed in the rustling palm-tops and a jungle-fowl called to its mate. An afternoon sun threw lengthening shadows over coarse sedges and swaying tree-tops. But these things, beautiful in themselves to those of us who watched the islanders prepare to mourn their dead, were unnoticed by the dusky warriors and their women and little pot-bellied children. *Mapuditti*, or the Evil Spirit, was the predominant thought in each aboriginal mind. At a distance of about one hundred yards from the grave a fire was lighted, on this being thrown much green foliage, so that dense columns of smoke arose. The acrid odour of the smoke was overpowering, and for the time being it rose superior to those inherent, characteristic smells that are part and parcel of a North Australian landscape where vegetation, by reason of humid heat and abundant rain, springs to wonderful fecundity.

The men, numbering about forty, stood in line to the fire, whilst the lubras and children clustered in a group near by. With bodies daubed over with coloured ochre, the noses in particular smothered with yellow and foreheads covered with charcoal, and with their long beards painted in sectional designs with white, so that they stood out, mask-fashion, round the contour of the face, the men looked a truly wild company. Then strode to the fire the father of him whose death was being mourned. Something of the pride of parent-hood, and defiance of the unseen Power that had wrested the living from his accustomed place among his kith and kin, was suggested by the bearing and mien of that wild, painted savage. He commenced to dance round the fire, and then he stepped boldly on to the middle of the smoking heap and stamped at ever-increasing rate, each foot being brought down on to the fire with a resounding "thwack". He was stamping on the Evil One so that no more, wherever his dead son had been taken to or had gone to, should he be under its malign influence. And as the man stamped thus in the fire, his tribesmen stamped in unison whilst with opened hands they struck their buttocks in perfect time, and gave voice to a wild chant—half song, half dirge; half wail, half a terror-stricken yell—that culminated in a long-drawn-out "E" which rang and rang again over forest and jungle. Time and time again man after man stamped upon the Evil One, then in an untrammelled stampede, with every native yelling in high register, the whole company rushed to the graveside.

The belongings of the deceased, such as spears, dilly-bags (made of gum bark) and other odds and ends lay across the months'-old mound or on top of some of the grave-posts, against the time when the spirit of the blackfellow, who had learned the last Great Secret, entered his happy hunting-ground where there was "full-up kangaroo, full-up wild goose, full-up all about plenty tucker".

For hours the weird, wild dance round the grave went on. At times one man rushed round it, then two or three followed close upon one another's fast-moving heels. Every few seconds these rushing, yelling, sweating figures halted and stamped the ground, all the time to the accompaniment of stamping feet and striking of buttocks with hands. Truly it was mourning at a tremendous tempo. In between the dancing evolutions, there were imitations, by men who were no mean actors, of animals of the chase. In mock actions they rubbed their shoulders against the painted grave-posts, as a hefty buffalo does against a jungle tree. From side to side, the painted human head imitated the sweeping action of the buffalo's horns, and the fact that in dumb show was given the unmistakable action of the buffalo lifting its hind leg so that it could be scratched by the tip of the huge horn to rid it, maybe, of some irritating insect, was proof that that particular aboriginal was a close observer of the great, lumbering brutes that now roam far and wide over Melville Island and parts of the adjacent mainland.

On our journey across Bathurst Island we passed through varying types of country. There were belts of cypress pine, a very valuable timber in the North, because of its properties, that render it immune from the attacks of persistent and destructive white ants (termites). Then there were deep groves of jungle where cable-like festoons of living green fastened tree to tree, and coral fern, in billowy masses, covered the moist ground. It was a well-watered land, for at almost every half-mile we came to pretty, gurgling creeks, on the banks of which thick vegetation gave sanctuary to plump wallabies and brightly-plumaged birds. In most of these streams, the black youngsters had a fine "play-about", for time and again during the morning or afternoon stage of the march they indulged in a "bogey" or bath. Ducking one another, dashing water with cupped hands, the fun was fast and furious. They are a cleanly people, these island natives, for they are almost as much in water as they are out of it.

Many interesting things we saw during our long tramp. Our carriers at every opportunity caught numbers of the very handsome but ferocious-looking frilled-necked lizard which, when enraged, throws out a beautifully-coloured frill that looks like an Elizabethan ruffle round the creature's neck. These lizards are "good fellah tucker" and they were often on the aboriginal menu. Then, as we got within easy distance of the western coast of the island, and having passed round the heads of small salt arms that ran in from the sea, we came across many nests of crocodile, or so-called "gator". The soft leathery eggs of this beast are deposited in a small mound, covered with leaves and grass, the resultant heat from the decomposition of which in due course incubates the eggs. Vicious little things the newly-hatched "crocs" are as they scuttle away to the nearest water. Even when they are but a few inches in length, if one unwisely puts one's fingers too near to the tiny, tapering jaws, rows of needle-pointed teeth will leave their marks in one's flesh, and the wound will give much trouble before it heals.

Owing to torrential rain having set in, we camped for two days and nights on high ground that overlooked a large mangrove swamp, and as the rain pelted down, thunder pealed, and lightning flashed, the boys gathered round a fire, which they kept alive by covering with large sheets of bark. At each successive clap of thunder all hands yelled and wailed in unison until the sopping bushlands resounded with their wild cries. And thus the terror of the tropical storm was reflected in the excitement of these ochre-painted nomads of the outer spaces.

We tramp-tramped to the north-western corner of Bathurst Island. This is the first part of Australia that is sighted by aviators as they wing their way across the Arafura Sea *en route* from the northern hemisphere. As we trudged along, with our long line of carry-boys with their loads, winding in and out like a gigantic serpent, we thought with what delight these daredevils of the air must have sighted the island over which "per boot" we made, comparatively, such slow progress to that of a zooming aeroplane. That far end of Bathurst Island, with its white, ribbon-like beaches, topside of which are clumps of casuarina trees waving in the breeze, is a picturesque spot. Thereabouts in the dense thicket not far inland, we saw large mounds of the jungle fowl, a remarkable bird with tremendously-developed feet, that kicks up huge mounds of earth and jungle debris, in which the eggs are laid. Although this northern megapode is the smallest of the three Australian species of mound-builders, it has the distinction of building the largest mounds. Sometimes 12 feet in height, these occasionally have an outside circumference of 100 feet. One observer, in fact, has noted that, "a specially large one has been estimated to contain 297 cubic yards of material weighing approximately 300 tons". In several localities we came across nesting-mounds of jungle fowl and crocodile within a few yards of each other, and thus was suggested again the long, interesting evolution, through passing aeons of time, of birds from reptilian forbears that possessed flesh-eating teeth.

We had proof, several times during our journey, of the contempt shown by the aboriginals towards the crocodile. In North Australia, as in all tropical countries, rivers and lagoons are alive with these dreaded saurians, but, generally, the native is immune from attack by them. On the other hand, there have been instances of their having been grabbed by the monsters. I saw two men on Bathurst Island who, having been attacked when they were swimming across the mouth of a salt creek, had lost a leg and an arm respectively, but in each case the victim had managed to reach shore though maimed and weak from loss of blood. Whilst, invariably, when we reached tidal streams that ran in from the sea between mangrove thickets, we deemed it wise to head them before attempting to cross over; the carriers, however, almost to a man and a boy, not forgetting the mangy dog, dived into the salt, muddy water unmindful of the fact that crocodiles were plentiful on the banks and in the streams. Only on one occasion did a native call out to his young son, "Murka, murka, alligator, him come up quick be'ind." The warning was eloquent in urging the boy to greater efforts, and there was no argument with parental authority such as is not unknown in white circles.

SIR ALBERT ELLIS

SIR ALBERT FULLER ELLIS, C.M.G., who was born in Queensland and educated in New Zealand, discovered the phosphate deposits on Nauru and Ocean islands in 1910. In 1920 he became New Zealand representative on the Board of the British Phosphate Commission. His *Adventuring in Coral Seas* (1936) is an instructive and entertaining account of expeditions in Australasian waters.

ROCKY ISLAND

ROCKY ISLAND deserved its name. It was the hardest place that we worked in the old days—hard in more senses than one. Most of its surface was bare rock; not the elevated coral reef of the ordinary low-lying islands we had experienced, but a species of sandstone, about two inches of which we found had been converted into phosphate guano. This was the highest grade material on the island; somehow it had escaped the notice of the company that had occupied the place some years previously. Our labourers were put on with mattocks at chipping over the whole of the bare area; the small rock thus obtained was ground up in a disintegrator and mixed with the lower grade, to average the quality.

Unlike the previous islands, where calcium carbonate was practically the only foreign substance to guard against, on Rocky Island there was a varying percentage of iron and alumina. This gave me a lot of extra work in the laboratory, and complicated our operations. Nevertheless the formation of the place was interesting; it was not a coral island, but appeared to have been built up by the hard gales and tempestuous seas of the Gulf, accumulating on a rocky base a mass of sand and marine debris which had become cemented together. The island was a mile in length, with a width of half a mile, and its highest point above sea-level was about fifty feet.

Shipping conditions too were difficult, though we did not

have to put down deep-sea moorings. The trouble was in the opposite direction: we had too much shallow water round the coast. Vessels had to anchor about a mile off shore; and the "holding ground" was not good, as some of the shipping found later on, the anchors dragging with disastrous consequences.

A long jetty of the usual type was built. Even this did not reach deep water; so loading operations at low tide had to cease. Then the lighters had a long pull out to the anchorage. Ultimately a large steam launch was engaged in towing them to and fro. In each section of the industry it seemed that Rocky Island was a hard place.

The climate was very hot in summer and cold in winter. During the winter there were occasional gales of extraordinary violence. These carried clouds of sand and little bits of rock with such force that no work was done out of doors during the height of the gale. The wind at such times was so piercing that we were glad to dress over our pyjamas. If the critical reader thinks that sounds soft, I can only say that he would have done likewise had he been in our place, with the rigorous conditions and the thin tropical clothing we were accustomed to wear.

Finances had to be considered a great deal in those days. The dwelling houses were of a flimsy nature, having been shifted from island to island over a number of years. Although well protected with stays to keep them upright, they seemed, at times, in danger of being blown over the cliffs. As a precautionary measure, a low strongly built hut was put up in an old railway cutting. There the staff used to take refuge during the height of a gale.

Then conditions were hard in the mess-room; and when anything is seriously wrong with the commissariat department it is decidedly disturbing. We had our meals in a low structure with corrugated-iron sides and roof, something like a large benzine tin with three divisions: one was the mess-room, the next the kitchen, and the third the cook's room.

The arrangement was not a good one. The sleeping compartment for the cook was too near. He was a coloured man of rather nondescript hue, resembling a half-caste West Indian employed years after at Ocean Island, and who puzzled the Gilbertese a great deal. He was neither a brown man like themselves, a black man like a negro, a white man like us, nor a yellow man like the Chinese. They decided he must be the only remaining appropriate colour, so he was spoken of afterwards as the "blue man".

One day a member of the staff going into the cook's room unexpectedly, found that worthy removing the dinner-plates from under the blankets where they had been stowed to keep them free from dust! We were much depressed at the news, and the cook was suitably admonished. But he was hopeless.

In the summer that mess-room was like an oven. A tea-spoon regularly did duty for a butter-knife. To this day it makes me smile grimly to hear people complaining of the butter in civilization.

As living conditions on Rocky Island were so rigorous, it was perhaps as well that there was no feminine society of any kind there—and we had no visitors. A miserable sort of life, some may say. But it all came in the day's work, and the staff accepted the position philosophically; the place had to be worked, and nothing could be gained by making a fuss about it.

There were no trees on the island—nothing to give shelter from the boisterous winds. A coarse kind of grass grew plentifully in some areas, and among this the pelicans built their nests. They were the only birds to be found nesting, possibly because they alone were able to repel the attacks of the wild cats; these animals were the descendants of tame ones left by the company operating there previously. At times they could be seen out on the rocks in the early morning, watching for fish in the pools, though we could not find out their method of catching them. The cats were not attracted to our settlement at all, probably through the activities of the fox-terriers, who had some great hunts; but the rocky formation was all in favour of the cats.

It was interesting to watch the fishing operations of the shags, pelicans, and cranes, and the systematic manner in which they worked a small deep bay. Shortly after dawn a number of shags would come flying along; spacing off in an orderly way, they would alight in line across the mouth of the bay; then diving they would drive the fish towards the shore. While they were thus engaged, a flock of pelicans would swoop down to shallower water farther in, and with their long bills and necks catch numerous fish without diving. They too worked in towards the shore. Then some white, and a few blue, cranes would put in an appearance, wading close to the beach and snapping up all the small fish there, or any which hopped out of the water. The three kinds of birds in their different capacities formed a singularly efficient fishing unit.

The small lake in the interior dried up during our occupation, so wild fowl were not as numerous as on our first visit with German Harry; but occasionally a flock of whistling ducks put in an appearance, affording a welcome change of diet. These strange birds whistled in a peculiar way while feeding in the grass, apparently hunting for insects or seeds.

Our Malay and Chinese labour accepted the rigorous conditions without undue complaint, and really behaved very well; they doubtless looked on the employ as a good opportunity to save money. One Chinaman in particular is remembered by the good evidence he supplied as to the harmless nature of the phosphate guano in the matter of health. He had been dubbed by the staff wag "Mouthy", owing to the fact that his mouth was always wide open under any conditions; shutting it looked like a physical impossibility.

A man was required for feeding the disintegrator, an exceedingly dusty job, and extra pay was offered for a volunteer. To our surprise Mouthy not only offered for the duty, but kept at the trying work month after month without any ill effects. We frequently lost sight of him in the cloud of dust, but he was always there with his mouth wide open, and shovel in hand, regulating the quantity entering the machine.

Sometimes it was a matter of speculation with us as to how much he swallowed in a day.

We were glad to finish up at Rocky Island. When operations there were closed down, it was not surprising that several of the old hands decided that they would try their fortunes in civilization, before getting too advanced in years. At that time there was very little in the business for any one —except perhaps the labourers; they were on quite a good footing.

ON MORNINGTON ISLAND

WORK was slack in the laboratory at Rocky Island, and the stock of firewood was low in the cooking department. The *Lizzie* was available for a few days and I suggested to my father (who was still managing for the company) that I should go across to Mornington Island with seven or eight Malays and bring back a load of wood. At first the idea was not approved, as the blacks there were known to be a wild lot. One of our staff had been speared in the thigh some years previously, when out with a party of prospectors looking for gold. At the time they did not even see the blacks; several spears were suddenly thrown from among the trees and long grass, and one reached its mark.

Then a manager at Rocky Island for the company that preceded ours had a narrow escape on Mornington. He had gone across with some men to obtain supplies of wood and water. While they were at work he wandered away unarmed. The blacks caught him, and in his struggle to escape he was being roughly handled, when suddenly his false teeth dropped out. That was enough for the blacks: a man who could shed all his teeth in such a manner must surely be allied with "debil-debil" and off they went posthaste. It is not related whether the white man even waited to grab his teeth before making a bee-line for the camp.

Mornington Island is the largest of the Wellesley Group, being nearly forty miles long and fourteen wide in places;

there are only two or three larger islands in Australian waters. It is densely wooded in parts, and from Rocky Island, about twelve miles distant, we could frequently see the smoke of fires lighted by the blacks. We had wanted to get an idea of its formation in view of the possibility of phosphate guano deposits there, so my proposal was quite a good one, and was finally agreed to. After various paternal injunctions to be careful and not run risks, we set off.

The leading Malay with me was known as "Big Alik", a native of one of the North African countries and a fine type of fellow. We took a shot-gun and several rifles, including a light Colt's magazine type, with which I had the credit of being a good shot. The object of the rifles was of course purely defensive, it being considered by those who had some knowledge of wild blacks that they would keep away if they knew we had guns; doubtless it was wisdom born of experience on their part.

At Mornington the cutter had to anchor about two miles off shore, as shallow water ran out a long way; a wide stretch of reef could not be crossed until the tide was at least half in, and it was therefore necessary to do tide work for boating the firewood off; a large punt had been taken for this purpose. While pulling ashore we noticed some blacks in the distance making off along the beach. In a short time I was banging away with the shot-gun, there being some white cockatoos about. Tough eating they proved to be!

There were plenty of trees suitable for our purpose quite close to the beach, and after setting the Malays to work, I took Alik and went off to have a look at the open forest country in the vicinity. It was soon evident that the island's formation did not suggest phosphate deposits; there was no need to spend further time over that aspect of our mission.

The element of sport and fresh food was more promising, and naturally appealed to me. Several large waterholes or billabongs were likely places for wild ducks, and we saw some kangaroos jumping about in their spectacular style—my first experience with them. Alik was very emphatic that they were good eating, so I fired at one, wounding it; we had quite a chase and then the animal went over on its back with the long hind legs drawn up as if ready to strike out.

"Get hold of it Alik," I shouted. But he knew more about kangaroos than I did, and exclaimed "No fear!" A billet of wood soon did what was necessary. Subsequently I heard that the animal had taken a fighting position and could easily have ripped any one approaching carelessly.

Another thrill was my first experience with a snake; one of the Malays poked it out from a hollow log while we waited with sticks at the other end. The snake didn't have a chance.

While at the island, our procedure was to have meals ashore during the day, and to sleep aboard at night when the blacks might have been troublesome. The plan went very well and I quite enjoyed the novelty of the experience, the Malays doing everything possible for my comfort.

Invariably I found when alone with different races of coloured people on various expeditions, that they are particularly attentive on such occasions, as if appreciative of the confidence placed in them. They seem to realize that the onus is on them to respond, which they do at times in a very full measure. Quite a pleasing instance of this occurred at Mornington Island, and touched me deeply at the time.

One morning after going ashore we loaded the punt and I sent them off at once to catch the tide, keeping one man ashore with me to cross-cut some logs. Within a quarter of an hour the wind freshened, and before the boat could return from the cutter it was blowing feather white. The Gulf seems to specialize in these sudden gales as well as in other weather phenomena, such as singular fog and mist effects; in waterspouts too—I have seen eight in a single squall, and they were decidedly disconcerting when viewed from a small cutter towards which they appeared to be travelling.

To return to Mornington Island. We went on with the wood-sawing, keeping a watchful eye of course for the appearance of the blacks, and with rifles handy. It was late

M

in the afternoon before the wind eased off, though still too strong for the boat to come ashore, so I thought. One could not but feel somewhat anxious with the approach of nightfall; the blacks would be sure to know that most of our party had gone aboard that morning. Then suddenly shouts came from farther along the beach, and we saw Alik and another with rifles walking towards the camp; the others were in the cutter's boat working it along inshore.

Though much relieved at their appearance, I started to rate Alik forthwith, telling him that in taking such a risk they might all have been drowned. He was quite worked up and said they had been very anxious for our safety; the captain was pacing up and down the deck watching the beach all day with his glasses. How could they go back to Rocky Island and tell the "Old Master" that his boy had been caught by the blackfellows, and there was a quaver in his voice as he said this.

My scolding ceased there and then, for that strange sensation known to most of us as a lump in the throat had suddenly developed. After leaving the cutter they had not attempted to pull directly against the wind and rough sea, but took them at an angle, reaching the beach several miles down the coast.

Early one morning when rowing to our camp-site, we were surprised to see a dingo padding along the beach at high-water mark, so intent on searching for food of sorts that it did not see us. My first impulse was to shoot the animal from the boat, but I refrained from doing so in case it might have been owned by the blacks. When about twenty-five yards distant, the Malays gave a simultaneous yell; the dingo looked up and was off like a flash, demonstrating the pace that these canines of bad reputation can put up.

We did not have any actual encounters with the blacks. We knew they were in the vicinity, because each evening they visited our camp after we had gone off to the cutter. Various odds and ends were left for them, but nothing to arouse their suspicions. Some comic illustrated papers, weighted down with pebbles, doubtless gave them some amusement, and possibly supplied evidence that we bore them no ill will. The element of humour is, probably, one of those features which help to make the whole world kin. The blacks no doubt realized the purpose of our visit and did not resent it. At the same time one never knew when they might be out to avenge some previous trouble with other people.

Just before returning to Rocky Island, several kangaroos and some ducks were shot; the billabongs near by proved a splendid place for game and I often went to them, taking one of the Malays with me. Once I caught sight of a big kangaroo in the distance hopping along for his evening drink. Bending down I ran to the opposite bank and under the shelter of a bushy tree. Thump! Thump! Thump! Along came the kangaroo, stopping four yards from me. He did not know what had hit him; I have never bagged one so easily since. This fresh meat proved a welcome change at the staff mess-room; a continual diet of tinned or salt provisions becomes very wearisome.

Our expedition was considered so successful both from the firewood aspect and the spoils of the chase, that I went over again, meeting with very similar experiences, though without having again to test the fidelity and pluck of Big Alik and his friends.

The worst feature about Mornington Island was the extraordinary number of flies, and the vigorous and pertinacious efforts they put forth to get into one's eyes, mouth, ears, and nose simultaneously. They were a pest. To take aim at a kangaroo with about three dozen flies engaged in this manner was a novel and exasperating experience. In order to eat my meals minus flies, I used to sit in the smoke of a fire, often with streaming eyes, and gulp the food down as quickly as possible. Afterwards I was very glad to lower the mosquito-net veil. However, there is usually something or other to put up with when one strikes out from the beaten track, and fussy people ought to stay at home.

The last I heard of Mornington Island was that a mission

had been established there. No doubt the blacks have ceased to be "wild" and I trust are less suspicious of the white man. I hope also that the missionary has found some satisfactory way of dealing with the flies. He certainly has my sympathy in that respect. To have to endure these pests day after day and month after month must indeed be a trial.

T. C. ROUGHLEY

THEODORE CLEVELAND ROUGHLEY, zoologist and author, Superintendent of Fisheries and Game for New South Wales, is the author of numerous scientific papers and several ichthyological works. His abundantly illustrated *Wonders of the Great Barrier Reef* (1936) is one of the most popular books on the subject so far published.

WE GO FISHING

ANGLERS on the Great Barrier Reef fall naturally into two classes. There are those who regard angling only as a side-line; who join a boat party bent on reef fishing because it is one of the things usually done on the reef; it is part of the programme and one must see and do everything possible in the limited time available. When preparing for the trip these novices in the noble art usually go to a fishing-tackle dealer and seek his advice as to the tackle required, but many rely on the skipper of the boat for their gear.

Then we have the real anglers who fish for the surface-swimming fish with rods and gear of the utmost refinement. There is nothing casual about these anglers; fishing is in their blood and years of experience have taught them how to match their skill against the cunning and fierce fury of the fastest of the ocean's denizens. For months before the trip they have discussed together the habits of the different species, for months they have argued about the respective merits of the various types of gear—the best kind of rod, the efficiency of reels, the breaking strain of lines, and the attraction of lures. To these men angling is a life's hobby; they talk eternally of the catches of the past, they dream of the greater ones to come.

We join a launch party about to start for a day's angling for fish that live amongst and in the vicinity of the coral at Heron Island. The skipper knows the best spots, and as he makes for a likely ground we rig our lines, some of heavy cord, others of gut, the skipper supplying sinkers and hooks if those we have come provided with are not of the right weight and size. A spot is chosen where there is a long, wide channel between coral reefs; the engine stops and the launch is left to drift along where the bottom is broken only by isolated coral boulders. The lines are baited with large pieces of fish caught the previous day, and over they go, the heavy sinkers taking them rapidly to the bottom.

Within a few minutes one of the party is hauling in the first fish. Quietly, but with obvious pride (for the competition for the first fish is always keen) he pulls in his line while all the other anglers peer into the water in an endeavour to catch a glimpse of the fish as it nears the surface. Shortly a coral bream of glistening silver is flopping on the deck; it weighs about three pounds, and, as the skipper approaches, the angler responsible for it holds up his prize for inspection. Never shall I forget the look in this man's face as the skipper takes his catch with the casual remark that such small fish "come in handy for bait". What sacrilege! Our friend's previous angling experience had been obtained in waters where a three-pound bream would be regarded as a rare prize, a fish to be talked about for long afterwards. And here it is regarded as rubbish, fit only for use as bait. But if a three-pound fish is so despised, there must be something worth-while in store for us. And there is.

Suddenly one of the anglers is hauling in a fish that is obviously heavy; although he knows he must get it into the boat as quickly as possible lest it take his line amongst the coral, which will surely cut it, he is several times forced to let it run a short distance before he is able again to turn it. Nearer and nearer he brings his catch till just beneath the surface we see a handsome fellow flashing pink and silvery; a final dash and it disappears beneath the blue water; slowly it is again brought to the surface, this time to be hastily lifted into the boat where it is determined as a king snapper of about fifteen pounds, its silvery sides ornamented with bright pink bands which take the form of a broad arrow and have been responsible for the name "Government bream" being sometimes bestowed upon it. "That's better," remarks our skipper, as he places the fish in the ice-box, "and we shall probably get a lot of these this morning."

Now we are properly amongst the fish; they are flopping everywhere on the deck. And what fish! Every one is an object of great beauty—coral cod up to thirty pounds, no two alike in colour, some bright red spotted with blue, others blue with red spots; snapper, a delicate pink with a flashing iridescence, red-mouthed emperors bluish-silver with blood-red markings about the head and on the dorsal fin and the bases of the pectorals; hussars, pale pink with a broad green-ish yellow band traversing the sides longitudinally; blue-spotted groper in a variety of beautiful liveries, some green along the back with blue fins and pale sides; others bright pink with multi-hued fins, many with opalescent blue spots along the back and sides. What an array of colour indeed.

In the course of a couple of hours we have landed fifty fish ranging from about two to thirty pounds, with an average weight of about six pounds. There is no art in landing these fish; they bite greedily, a sharp pull on the line to drive the hook home and a rapid hauling from the bottom to keep the fish away from the coral with as tight a strain as the line will stand—and in a short time, measured usually in seconds only, the fish is on the deck thumping the boards heavily with its tail as it continues its swimming movement.

It is interesting to see how in the space of an hour or two the merest tiro develops into an experienced angler. Not only can he tell you the species of fish he has on his line long before he sees it, but often he will distinguish between the various kinds by the manner in which they strike his bait. "Ah, another sweetlip," he exclaims, and four times out of five he is wrong; but it savours of the experienced angler and just that far serves its purpose.

Curious that it should happen that way, but the sweet young thing of the party, enjoying her honeymoon in the romantic setting of a coral island, hooked a Queensland groper. Squealing excitedly she calls to hubby to help her—

she has hooked a giant shark or a whale or something. Hubby grabs her line and, after a strenuous tussle, his wife dancing round and giving instructions what to do as the fish begins to throw its weight about (instructions which hubby, experienced angler that he is, invariably ignores), the fish is brought to the surface, gaffed, and hauled on board. Then ensues the usual argument over its weight. It is probably fifty pounds, but who would deny the gentle angler's estimate of a hundred pounds? Hers is not alone an angler's prerogative. And so that hundred-pound groper will go down in history as the best fish, the best bit of fishing, of the day. Any one can haul a fish aboard; that's simply a matter of brute strength —it's the hooking of the fish that counts. She said so. Many times. And now that I have related its true history I feel ungallant, ashamed, and sincerely hope our fair angler never reads this book.

Such is a typical day's fishing on the reef. Of course, there are times when very few fish are to be had, but they are the exception rather than the rule, and in many parts of the Barrier the boat rarely returns without a good haul. Winter or summer, day or night, coral fish bite freely.

And now we shall spend a day with the rod fishermen at Hayman Island in the Whitsunday Group.

We are astir before daybreak because the early morning fishing is usually the best. Making for the mess-room we find some of the party already preparing a cup of tea, while others are overhauling their rods, oiling their reels, or attaching their lures, some of feathers, others in the form of automatic strikers. No time is lost over refreshments; a few sandwiches are washed down with a cup or two of tea and the party makes for the beach to the accompaniment of the melodious chatter of currawongs and the boisterous laughter of kookaburras as they greet the dawn in the magnolias and beach oaks fringing the shore.

The day has broken fine and clear; but a fresh breeze from the south-east, unusual during July, causes some concern. We pack into a dinghy till there are but three or four inches of freeboard and, although one of the party puts his whole weight behind the oars, we make slow progress against the choppy sea. The dinghy is overcrowded with rods, legs, and cameras. All safely aboard, the engine kicks over in an instant and we head for the channel south of the island, for we intend to fish off the eastern shores of Hook Island. But the fish may be anywhere, and this channel has frequently provided great sport, so the lines are dropped overboard. Four anglers make themselves comfortable, their rods secured by a strong harness encircling their backs, their lures trailing from fifteen to thirty yards astern according to the whim of the individual angler. At last the day has arrived that has rarely been out of the anglers' minds for months past—a whole year's work has been done to win this holiday. Surely the guardian deity of all anglers is watching over them; surely he will realize what this day means to his devout disciples.

And so we troll. One hour, two, three hours pass, and not a sign of a fish is seen. This is unusual, but our anglers show no sign of despair—hope springs eternal in their breasts. But why no fish? After the same time on their first day out last year a dozen fish were scattered about the deck. But the tide is on the ebb and the water, churned up by the breeze as it comes from the shallow water inshore, is slightly milky. Perhaps when the tide turns, bringing in the crystal clear water from deeper regions, the fish will be attracted by the lures dancing along the surface in the wash astern.

To those of us who are not fishing time begins to drag; our eyes cease to watch the lures for the swish of the strike and we gaze over the water reflecting from the sun a silvery sheen which scintillates with a myriad points of light. And as we cruise along the coast of Hook Island with its lofty peaks now obscured as a fleecy cloud drifts over them, we find our interest transferred to the grandeur of the scenery about us. Rugged lichen-covered rocks, mottled grey and brown, rise hundreds of feet sheer from the water with here and there a pine-tree apparently growing in the solid rock; now we pass a dense forest of pines with trunks as straight as match sticks, while on the summits of the ridges great walls of rock stand gaunt like the ruined castles of some giants of the past. Here the vegetation is dense but stunted, and an occasional pine-tree towers, sentinel-like, high above it. An osprey's nest, a crude affair of interlaced sticks about six feet in diameter, is perched on the summit of some barren rocks fifty feet or so above the water, the owner peering at us over the top, apparently wondering what we are about.

Engrossed by the beauty about us, our reverie is interrupted by one of the anglers coming forward. He had a strike and missed, and now he must give way to another until again his turn comes round. Disconsolate, he lies on the deck to ponder over his mistake.

There is a swish astern, a fish flashes momentarily at the surface, a reel screeches, and a Spanish mackerel races away with incredible speed. Far in the distance he leaps high in the air, throws the hook, and bounds away to freedom. Another angler joins us amidships and complains that he allowed too much slack; he is out of touch, but some fish will pay the penalty when he gets his hand in.

And so the morning wears on with a faint promise only of the excitement we had been told was in store for us. Then from out of the galley a faint sizzling greets our ears and the smell of fish frying fills our nostrils. The morning on the water has sharpened our appetites, and the sizzling and spluttering below is music in our ears. It seems a long time before that fish is cooked; but at last, with palates moist and keen, we accept the invitation shouted from below, "Lunch is ready." A liberal helping of Spanish mackerel caught the afternoon before is devoured with a relish that is but due to a fish of such fine flavour and texture. The mackerel is not only the best sporting fish but is also one of the finest eating fish of the Barrier Reef; though just a trifle dry its flavour and the firmness of its flesh are a real delight.

During lunch there are but two topics of conversation—the excellence of the fish and the cause of the morning's poor sport. Alone amongst us the skipper retains his confidence; he goes so far as to guarantee good sport when the tide turns; moreover, he reminds us that the breeze has dropped. Somehow, we have great faith in our skipper; he has angled over the reef since boyhood and he impresses us that he knows all its peculiarities. And so our anglers, refreshed and inspired with renewed confidence, again take up their stations.

It is about half-past three when the fun begins. We run into a great school of giant mackerel; they appear excited at our coming and leap into the air as if to signal their delight. Wherever we look there appears to be at least one fish out of the water. The anglers stiffen their backs, take a firmer grip of their rods, stare intently at their lures. A flashing green back momentarily breaks the water, a reel screams, and the fight is on, the other anglers winding in their lines to give their more fortunate companion a free field to work in. Instantly the fish strikes, our skipper throws the engine into neutral, ready in a moment to race it forward or astern, to manoeuvre the boat this way or that in order to prevent the fish from making to the front of the boat and so fouling the angler's line. The first mad rush over, the fish turns, then plunges down, the angler putting more drag on his reel to prevent the fish sounding too deeply; realizing the futility of its downward flight the fish now makes for the surface; with a great bound it leaps high in the air, hitting the water on its return with a resounding smack, to race away again just beneath the surface at a speed that fills us with amazement. Now it rushes towards the boat and the skipper gives the engine full throttle; no orders are necessary from angler to engine-room; the skipper has manoeuvred his boat in similar circumstances hundreds, thousands of times, and knows what to do in every emergency.

And so this infuriated fish fights every inch for its freedom, with the angler using every resource he knows to keep it where he wants it. Again it goes down; again more drag is put on the reel; over bends the rod at an alarming angle. The angler now begins to pump; throwing his body back he heaves on his rod, then leans forward and winds in the slack. This is hard work and beads of perspiration begin to gather on his forehead. The fish is stubborn; but foot by foot it is brought closer to the surface. Is the fight over? As the fish sights the boat it tears away in another mad rush, taking about fifty yards of line out. And then the fish, five feet of fighting fury, turns again towards the boat; with a mad rush it leaps clear over the stern and we see its glistening black eye staring at us, we see a row of sharp, vicious teeth as the fish, stiff as a ramrod, cleaves the air above us. As it hits the water it sends a shower of spray over us and when next we sight it, it is thirty or forty yards away.

But it now shows signs of tiring and gradually the angler becomes its master; its rushes are shorter and less speedy; each is nearer the boat than that which preceded it, until at last, every ounce of its fighting strength exhausted, it is brought alongside; a gaff is thrust into it and many willing hands haul it aboard. There it lies, its handsome green back and silvery sides glistening in the sunlight; reviving a little, it flings itself about the deck fiercely snapping its pointed jaws. It is a noble fish whose fighting spirit was subdued only when it was exhausted beyond further effort.

And as we admire it our angler takes off his shirt and with a towel wipes the sweat from his body. He is tired, very, but his countenance is aglow. He has had his thrill for the day and is content.

Of course, there is the usual conjecture about the weight of the fish, but no angler's exaggerated estimate is allowed to pass in this company. There are rules governing the strength of the line to be used, the length of the trace, the length of double line connected to the trace, and all records of weights must be accurate, for trophies are allotted for the heaviest fish caught in various classes. This mackerel is found to turn the scale at fifty-three pounds.

But we are still in this school of fish and all four lines are again over the stern while the boat circles about amongst them. In a few minutes a reel begins to spin, followed by another, then another; yes, the fourth goes also. All four lines are tearing away together. Each angler concentrates on his own fish; as one winds his reel to draw the fish nearer the boat another pays his line out as his quarry dashes away in an irresistible rush. Two of them, swimming in opposite directions, cross, and the anglers change places, their right hands on their reels, their eyes on their lines. For fully five minutes the combined fight is on when one of the four finds his line slack. Thoroughly sorry for himself he reels in and discovers that another fish has bitten his line at the swivel. The three remaining anglers scarcely notice his misfortune; this is no time for sympathy. The skill of the skipper is now tested to the utmost; he must manoeuvre his boat to give each angler a fair chance, and this calls for fine judgment when fish are tearing away in opposite directions. For about a quarter of an hour the fight continues when one of the anglers brings to gaff a mackerel weighing twenty-seven pounds. This leaves more room for the remaining two who, aided by the skilful movements of the launch, manage to manoeuvre their fish out of each other's way. At the end of twenty-five minutes the second fish, weighing thirty-six pounds, is landed, and our sole remaining angler continues the fight against his fish which, judging from the tussle he is having, is the heaviest of them all. Eventually he brings it alongside. It turns the scale at forty-four pounds.

And so the afternoon passes. Before the sun's last rays are fading into twilight fifteen large mackerel can be counted strewn about the deck. One might reasonably assume that after such a strenuous afternoon's work (for hard work it certainly was) our angler friends' lust for game would have been completely satiated; but there is no satisfying an angler whose pulse quickens to the run of the reel, and after tea and a consultation with the skipper it is decided to moor the launch in a quiet bay and angle for reef fish.

The night air is balmy but cool and we wrap rugs about ourselves as we lie on the deck above the wheel-house. No longer the thrill of the screeching reel, but quietly and efficiently the anglers haul their catches to the surface, and we have difficulty in determining what species they are as they are freed from the hook by the light of a hurricane lamp. The silence of the night is broken only by the lapping of the water against the boat as she rides at anchor, by an occasional flopping of the fish about the deck, and by the plaintive cries of curlews from the wooded depths of the island, dark and mysterious, towering high above us on our starboard quarter.

Suddenly one of the anglers stumbles as he makes a dash for a heavy line he had left unattended as he fished for smaller fry. Into the night his line is drawn with a strength which his bare fingers cannot check, and, handing the line to the angler nearest him, he hastily dons his gloves to save his fingers from scorching and cutting. No spectacular leaps, no rapid skimming over the surface of the water, just a dead weight as the monster (obviously a shark from its movements) sulks at the end of the line. Now the angler gains a few yards, now he is forced to give way as the shark moves away from the boat. And thus the tussle continues, each opponent momentarily gaining an advantage. At the end of an hour the shark is alongside, subdued but still unconquered, and three shots are fired into its brain or at least where its brain is conjectured to be. In the dim light of the lamp it is turned over on its back, its mouth, bordered by a row of vicious triangular teeth, grinning even in death. Shall we haul it on board or cut it adrift? It is left to the angler who caught it to decide, and we find him quite indifferent, for hand-lining does not count in the records of this august band of fishermen; and so the line is cut and we watch the ugly brute sink slowly out of sight.

It was a tiger shark about ten feet in length, and the ocean has been bereft of one of its greatest marauders. Somehow everyone felt intense satisfaction at the capture of that shark. One can easily feel sorry for a mackerel or any of the other food fishes as they lie gasping on the deck, but a shark—sly, repulsive, cowardly—who can show the slightest sympathy for its suffering? Yet, after all, there is no blame attaching to it for its apparent misdemeanours towards mankind; if occasionally it attacks us it does so in the ordinary course of its feeding; we are perhaps too apt to attribute it to malice, and in doing so frequently treat the creature with unnecessary harshness.

Again the anglers settle down to their fishing, but the fish have apparently been scared by the presence of the shark and the bites are now few.

Drawing our rugs tightly about us we turn on our backs and gaze up into the heavens. The night is dark but clear, and the stars above appear far more numerous than in the southern regions whence we come. The lap of the water against the boat is very soothing; the curlews appear to be retreating farther and farther into the island, the sounds of voices grow dimmer and more confused till at last they die completely away.

H. H. FINLAYSON

HEDLEY HERBERT FINLAYSON, Honorary Curator of Mammals in the South Australian Museum, Adelaide, has since 1920 conducted annual field studies in mammals in all the Australian States. In *The Red Centre* (1935), he deals with animal life in the heart of Australia.

THE RANGES OF THE CENTRE

OF the many misconceptions which find a place in the popular estimate of Central Australia, the idea of its flatness, of its treelessness and its monotony, is probably the most persistent. Even amongst those who have read widely in the literature of Australian exploration and have seen something of inland conditions, such impressions are often to be found. On reflection, it seems probable that the cause is two-fold.

First, the frequent use of the word "desert" by some of the early explorers for all the country away from the ranges, has been adopted by some of the later geographers. No doubt the use of the word for an area of low rainfall and few surface waters is justified when applied to most of the interior; but it is most unfortunate that the popular idea of a desert is very different from the scientific one, and usually takes the form of a wind-tortured Sahara of drifting sand, whose chief function is to provide material for the "brick-fielder" dust-storms which occasionally cloud the towns.

The second cause of misunderstanding arises from the fact that from all the settled areas of the south and east, the Centre must be approached through a belt of some hundreds of miles of pastoral country which, to a greater or less extent, has been wrecked by overstocking and other amenities of the white man's occupation. The traveller from Adelaide, for example, having cleared the Flinders Range, gazes out from the carriage window on the goat-made desolations which follow. He consults his time-table, and, finding that his change from the parklands has been wrought in four hundred miles, and that the Alice is still six hundred miles away, does some mental arithmetic, and concludes that Hades itself awaits him.

It is true that parts of the country, particularly of the Lake Eyre basin, come close even to the popular conception of a desert. But the Luritja Country—the south-west portion of Central Australia and contiguous tracts in the adjoining States—is totally different. Though the climate is rigorous, and the rarity of surface waters made the lot of the first-comers a hard one, the face of the country is varied, often attractive, and sometimes highly picturesque. The drabness which characterizes the more southerly dry country—the greys and dull greens, the fawns and faded browns of the saltbush tablelands, for example—have little place here; and it might well be known as the Red Centre. Sand, soil, and most of the rocks are a fiery cinnabar, and the grey mulga is liberally splashed with the clear green of ironwood and sterculia.

The country presents two very distinct environments— the ranges and the tracts surrounding them. First for consideration are the ranges, since from them the whole country is naturally orientated, and the permanent waters which they hold are the pivotal points from which the country is worked over.

Judged by the standards of other lands or even of eastern Australia, they are but minor features. Few of them have a longitudinal extent of over a hundred and fifty miles, their breadth is usually less than fifty miles and their highest peaks rise no more than three thousand feet above the general country level. Yet in spite of their insignificant dimensions they are curiously impressive; and the first sight of a blue line of distant hills breaking the horizon of scrub is seldom without a pleasurable thrill. One enters their valleys as a refuge, for here is water and ease, and for a space one's eyes may rest upon sheltered scenes the nearness of which is a welcome relief from the vast prospects of the outside world.

N

They are bare, rocky chains, for the most part broken and weathered into wild and arresting contours; destitute outwardly of soils on their main ridges, timberless or with scattered cypress pines and mulgas, but supporting an interesting small flora in sheltered nooks and gorges.

Finest of all the Central ranges is the Musgrave. Although it appears to consist very largely of granite, the rock is fractured and altered over large areas, and the chain from the north or south presents contours totally different from those of the Everard, for example, which preserves the characteristic rounded, smooth bulges of the original granite intrusions. The southern front of the range is especially fine; one may ride for days along its foot with an ever-changing panorama of jagged peaks and ridges, which never palls. From the far-famed Glen Ferdinand on this side issues the Ferdinand Creek, which, within a few miles of its exit, is joined by the Currie and other streams, together forming the Officer. The Officer is by far the largest channel in the Centre west of the Finke. For a hundred miles or more it sweeps on through the sandy country south of the range with an avenue of tall brilliant green gums fringing its wide bed. At fifty miles from the opening of the Glen, where it crosses a patch of spinifex and loose sand, it is still a hundred and fifty yards wide and with a clearly defined channel—a striking testimony to the immense volume of water which the range has shed at some former period of its history.

At Ernabella in Glen Ferdinand, the pioneers of the Musgrave have an outcamp which was my base for six weeks in a series of expeditions into the surrounding country over a radius of three hundred miles. The camp is in the heart of the hills and I left it, and came into it, from half a dozen different angles. After weeks in the scrub country outside the range, those home-comings to Ernabella are amongst the pleasantest recollections I have of the Centre. There seems to be no single vista round about it which lacks an element of striking beauty, or becomes commonplace or dull. The peculiar feature of the Musgrave landscapes is the great development of grasslands. In amongst the hills, and frequently enclosed on all sides, and accessible only through rocky passes, are little plains of varying extent, and broad valleys, entirely free from bush growth, but with an even carpet of grasses and herbs.

The large open space of true "waving in the wind" sort of grass is a rare feature in this country of scrubs and thickets; and when they are backed by long vistas of blue hills falling away with a gently graded softening of outline into the distance, a combination is presented which stirs memories of a softer clime.

To Giles the Englishman—after weeks of bush-whacking in the mulga farther north—these views appealed with special force, and his descriptions of them are pathetically filled with a homesick longing which found expression in the nomenclature of the place. His maps are studded with glens and passes, tarns and vales. It must be admitted that Giles carried the matter rather far. Farther up the country some of his "vales" and "passes" are plains miles wide with scarcely a bump of any kind breaking the horizon. Twenty years after, Sir Baldwin Spencer was so disappointed with the Vale of Tempe that he was constrained to remark rather testily on the "ridiculous" character of Giles's names.

So far as they apply to the Musgraves, however, they are appropriate enough. Basedow, in the winter of 1903, was similarly impressed by the "unaustralian" character of many of its views—if one may put it so unpatriotically. Writing of Glen Ferdinand he states:

When the mists of evening rose and the light in the Glen grew dim, the blue-black thickets of mulga on the plain could no longer be distinguished from the pines on the hills, and I could scarce persuade myself to believe that the landscape before me was part of arid Central Australia, and not Thuringia or Tyrol.

I saw it all in the height of midsummer, when the green swards and wild flowers were no longer there to help the illusion, but even so the old-worldliness of the place was very evident.

Each range has special characters which give it an individuality of its own: the low rolling outline of the

Everard, with its bare smooth domes and rock slides; the grassy mounds and conical peaks of the Musgrave; the extraordinary mural cliffs of the Petermann; the canyon-like gorges with their smooth rock basins which give the George Gill the finest waters in the centre; and the glistening quartz screes that lie like a mantle of hail under the dark mulga, round about the Rawlinson.

When one reflects on them individually, these features come first to mind; but about them all there is the same curious atmosphere of aloofness from the surrounding country. They look out, as it were, over a world which has seen great changes in which they have had no part. To walk alone into their gorges by moonlight; to look into the clear depths of their splendid pools when the noon sun flares on the rocks and the world is unbelievably still; or to listen to the dawn wind singing in the pines on their tops, brings always the same suggestion: a sense of things about them once familiar, but now long forgotten; a haunting nostalgia that will not be shaken off.

The feeling is stirred by many parts of the Centre, and is the secret of much of its rather melancholy appeal. It needs no fore-knowledge of its geological history to see and to feel, for example, the influence of the old-time seas in shaping the contours of some of the lower lands. This impression of things anciently marine is especially strong about the George Gill Range. It rises as the scarp of an old plateau from a sandy mulga plain, which stretches away south two hundred miles to the Musgraves. It still retains its flat-topped outline, except where it is broken by steep little gorges and gullies, which, opening out suddenly on to the flats, are flanked east and west by bold crags and bluffs. As one rides west along the foot of the range, the feeling of something familiar about the whole scene recurs with tantalizing frequency. In the heat and glare of the sun the red rocks hold their secret well, but on the rare grey days when a fresh wind piles the clouds behind the hills, the changes of a million years fall suddenly away, and one remembers. Even as the light is fading, the mouths of the gorges have become little bays, the mouths of the gullies shingly coombs, and the crags and bluffs of the range are now the capes and headlands of a rocky coast-line streaming away into the west.

Wondering at the transformation, one yet remembers the desiccation of the land. Surely no imagining could ever bring back to the thirsty sands the element whose waves would make the change complete? But as if to mock comes a vast whispering out of the south, and the stirring of those miles of usurping mulga is the very voice of the ancient sea, come into its own again.

R. H. CROLL

ROBERT HENDERSON CROLL, naturalist and member of the administrative staff of the Victorian Education Department, made four journeys into the interior of Australia. On the first he assisted Professor S. D. Porteus, Professor of Clinical Psychology, Hawaii, to test the intelligence of the natives. The following passage, from *Wide Horizons* (1937), exemplifies the nature of his impressions.

HERMANNSBURG

OUR headquarters we fixed at Hermannsburg, where the Lutheran missionaries rule and where we found not only hospitality but abundant material for our researches. It is about ninety miles west of Alice Springs, the terminus of the north-south railway line built by the Australian Commonwealth. Camel trains plod in and out to carry supplies to Hermannsburg, and to cattle-stations even farther out, but the camels take three days to travel the ninety miles. A motor-truck reduced the time to six or seven hours.

The train to the Alice ran once a fortnight. A notice board had caught the eye at one remote spot where a dusty track showed that sometimes vehicles crossed the line at this point. All around lay unpeopled desolation. The notice read: "Beware of Trains!"

A fierce wind had raged a few days before our visit, and its effects were still visible. It had carried the desert sand, sand as fine as any in an hour-glass, as far as the coastal towns where it had fallen as "red rain", charging the Spring showers with a pigment which marked the streets and the dwellings as with stains of blood. Soft and almost impalpable as this sand was, it stopped our train twenty-six times in one stretch of ten miles. Each time a gang of men, travelling ahead for the purpose, had to dig the line out to let us through.

Alice Springs was reached on the third day. We came to it by way of one of the amazing gaps cut by Nature through the Macdonnell Ranges. These mountains, as I have said, extend east and west for some 300 miles across the centre of Australia and they are pierced at irregular intervals by deep ravines, really river beds, which provide the only means by which north and south traffic may pass through such a mighty barrer. The ravines, or gaps, may be no more than a few yards wide; their walls may tower up seven or eight hundred feet. The rivers which have made them are usually destitute of water, but floods course down from time to time and turn them into formidable streams, often miles across.

Ours was the second passenger train to reach Alice Springs, so the people turned out, almost *en masse*, to welcome it. The population then might be 200; the shops and houses formed a long straggling main street, in the sand of which still stood some fine eucalyptus-trees. Deep indeed must the roots go to derive sustenance from such soil in such a season. A cool hotel, some official residences with deep verandas, an hostel maintained beautifully by the Australian Inland Mission, a few stores, a tiny school—and one had seen Alice Springs.

Some half-castes and a few natives living in diminutive humpies on the far side of the Todd River were all the aborigines visible in the settlement. We chartered a motor-truck, loaded it with our measuring and testing apparatus and set out along the Macdonnell Ranges westward. We travelled most of the day; through Heavitree Gap, across plains covered with dusty mulga and desert oak and some Hakea, or over low hills rough with spinifex and porcupine grass, now rushing across stony river beds with never a drop of water in them, always with the mountains, now close, now distant, towering up on either side. Then from a sandhill we saw the Krichauff Range, standing a purple bar across the sunset, and in the middle distance the cement houses of Hermannsburg.

The Germans of this outpost in the wilderness have toiled long and faithfully as missionaries to convert the native people to Christianity. I shall not question the results; I shall only bear witness to the earnestness of the endeavour. Here it was that the missionary Strehlow laboured for so many years and from here he supplied the material of his monumental book on the Australian aboriginal.

He compiled, too, certain word-books of the Arunta, Dieri, Luritja and other native languages. It is a pity that these are still unpublished manuscripts, for the tribes are going or have gone, and their languages have gone with them. Strehlow's writings were in German; here is an opportunity for a learned society in the Fatherland, or elsewhere, to publish, and so place in permanent form, some unusually interesting work of scientific value.†

About 300 men, women and children, mostly members of the famous Arunta tribe, were listed in the books of the mission, and a number of these was always available for testing. So for three weeks we worked every day and eventually put together a valuable set of records which Professor Porteus has since worked out in Hawaii and published in his *Psychology of a Primitive People*. Very friendly was the general attitude towards us and we were gratified when after a short period of close association we were told that we had been admitted as members of the tribe.

This can best be described as a kind of honorary membership; mercifully it called for no participation in the customary initiation rites, embracing as they do the knocking out of a front tooth, the ceremony of circumcision and the still more painful practice of subincision.

Nevertheless we were members, and it was soon apparent that every one knew exactly his or her relationship to us. Tribal kinship goes further than the white man's limited relationship by marriage or by blood. We found we had numerous brothers and sisters and even, absurd as it may seem, a number of (for want of a better name) fathers and mothers apiece. A little girl, Angeluka, was brought to me and introduced as one of my mothers. She was possibly nine years old. Eight others were later to claim similar relationship.

There were nearly a hundred children at the mission, bright-eyed smiling youngsters with whom we were soon very much at home. In the day-time they were our com-

† See *Aranda Traditions*, by his son, T. G. H. Strehlow.

panions as often as we could have them; in the evenings they invariably sang to us. This is what used to happen on those spring nights. I wrote it at the time:

> Jinga arbalama
> Larberinja nuka
> I mankilna kuta
> Jinga ilbaukama
> Ara ntjara indora
> Inka kat mugala
> Lata bula ta itja
> Ninteula juntama.

The soft desert darkness is all about us, the little fires of the children are lighted, they sit in circles round them singing. "*Jinga arbalama* . . . " What is this haunting new-old song? I feel like Wordsworth regarding his solitary reaper:

> *Will no one tell me what she sings?—*
> *Perhaps the plaintive numbers flow*
> *For old, unhappy, far-off things,*
> *And battles long ago.*

Yet the language should not, maybe, sound foreign to Australian ears. It is pure Australian. The singers are the youngsters of two native tribes, the place is almost the exact centre of our huge continent, and the tongue is Arunta, made world-famous by many scientists. The voices rise shriller than the cicada chorus of a still day in summer and with much of the vibrant quality that is in the high-pitched strains of those fairy fiddlers. But what is the air?—the words may be Arunta and strange, but the tune is familiar. Ah, I know; it is the ancient German *Lorelei*, transported to these wild surroundings, and words given to it to voice the feelings of a people who are doomed. They see their land taken from them, they see their native animals passing down a road on which their feet too are set, and a teacher, with rare poetic insight, has put into their mouths this version of the old-world song . . . *Jinga arbalama*. . . . They are saying: "I do not know the name of my sadness. I often think of the olden days when plenty kangaroos sat on the hills. To-day I cannot find a single one."

Sad it is, but they are not deeply affected, these happy

children of a naturally smiling race. *"Mara indora!"* (very good) we cry, and with flashing white teeth, as yet unspoiled by the Arunta practice of knocking out an incisor, and with the merriest laughing eyes, they echo, even more shrilly than they sang, *"Mara indora!"*

Just as they have no form of salutation, so they appear to have no folk songs truly their own. The corroboree chants, at once monotonous and gripping, are not for these infants. Their world of music is a European one and they have adapted themselves to it wonderfully. Sometimes, too, they sing the English words. "Three blind mice!" announces the superintendent, and they are off, at a pitch I have never heard approached by any other human beings, in the repetitions of the adventures the farmer's wife had with the afflicted rodents.

It is hard to say which soar highest towards heaven, the boys' voices or the girls'. We chance it: *"Warra mara yielima!"* we proclaim in our best Arunta. There is a shriek of delight from all, but mainly from the boys, for what we have said is: "The boys sing nicely!" An excited yabber is followed by an unintelligible request from two of the older girls who have stolen up close, emboldened by the darkness. We guess its import. "Three blind mice, three blind mice," we chant and they are in full cry once more. This time we again applaud with vigorous *"Mara indora,"* then, diplomatically, *"Quarra mara yielima,"* signifying that it is the girls now who have excelled. Tumult greets this, laughter predominating.

A young moon hangs in the west, paled by the amber glow that lingers from the sun. Above is the great arch dwarfing us all to insignificance. The little fires die down and the little people creep towards us, less shy in the night than in the light of day. They come closer and closer till we are standing in a stirring pool of dark forms. "Quiet!" commands the superintendent. They have been served with fresh clothes to-day. "Are you all still clean and tidy?" he asks. *"Aua!"* they chorus, all safely agreeing to that in the dark. Then, for he is also schoolmaster, he attempts to display their

mental paces. "What does 'untidy' mean?" he inquires, with
strong emphasis on the "un". The bright boy, as much in
evidence here as in any white school, knows and answers
promptly. "Breakem trouser!" says he.

But they're off again. Someone has hummed "Abide With
Me" and to hint at a known air is to start the whole pack.
What vigour they put into it; still the rendering is not with-
out a certain light and shade. Withal it is musical.

We find that they are always wanting new songs. So we
rack our memories for fairly simple examples and presently
they are following us in the Hawaiian "*Mokehana Lei*". It
is astonishing how quickly they learn both the music and
the words. Before the session is over they are giving a colourful imitation of our rendering, and next day, wherever a few
of the younger natives gather together, we will hear solos
develop into choruses:

> *Mokehana Lei with its sweetness*
> *Bringing happy memories of Kauai,*
> *There are all the valleys,*
> *There are all the palis,*
> *Mokehana Lei that I love!*

One cannot help wondering what will be the speculations
of the first visitor from Honolulu to encounter the song in
these surroundings.

More popular still is "Old Macdonald had a farm", which
they find humorous to a degree. They delight particularly
in the turkeys—"With a gobble gobble here, and a gobble
gobble there, here a gobble, there a gobble, everywhere a
gobble-gobble" and while still in the learning stage they
keep on asking for "Mo' tuckey". An additional gobble
thrown in never fails to convulse them with laughter. We
teach them also "Good Night Ladies", which they sing with
fine effect.

Soft little hands are touching us by this time, timidly at
first, then more boldly as they feel no repulse. A few wild
children are amongst the others to-night, Luritjas from the
naked tribe newly camped on the Finke River below the
station, and they hold aloof; but it seems as if all the rest,

every single one of the eighty odd, have attached themselves to our hands or our clothing. I did not know that an ordinary number eight hand could be so expansive—I must have at least half a dozen tiny grubby paws in each of mine. There is something attractive in every young creature, and these helpless babes of the Stone Age, thrust as they have been without any preparation into a world in which they have no place, make a special appeal. . . . How close are tears and smiles! Sentiment is strong within me as I stoop towards the dark heads. One small fellow of about nine years lifts his face with a brilliant smile to meet me. "Me you fader!" he says. I laugh, but he is right: we two white men were made members of the Arunta nation a few days before. He is one of my several fathers. As we have each a number of mothers-in-law (who, by the merciful laws of our people, may never speak to us!) it follows that we have many wives. Personally I have recorded the names of nine belonga me. "How many wives this pfella?" I ask, anxious to learn my full responsibilities. A blackfellow readily counts up to ten by means of his hands; anything over that is "mob". "Oh, mob wife!" is the cheery response, the stress on "mob".

They don't know how comical their next selection sounds to our ears. It is Harry Lauder's "Roamin' in the Gloamin'," learnt from a gramophone record and reproduced with ludicrous imitation of the broad Scotch. In swift succession come "The Song of Australia" (their birthright song, if they only knew it!) and two war memories (though not for them) in "A Long Long Trail A-winding" and "Tipperary".

I flash my torch to see the effect. They are too much accustomed to fire to be impressed save by the ease of the lighting. "Blow!" I say, in an incautious moment, and set the example, switching off the light as I do so. Wild excitement follows. All must blow it out in turn and the circle of light reveals each time an eager young face, dark brown rather than black, surmounted by hair of the tone of ebony and relieved by a pair of the brightest of bright eyes and a set of the whitest of white teeth. How quick they are to smile, how readily they laugh! I feel a great liking for these, my own people of another colour and another Age.

"*Kalla!*" (enough) calls the teacher. It is bed-time. The little fires are dead, the moon is low, though the night is yet young. Everybody is vocal at once; a babel of rapid talk mingles with snatches of song. The song has it and all are united again in one melody. But what is it? This is something new, even to the teacher. The leaders are obviously two girls of about fifteen. We ask for it again and find it a song composed, words and music, by this pair of young people partly in our honour and partly in that of an Adelaide University party which had visited the station some months before and had done some fine medical work. The individual to be honoured is named in the last words of the verse. As Professor Porteus and I are present it is his or my name to-night, coupled with a reference to our projected departure from the station:

> Jakkai, jakkai, angai
> Erareramanga,
> Lena atua tjulkaraka,
> Reka ekara Mister Croll

is what they sing, meaning that they are sorry to think that the white man has gone from them whose name is Mister Croll (or Professor Porteus if it were his turn).

"A last song," says the teacher, "*Era rella . . .* " and with the vim that is too generally absent from more civilized gatherings they burst into:

> Era rella mara indora,
> Era rella mara indora,
> Era rella mara indora,
> Nuna allmelama.

In other words "For he's a jolly good fellow, and so say all of us!" For the "Hip Hurrah" they substitute "*Jakkai! Ndurbai!*" which being freely translated, says, "Yes! He certainly is!"

To a medley of "Good Night Ladies" and "*Mokehana Lei*" the girls move off to their quarters. The boys turn towards theirs, some fifty paces away. We find ourselves each with an escort of closely clinging forms, much as a queen bee centres a swarm. From one of those unable to secure attachment comes a burst of familiar song. His accent is quaint but the air is unmistakable.

"Mara, Mara, quite contrara," he sings, and "How does your garden grow?" I break in. It is delightful to hear them finish the old nursery rhyme.

They pass into their long cement house bearing armfuls of wood and many lighted sticks, for they must have a fire these cool nights. "Goood night, goood night, goood night" comes from them all; then, as the door is shut, a final call, in a voice so young as to be almost babyish, reaches our ears: "Goood night, Mister Croll, my son."

It is one of my youthful fathers bestowing his blessing in all seriousness upon his very much older tribal offspring.

"Bush tucker" could hardly be called plentiful about Hermannsburg; there was too great a congestion of natives for many food creatures or much edible vegetation to remain in the neighbourhood. I wanted honey-ants, and I thought, till I saw them, that I wanted to taste witchetty grubs. No ants were available on any of my visits; the grubs, the living ones anyway, I could not manage.

My young friend Urabulla had something in his hand. He held it out. "You eatem witchetty grub?" he asked. His dark pleasant face was serious; but there was a hint of humour in the bright brown eyes, and the hint grew to a definite sparkle of pleasure as I examined his offering. It was a wood-grub about four inches long and as thick as my finger, resembling a very faintly animated piece of suet. In Scotland it might have passed as the young of an anaemic haggis. A slight wriggle, as I took it, assured me that it was alive. Urabulla regarded it as a white child would look upon a stick of chocolate. He was evidently "treating" his friend.

"You eatem?" he asked again, and I remembered that I had asked for this, that I had said I should like to taste more of the native food—indeed had specifically named the

witchetty grub. The thing wriggled again. Urabulla looked
expectant; I think his mouth watered. No, I couldn't face it.
"Urabulla," I said, "no eatem now; plenty dinner: no more."

A native youngster will masticate the grub *au naturel*, with
the gusto of a white child chewing a lump of toffee. Urabulla, however, lit a small fire, browned his sample nicely,
and in that way made an excellent *hors-d'oeuvre*.

I was reminded of this, and of happy days spent in Central
Australia, by the arrival yesterday of a box of honey-ants—
another aboriginal delicacy. As an article of diet they do not
offend white man's ideas quite so much as the grubs do, but
all the same some courage is needed to tackle them. A live
ant, whose head you grasp between finger and thumb in
order that you may bite off its swollen body, cannot be
regarded as attractive. This consignment, however, sent by
Rex Battarbee, the artist whose work has done so much to
make the Inland known, is not intended to serve as a meal.
Several of the insects are alive, and these favoured specimens
of *Camponotus inflatus* are now enjoying a luxurious existence at the Melbourne University, while those that have
died have been added to several entomological collections.

Tillyard is responsible for the statement that the genus is
represented in Australia by something like a hundred species,
but apparently only a few of these have the honeypot habit.
That habit is surely among the most extraordinary of Nature's
many queer provisions. *Inflatus* is in appearance just an
ordinary ant, a creature somewhat smaller than our common
red sugar-ant, and there is nothing about the worker, following his lawful occasions in the mulga, to suggest his
unusual method of storing the honey he is gathering. He has
apparently found it beyond the ability of his people to build
suitable storehouses, as the bees do of wax, in which to keep
safely such chancy stuff as honey, so he has invented a living
storehouse—the body of a fellow ant.

How the choice is made of the fortunate, or unfortunate,
creature which is to spend the rest of its days inert, a mere
helpless bag of sweetness, is not known. Seemingly any

ordinary member of the community is eligible. Once selected, the workers bring to it their daily gains of nectar from the exudation of insects, from the flowering mulga or other plants, or from wherever it is they find their supply. John Shaw Neilson wrote of the bees:

> *All their day's love is sunken*
> *Safe in the comb—*

The poet who would sing these other wonder-workers must find a rhyme for "abdomen", for that is where the "day's love" of the honey-ant is sunken. The "honey-pots" swallow the nectar brought to them, but keep it for the general use of the colony. They have two stomachs—the one private, the other communal.

I have a series of the ants before me as I write. The larva is a flabby, wrinkled, cream-coloured object, with but little definition of head; the adult worker is black, save for bands of brown across the back of the abdomen. The various stages of inflation are well illustrated in the next nine specimens. As the body swells, the brown bars (really a thin membrane) stretch until they present the appearance of a shiny deep-toned cherry, a cherry reinforced with dark bands of chitin, that horny substance which helps to form the overcoats of invertebrates. As the head and thorax remain unaltered, the animal looks ludicrously disproportioned.

Baldwin Spencer says that honey-ants similarly modified occur in certain parts of America, and suggests that the modifications may be connected with the fact that all these ants, including our Australian species, are found in dry, arid country.

When a member of the ant community requires nourishment, it caresses the honey-pot with its antennae, and the living pantry, this sentient storehouse, passes out from its mouth a drop of the desired food. One speculates upon how much of the precious substance the trusted guardian is permitted, or permits itself, to absorb for its own nutrition.

The aborigines are fond of the *Yarumpa*, as the Arunta tribe call this black honey-ant, and gather it, whenever they

LAMINGTON NATIONAL PARK

"A wild and lovely spot"

MACDONNELL RANGES

"A refuge, for here is water and ease"

can, in great numbers. There is no mound on the surface
to indicate where a nest is located; a small hole leads vertically
to the passages and chambers in which the home life is led.
Mr. Battarbee, writing from Hermannsburg, records that
these present ants were down in the earth about three feet
and that the living honey-pots were stowed away in rows,
the big, full dark ones being at the bottom in far corners, while
the eggs were near the top. He added that the natives sometimes bring in the equivalent of a billyful, and I remember
reading in Spencer, somewhere, that he had seen the surface
of a stretch of country turned over for these ants so
thoroughly that it looked as if it had been prospected for
gold.

I was interested to know that it was an old acquaintance
of mine, Titus (habitually pronounced Tittus), who had
dug out this lot for me. He it was who looked so incredulous
when we walked the bush together and I could not see
certain tracks which were so obvious to him; but I remember
him best because it was with him that Professor Porteus and
I entered a certain sacred corroboree cave, once a storehouse
for Churinga. It was black as midnight inside; we had to
crawl with our heads close to the ground, and we had no
torch. Very carefully did I sweep the floor ahead of me with
a stick—I had no desire to meet a snake at face level. Then,
as the roof lifted and a match was struck, something sprang
at us suddenly and swiftly from the shadows and passed so
close that our light flickered and all but went out.

It was only a bat; but I never did care for caves, so we
crept out again (I hope with no undue haste) to sit in the
blessed sunlight and eat the lunch provided by the hospitable
missionaries of the Finke River, a lunch, I need hardly say,
which contained neither witchetty grub nor honey-ant.

FRANCIS RATCLIFFE

FRANCIS RATCLIFFE, an English biologist, came twice to Australia, the second time to stay. In 1929-31 he made investigations into the life of the flying-fox, and in 1935-36 studied soil erosion in Central Australia under the auspices of the Australian Council for Scientific and Industrial Research. Events of his travels are described in popular language in *Flying-Fox and Drifting Sand* (1938), from which the following extract is taken. Ratcliffe now lives in Melbourne.

LAMINGTON NATIONAL PARK

My final fling in Queensland, my last bush trip of all, was a visit to the Lamington National Park. It is a wild and lovely spot. I had strayed over its boundary once before, when Romeo Lahey took me up to inspect some hoop-pine stands which his firm had acquired and was planning to fell. They bordered on the Park. I remember that we walked along a narrow track brushed through the jungle on the brow of a precipice. Through the gaps between the trees we looked up a deep valley, pine-cloaked and shadowy, ending blindly in a straight sheer slope. Along the top of this slope ran the New South Wales border. Sometimes, Mr. Lahey said, when a wet wind blew from the south, clouds would pour over this ridge into the valley below. They would always dissolve away, however, before they reached the lower levels, and because the flowing movement of the misty curtain was more obvious than the disappearance of its hem, the phenomenon had a touch of the miraculous. It was as if the gods of the mountains were amusing themselves with a vast conjuring trick. R.L.S., my guide told me as he stood gazing up that lovely lost valley, had seen clouds behaving in just such a way in Samoa, and had described it in one of his essays.

I visited the Park with two very good friends of mine. The journey started in the little town of Beaudesert (pronounced "B'desert"), where shortly after midday we were

picked up by a lanky red-haired youth in a big Dodge car.
In this car, packed between our luggage and sundry pro-
vision sacks we were sped southward through pasture
paddocks and scattered farms toward the distant hills. We
pulled up in a narrow valley beside a roughly made stock-
yard. Here half-a-dozen ponies were waiting, while an
assortment of disreputable saddles hung on the wooden rail.
The car was unloaded, backed into a natural garage which
had been chopped out of a thicket, and covered with a green
tarpaulin. The ponies were caught and saddled, two with
packs to which our luggage and the provisions were tied,
while we three and our guide mounted the others. Thus we
started on the next lap of our journey.

Of that great ride up to the guest-house on the plateau I
can remember only two or three isolated scenes. We began
by following a creek running through a belt of semi-jungle
in which grew tall scrub boxes and a few giant Moreton Bay
figs. The undergrowth rang with the calls of stockwhip
birds. We followed the track climbing up a great grass-
covered spur. There was no jungle here, except on the ridges
round about. On the steep sides grew little bloodwoods and
delicately tinted mountain gums. Grass trees, some of them
overtopping our heads as we rode by, stood beside the trail.
We saw some Parry's wallabies (usually called whiptails or
pretty-faces), and disturbed a flock of crimson lories. At
one point the track became so steep that we dismounted,
and led our horses upward on foot. After traversing a razor-
back ridge the pad disappeared behind the shoulder of a
summit. I can shut my eyes now, and see every yard of
that climb to the strangely shaped peak, where the clinging
trail was so narrow that the pack-horses found it awkward
to round the bends. Then my mind becomes a blank. What
was beyond the ridge I do not know.

My next memory is of passing through a gate and riding
out into a group of stately ring-barked trees. It was by now
late in the afternoon, and the golden sunlight warmed the
bare trunks and the straggling branches. I believe that a

deserted hut stood near by, and I seem to recall that there was a view, though the dense forest was very near.

Then after another mental blank comes the most vivid memory of all, and the beginning of the last lap of our journey. This, a night ride through the jungle, comes as the realisation of one of my greatest desires. I had always wanted to be in a tropical scrub at dead of night, but had never raised the courage when alone to leave a well-trodden track and risk the caresses of stinging trees and the siege of age-old fears. Now I was mounted on a beast which knew the narrow trail as thoroughly as I knew the few yards between the light-switch and my bed. I had only to sit tight and enjoy myself.

We were in another clearing, but this time the wall of the uncleared jungle hemmed us closely round. We were riding in Indian file, the guide and pack-horses in front, while I brought up the rear. The sun had nearly set, and its almost horizontal rays were trained, like a theatre spot-light, on to the forest edge into which our track disappeared. I watched each horse and rider pass between the two ash-grey trunks which stood as gate-posts on either side of the trail, watched each pass out of daylight into the gloom beyond. For a second or two they retained their solidity, and then faded into unsubstantial ghosts. I waited in the open until the darkness had swallowed them up completely, then, kicking my pony into a trot, I followed on their heels.

Inside the forest it was not as dark as I had expected to find it. I could recognise the backs of my companions, though I sometimes found it hard to distinguish the obstacles which my mount was so skilfully avoiding. To tell the truth I was not much interested in the track, but for the most part kept my eyes glued to the canopy overhead, enthralled by watching it pass behind. Every now and then there would be a gap in the leafy roof, and through it I would catch a glimpse of the head of some tree taller than its fellows, which shone a golden-orange in the light of the setting sun. I would stare at it for as long as I could, turning my head to keep it in view. Patterny things would pass across the bright window—a net of vines, perhaps, or a branch decorated with a shapely staghorn fern.

Soon the twilight faded, and we rode through utter blackness. I could see nothing at all of the riders in front of me, but now and then the jingle of a bridle, or the snort of one of the ponies, told me they were there. Sometimes, too, a shouted warning, of a jutting branch or a low-hanging liana, would be passed back along the line. This, at last, was what I had been longing for, night in the deep jungle! It was a wonderful experience, but I fully realised the wisdom of my past caution. It was only the knowledge of the presence of other beings, and my trust in the horse which carried me, that kept my mind at rest. And once, when the trail divided and my mount took an alternative route, so that for seemingly endless minutes I rode without human company, even my trust in the pony's instinct could not quite dispel a growing disquiet.

It was largely on account of the lyre-bird that we were visiting the Lamington Park. (Both my companions were keen ornithologists.) Remembering my success with the bower-bird at Meteor, I had brought my movie camera, picturing in my mind some clearing in the jungle, lit by a kindly beam of sunlight, with a lyre-bird dancing and displaying himself quite unworried by the whir of my machine. Little did I know *Menura alberti*. During our whole stay on the plateau, ranging through the scrubs every day, we caught sight of only one lyre-bird. We were riding along one of the jungle trails when a reddish bird about the size and build of a small pheasant, and trailing an untidy assemblage of long feathers behind it, flew up suddenly from the ground beside us. It rested for a brief second on a branch above our heads, and then dived swiftly into a patch of deep shadow. In the case of this, the northern species, the name lyre-bird is not particularly applicable, because the two long tail feathers do not form a lyre.

Although we saw only this one, the Park teemed with the creatures. Rarely were we out of sound of their voices

—and what voices! They say the Queensland lyre-bird is
an even better mimic than its southern cousin, and that is
saying a great deal. The forest seemed to be neatly divided
up among the individuals, each male having a recognised
beat. Walking along a scrub trail we would pass from one
beat into another, each occupying about a hundred yards
of frontage. The difference in the quality of the voices and
the mimicking power of the individual birds was quite
noticeable to anyone who listened carefully. The male
carries on his performance in the intervals of grubbing
around for food. Each seemed to have a regular sequence
of calls, most of them being recognisable imitations of some
familiar bird song or forest sound. When the repertory has
been completed, the performer signs it with the "natural"
call of his species, a penetrating and ringing but very sweet
whistle. The lyre-bird's hall-mark is quite unmistakable and
at once brings to mind an exuberant errand boy putting his
fingers to his mouth and emitting the shrill clear whistle
which only errand boys seem able to blow. It is a sound
which could only come from the resonant throat of a large
bird.

Having thus written "finis" to his act, the lyre-bird immediately starts an encore, and so far as I can discover, he
is quite happy to repeat himself for fourteen hours out of
the twenty-four.

The various imitations have to be acquired, one presumes.
I once had the luck to hear an unseen performer practising
the call of the stockwhip bird. Now this is such an incredible
noise that even the vocal cords of a lyre-bird require some
drilling to get round it. This one started off with an attempt
that was definitely poor, a mere clumsy caricature of the
long clear whistle and the echoing crack. (He got the whistle
easily enough: it was the crack that beat him.) There followed an obviously dissatisfied silence. Then he tried again.
This time it was better. Again a thoughtful silence and again
a new attempt. Now he had succeeded in capturing some of
the mechanical venom which marks the stockwhip's crack.
He repeated his attempt some dozen times, each essay being

quite noticeably more nearly perfect than the one before. At last he was satisfied. The miracle had been achieved: it would have taken an expert to spot the fake. He signified his pleasure (it was his only way of throwing his hat in the air) by letting rip the lyre-bird larrikin whistle as loudly as his well-trained lungs could blow it. It was nothing less than a wild proud paean of triumph, and I somehow felt disappointed in the absence of applause from the forest shadows. I know I instinctively raised my hands to clap.

Our lady of the fireside anecdotes had paid calls on all the lyre-birds near the guest-house, and had carefully compared their several performances. None, she told us, could quite reach the high standard of "Whistling Rufus", whose beat was beside the top of the track by which we had ridden up to the plateau. This accomplished performer was worth listening to at any hour, but was undoubtedly at his best in the early morning. So she, keen connoisseur, made a regular habit of getting up at five o'clock and walking the short mile down to his concert hall. Rufus, I feel sure, was fully aware of the honour that was being paid him, and set himself out not to disappoint so appreciative an audience.

It was hard not to think of the Lamington lyre-birds as disembodied voices, so invisible were they. Hard also, after listening to their rehearsals, not to attribute to them some human characteristics—a sense of fun, for instance. One day the three of us decided that it would be absurd to leave the Park with nothing more than a fleeting glimpse of a single lyre-bird, so we set out on foot, determined to be patient and thorough. Not far from the guest-house was a fine bowl-shaped valley, of which the edge on one side had been roughly cleared. Standing there we could look down on acre after packed acre of virgin jungle lining the slopes of this natural amphitheatre. And we could hear the voices of the lyre-birds. It did not take us long to find a path which led into the heart of the scrub.

We really were patient and thorough. Bird after bird we located by his whistling, and carefully stalked. We moved a few steps only at a time, taking great pains to avoid disturbing dead leaves or snapping a twig. Sometimes the voice of the songster would seem so close that we expected him to walk into the open under our noses at any moment. Then we would stand frozen into statues, hardly daring to breathe. The performance would suddenly stop, and then, after an interval of silence, we would hear it start again a score of yards away. Toward the end of the afternoon we had to admit defeat, and found our way back along the path to the high clearing. It was then that the lyre-birds demonstrated their sense of fun. It almost seemed as though they had been laughing at us all the time. We had hardly taken a dozen steps into the open when a bird at the edge of the forest let fly with his ringing whistle. There could be no doubt about it, there was a jolly jeer in it, and it said, "Sold, poor clumsy fools, sold!" as clearly as a whistle could. Then a second, and a third, and more and more took up the cry, until every lyre-bird in the valley was thumbing his nose to us in our discomfiture. The whole wide green bowl was echoing to their laughter, and we did the only decent thing —sat down on a prone trunk and joined in the joke.

FRED BLAKELEY

FRED BLAKELEY, prospector and wanderer, left Broken Hill at the age of fourteen, and has since followed the track in all parts of the continent. His experiences are described in *Hard Liberty* (1938).

"PIONEERS! O PIONEERS!"

WE counted thirty-two old graves on the way we took to the salt lakes lying between us and Moolowurtana, but only on rare occasions was there any other sign of the track known as the Old Hawker Road. The graves gave evidence of the haste and weakness of the retreating miners, for in their efforts to give decent burial to a mate men could not stay to make his grave deep, nor had they material to stone it securely. Where the sand had moved the skeleton was exposed, and I remember seeing the remnants of hobnailed boots adhering to the bones of a man's feet. Fragments of drays and waggons showed where the animals had failed. With their death went all hope of an orderly retreat, and also the chance of life. Men could not make on foot in drought-time the waterless stretch of sixty miles from Crozier's Well to Moolowurtana.

If a man talks about being two or three days without water in this country and travelling all the time you may know him for a liar. I have had two close calls, and neither time lacked water longer than twelve hours. The last occasion was so serious that I took a month to recover. There are still marks on my tongue where the teeth pierced it when swollen; for eight days I had to use warm wet bandages over my eyes because they had no moisture left, my hair came out and the skin scaled as from frost-bite in New Zealand when after taking a chance I got nipped and was in bed soaked in oil for nine days. A gallon water-bag will dry up in seven hours in summer-time, so what chance has a man?

Fifteen hours is the longest he can go, and less than that if walking.

It was never known how many perished on that track, but in my boyhood old settlers on the Barrier still told stories of the Mount Brown gold-rush and disaster. Mount Brown is in New South Wales, just within the north-western angle of the state, but the rush was from South Australia to this place. The nearest town was Hawker, in the north of South Australia, three or four hundred miles from Mount Brown, and a man has to take his hat off to these old diggers for blazing a track across such country—all right as long as rain came, but a death-trap when it failed.

I don't know the date when water cut out on Mount Brown, but the men were compelled to leave in droves, and the suffering must have been terrible, as the graves on the old Hawker track made plain. It was at this point, so pioneers have told me, that the South Australian Police sent out rescue parties, packing water and tucker hundreds of miles, and saving many from the worst death of all. Some of these officers, it was said, did not come back, but in the endeavour to pick up the straggling last got out of bounds, and the relief found only dead men. I have never read a record of that awful rush back for life, so mention it as a remembrance of those early pioneering days.

Had it not been for the artesian bores we should probably have added three more graves to that Old Hawker Road, and for the same reason—lack of water. As things went, however, the bores proved our salvation, but nearly our destruction too. We reached the first at midday, when we were hot from riding, and the big waterhole under the outflow looked inviting for a dip. It was a clear pool, four or five feet deep, and most attractive for a shallow dive. So we decided to have a bath, and nearly made our last mistake.

Dick put his foot into the pool to enjoy the coolness before he dived. It was nearly boiling. We had to go fully three hundred yards down the drain before we could take our bath.

The second bore made a good camping place that night.

The hot water and steam rendered a fire unnecessary, and just as well, for it would have been hard enough to get sufficient salt-bush stumps to boil our quart pots or to keep us warm. We carried little nap, and were usually obliged to sleep Blackfellow-fashion, with small fires around us.

We reached the third bore after dark, yet it was not so dark but we could see where everything was situated, for the starlight in that country is equal to the radiance of a new moon. The outflow was on the bank of a steep creek, and down this Jim and Dick set off to find cool water. I saw a big notice-board, and because the light was not sufficient to read by I struck a match. There was a great, dull explosion overhead. Jim and Dick came running back to see what had happened to me, for a cloud had formed over the bore.

I struck no more matches to discover what that notice had to say, but in the morning we found it warned one not to use fire near the bore, as the gas was highly inflammable. I suppose the chap who put that notice up never thought it might cause people to strike matches in the dark.

It was this inflammable gas escaping from the bore which first set me wondering about oil in Australia, and though I have since learned that the gas was not necessarily an oil indication, I have never ceased to ponder the question. The sandhills country may not be as useless as it looks. If there is commercial oil in Australia, I believe it lies below this great basin, probably larger than that of the American oilfields. I have traced the depression's rim for five hundred miles, and know it for three hundred miles in width before it runs out to sea. Nowhere have I seen indication of oil on the surface of this basin, and from observation of the dip of sedimentary bands I should not expect to find oil above five thousand feet, and maybe it would be lower than seven thousand. If my estimate of depth is correct the oil-bed is under great pressure, and the oil already found in Australia is seeping from this basin. The boundaries of the basin would take years to survey: its curve may stretch three thousand miles from Lake Eyre country to the Timor Islands. Aerial observation cannot take the place of ground-work. Floating about in the clouds to look for oil is bunkum. It is like the doings of some whispering angels who might stunt about in toy 'planes to find gold-bearing reefs from the air, and who on earth might never know a reef from any other kind of rock.

Although a good season, this country looked hungry and dry with whitish sand in drifts, and we wasted no time next morning in getting away, for tucker was down to a few johnny cakes. From instructions we knew the Salt Lakes country might be difficult, but till we came abreast of the first lake there was enough hard clay-pan ground to make riding fairly easy, and we covered it at the rate of eight or nine miles an hour. It was our habit when we had tucker to take a snack every fifteen miles, but to-day there were no snacks. We were anxious to know whether we could get through the lakes on a narrow spit of land which ran between them, for if the track was too soft it meant we must go round, and at a cost of forty miles' additional travelling.

I learned more of the Salt Lakes country later, and should not again go anywhere near it, as one is likely to drop into a soft spot with no surface indications. When the north-south railway was being built, a riding ganger rode over one of these soft patches, and both he and his horse were lost. The only evidence of what had happened was the track and the ganger's hat. A vehicle of any weight would just plunge out of sight, and those on board would have their wings for keeps, but we thought it worth a chance on foot and lightly loaded.

It looked very forbidding, but we carefully picked our ground, testing the salted crust with the front wheel of the bike to judge if it would take our weight. Of course, we did no riding that stretch of five or six miles. On both sides was water flat as a sheet of glass, and I am doubtful if any wind could have ruffled its surface, for it must have carried fully sixty per cent salt. In dry times those salt lakes would have been as hard and smooth as glass, and we could have ridden across in less than thirty minutes; but with moisture about we had to be very careful, for if the crust were broken once it would keep on breaking, and ground that had stood as one approached would crumple up. So we walked thirty or forty yards apart, for we all knew that the one who went through the crust must get out unassisted, if at all. A rope would have been handy to throw to him, but we had no rope, and were obliged to chance it. Within sight of solid ground on the western side we thought it would be necessary to turn back, for wherever we tried there was no solid footing. Even the pup was going through the crust.

There was a chance that the old salt-bed on the edge of the water might be firm, and as it was only some four hundred yards to the rising ground, we tried it. Without boots we walked, treading gingerly in two inches of soft salt, and the foundation underfoot seemed sound. It was necessary, however, to feel one's way very carefully, and when at last we stepped on solid ground, I can assure you we were very much relieved. Had it been necessary to go back, each one of us would have preferred to go forty miles around the shore, for those three hours of walking upon the glue-pot had proved very trying.

We all felt inclined for a good rest, but only stopped to boil the quart pots. There had been three johnny cakes for breakfast and two each for lunch. Unless we could make the station there would be nothing for tea, as those two each were the last. Nor, although the riding was good, did we make fast time; tightening the belt is all very well when you are sitting down waiting, but it is a poor thing to push a bike on. It soon grew dark, and that meant walking, for there was practically no track, and it had been hard to see one's way in daytime.

We kept direction, and it was wonderful how our spirits rose when we saw a light ahead. As we approached the station there was the usual bedlam of barking dogs, and the door-ways were darkened by men who wondered whoever was coming up the old track, for no one had been over it for months. But we had arrived at Moolowurtana, our first South Australian sheep station.

After the usual good-night greeting—and they were all surprised to see three bike-men and a yellow dog on a chain —one big man stepped out.

"Where have you fellows come from?" he asked, and when we told him he added, "Ho, well, if you have come across from Yandama you must be pretty hungry! Come inside and the cook will get you something."

While we were eating at a great pace, questions and comments flew right and left. What madman had directed us across the lake track? In the history of these lakes no one had got across while there was water in them! We could think ourselves lucky, for it was believed a fly could not walk that track without getting bogged. Although that last bore was on Moolowurtana, it was considered a three days' journey round by horse.

When they learned where we were making for, their interest increased, and questions again flew, for most of the men here were miners on the Flinders Range when the conditions were right. Their speculation centred in what might be moving up north that we should be making there by all the short-cuts, and on bikes at that.

The big fellow was Mr McTaggart, who owned the station.

"It's a trip I've always promised myself," he said, when he heard our plans, "and I envy you, but horses seem the only way to me. I am doubtful if you can get through on those gridirons." He added later, "Well, you came across from Yandama here, and I'll bet you will not strike another patch of country as bad as that."

He sent us off to bed, for he knew we had been through a hard day. "You chaps will need a couple of days' rest," he said, "and you are quite welcome. We seldom see anybody here."

We rested our legs next day, but our tongues worked on ball-bearings, for Mr McTaggart proved a very fine host, and as we had come over country he knew well, and could give him news of other sheep people, his interest was great.

Moolowurtana was noted for the fine horses that were bred there, and every year a nice lot was sent to the market. They were getting some ready then, breaking them to the halter and trimming up their hoofs. It was an interesting sight for us to watch those stock-men handling their colts.

Dick did a lot of barracking with the head horseman, a little wiry fellow that looked as if he had been bred specially to ride horses, and issued a general challenge that he would ride anything on the station, but the little fellow grinned and gave Dick some good advice that he should stick to the bike because he would not have so far to fall; also, said he, the station did not breed buckjumpers—everything was as quiet as a lamb. They were rather curious about our dog, which they thought a strange combination, but McTaggart sized him up correctly.

"Keep him on the chain," said he, "till you clear my country, for I can see the killer in him."

"Not a bit," Dick assured him, "he is as quiet as your horses."

McTaggart laughed. "I know more about dingoes than you do," he said, "and that fellow favours his dingo ancestors. The carriage of his tail shows his breed."

We had a jolly evening playing cards and swapping yarns, and felt that the extra day's rest to which we were invited would be just as pleasant, but we were on a trip and wanted to get on. Still we did not get away till after next morning's smoko, for McTaggart's hospitality was something special, and we felt that it was worth crossing the Salt Lakes to enjoy it.

So, leaving that very pleasant station and its friendly men, we made for the Flinders, and were soon on rising ground.

Climbing the first low spur of the mighty Flinders Range we could from the start see indications of minerals in the rock, and as the three of us were miners and prospectors we soon forgot in interest how hard the going was. We knew these mountains carried rich deposits of mineral, for many of our opal-mining mates had made big rises there, chiefly in copper. The deposits were small but very rich, and I have heard men talk of getting in a month a hundred tons of ore worth fifty pounds a ton. The richness diminishes as the mine cuts deeper; besides, the ground is very hard, and so the order of the Flinders was to get the quick easy stuff, for all those miners knew by experience that copper boom prices do not hold long. This rugged country, therefore, had been run over, and where it was possible the eyes picked out of the rich mineral outcrops. Some miners worked at a profit when the copper boom had burst, and I have no doubt that most of these old mines will work again when the price of copper goes over fifty pounds a ton.

Mining in the Flinders is a difficult game, and only those men get through who know the meaning of hard living and rough work. The Flinders is ruin for the new-chum miner, because unless a man is equipped with a good string of donkeys, good pack-saddles, and twelve months' tucker he is likely to fail early, for it requires a considerable amount of skill to locate this hidden treasure. He needs, besides, solid capital to get his plant together. Each pack-saddle costs over two pounds.

The donkeys themselves are an easy matter. They can be bought for a few shillings a head, as there are thousands of wild donkeys running on different parts of the range. Some prospectors have succeeded in working camels there; but, again, a man needs long experience to drive camels on that stony ground. They are almost restricted to level places, for if you attempt to work them on a steep slope they will fall on their sides. Immediately two feet are twelve inches below the others this beast loses his balance, and that is why camels have never been popular in the region. Horse and bullock teams were very successful in the early days, but with dry and drier years, work was gradually left to the donkeys.

It is marvellous how these little animals can forage for themselves. There have been many years when the goats were too poor to kill, yet there was no trouble in getting well-conditioned donkeys, for the donkey is the beef and

above: HACKETT HALL *"A style adjusted to the climate and traditions of the new world"*

below: PERTH FROM KING'S PARK *"The most Australian of the big Australian cities"*

Above: AUSTRALIAN ALPS (SUMMER) *"The silencing snow-grass and black-green heather bush"*

Below: AUSTRALIAN ALPS (WINTER) *"A long narrow ski-track winding up the valley floor"*

mutton of the mineral belt of the Flinders. I do not mean
that donkeys are easily caught, for it is only those men
skilled in hunting the wild donkey who can secure good
meat. These little fellows with the long ears can hear the
lightest footfall, and if the mob happens to be small, as it
mostly is, they plant themselves at once. If it were not for
the flies, they would seldom be found, for it is remarkable
how scanty a cover they need for concealment, nor do their
little feet leave much of a track; but flies are a plague the
old donk does not understand, or cannot deal with. They
cover themselves so neatly that only a few feet away the
family cannot be seen, and yet above them hangs the swarm
of flies showing the hunter where they are hiding. So the
prospector gets his meat.

Flies are a principal plague of the country life, and this
is one of the rare cases when I know them to be of use to
man. Aboriginals have always used fly signs in hunting, and
a little farther north the Natives discover water by them. At
a later date I was travelling in that country with camels. Our
good drinking water had run very low and the camels were
thirsty, when Micky, my black boy, saw a water-fly.
Appearing to be quite excited, he soon put his camel down.

"I see 'em fly," he said, "me track him. Him got a water-
hole along here somewhere."

Squatting down on his heels, he watched till he saw a fly,
and, quickly taking its direction, he would go thirty or
forty yards and squat down again to watch. By this method
he found where the flies were coming from. Of course, I
was interested in his manoeuvres, and followed, but I felt
like laughing when he showed me a little hole in the ground,
smaller in diameter than the top of a lead pencil.

"How deep is the water?" I asked.

"I been look," said Micky, "when him been go down
again."

Soon a fly came to rest at the edge of the hole. It was something like a small bluebottle fly, only this chap was striped
and longer in the body, coloured a bright bronze-green. He
went down his hole and soon came up again, evidently full

P

of water, for the insect appeared almost twice its former size.

"Him water that deep," said Micky, holding out his hands to show me a length of some three feet. I got the shovel and dug down. Sure enough, there was a good supply of cool fresh water, a soak in a deposit of chalk!

How extensive the soak was I had no idea, but we were able to fill our two twenty-gallon drums besides giving the eight camels two good drinks. I took particular care to measure the level of the water, and the amount we drew made no difference to it. But for that water-fly we should not have known such a supply existed. We were on a very dry belt, and knew that no rain had fallen in that country for at least three years. I have often discussed this insect with good bushmen, but none had ever been able to locate the water-fly without a Native's aid, so this bushcraft is vanishing with the Natives. It is a pity!

The Flinders Range is fairly well off for water; but, as in most other parts of the bush, it is not safe to drink raw water, and old hands always boil it, even though this means waiting on a forced journey. These men know what a violent illness dysentery is, and how, if not treated skilfully, it may turn to the dreaded typhoid fever, and they know, moreover, that once they take that for their pet complaint it is a million to one that they will acquire their wings.

The bushman judges by the appearance of the water. If it is covered with green scum it will be safe to drink when boiled, though it is often wise to boil it again after some thirty hours. It is the crystal-clear water which requires great care: no insects, no signs that the little birds have taken a bath! Here is danger, and, as most travellers have no means of testing its properties, the only safe way is to condense it. The Flinders had many of these crystal-clear pools mineralized sufficiently to make the drinker very ill for a few days, even if the consequences were no worse, and they often brought disaster to the new-chum miner. He might chance a dozen of them and think himself very clever; but if he kept on taking chances he would be surely caught.

These statements apply to that part of the range which is familiar to me, a part known as "the Flinders". The range is fifty miles in length, and in some places it must be forty miles broad, so that local conditions may vary, but as far as I can learn the wild donkey is everywhere.

A few years before a group of foreigners had thought to make a fortune by purchasing rights over all the brumby donkeys of the range, and they ultimately managed to get these rights in a given area. They set about building a trap consisting of two long fences in the shape of an extended V, and then employed some experienced stockmen to hunt a mob of donkeys and drive them into the enclosure. A mob was got together after much trouble, and three hundred donkeys were driven into the trap, but, donkeys or no, they knew their peril and found a way to meet it. They knelt down, trying to push out under the lower rail; unable to do this, they found out somehow how to lift together, and heaved the fence two feet or more till the whole party got away. The next mob rounded up had evidently some members of the first among its leaders, for they would not be driven into the yard but milled around, keeping the pressure on the wing fence till it collapsed and all went free again. When the company had spent a small fortune on trying to outwit the donks they were obliged to give up; but had they watched hillmen at work they might have caught a few hundred of the beasts.

These hillmen borrow, or take the loan of, a mob belonging to a teamster. The animals are driven to the foot of the hills and held at some runaway of brumby donkeys, while a couple of horsemen go out on the flat country and soon start the brumby donks making for their hills in an alarm which suddenly abates when they see a mob that shows no fear. They pull up, and quietly, without haste, are driven into yards, where the process begins of picking out a team or string of carrying donkeys.

Jinnies are usually selected, for they are easier to break in, and not so apt to break away, but a few Jacks are always included in a plant. These Jacks are not newly taken donkeys, but quiet, experienced old chaps who inculcate confidence. The female animals seem quite content as long as the male shows no sign of fear, though his constant braying seems to surprise them. Tame donkeys are a noisy lot, but in their wild state they seldom indulge in a *hee-haw* concert. Teamsters breed more than they know what to do with. In a plant of eighty, more than half are Jinnies, each with a foal a year, and it is a common sight to see three times as many following the team as the number working it. In fact, it is a problem what to do with them. Butchers will buy the young ones up to two years old, and wild dogs must take heavy toll from the herds ranging the hills.

When settlement in the Flinders first began it was regarded as safe country, and great flocks of sheep were run there; but with the coming of the rabbit came the dingo, and soon the sheep stations were in trouble also, so someone got a brain-wave and imported the mastiff and bloodhound to hunt and kill the dingo. It was not long, of course, before the cross-breed began to run in the hills, a most expensive business, and the ruin of practically all the properties adjoining the hilly country. They were rapidly eaten out, nor was it till long after that squatters and Government combined to exterminate this cross-breed. How much it cost I do not know, but the country was sheepless for many years. The last of these dogs were very hard to get, as they lived on the young donkeys. They were considered very dangerous when we were in the Flinders; no man ever ventured out without his rifle, and although I never heard of one attacking a man, there were dozens of instances when men were bailed up.

Once far enough into the range we found good roads for cycling, as copper mines were active and donkeys the order of the day. Nothing could be finer from the bikeman's point of view, for their little feet make good smooth riding-pads, and they travel eight to fifteen abreast. We came upon two teams of great size, one of seventy-six and the next of ninety. They are the most pleasant slow things on earth. One little foot is placed deliberately in front of the other, and so close that they seem bent principally on pressing firm each inch of soil. They never stop and they average two miles an hour. Never over two hundred pounds in weight, they are very small, and stand little higher than the saddle of the bicycle.

The teamsters are slow, humorous fellows, and their whips never wear out. They talk to the donkeys as they work, and the donkeys talk ceaselessly to one another and to the drover, who knows their language.

One old Jack lifts his head and frowns along the row. The others imitate him. One of the Jinnies is loafing, and half a dozen pairs of twitching ears accuse her.

"Now then," the teamster growls, "I can see you loafing there! Get up, you . . . !" And, rebuke administered, the twitching ears are busy giving other news in their sign language. Far on the road ahead someone is coming—the ears have heard him, and half a mile away the teamster has been warned.

Yoking a team of ninety takes some patience. The breastplate is made to individual measurements, and all the donkeys must be given their correct places.

"Now then!" the teamster admonishes some young thing trying a new place where she will not fit, "Now then! You weren't there yesterday!" The donkeys understand, it seems, and gradually the team is yoked. Ninety!

At a mining village we stopped for supplies and bought young donkey-meat for one shilling a pound. In the butcher's shop we thought it looked dark and unpalatable, but found it the tenderest and sweetest meat we had ever eaten.

Before leaving the range we camped at a place kept by two women, a mother and her daughter. Here they ran goats and somehow made a living—even managed, so they told us, to get trips to Adelaide now and then. But it was a solitary place, one of the loneliest outposts I have ever seen, planted upon a flattened spur of the mountain amid the roughest and most rugged country of Australia. A teamster's track ran close to their house, but it was not a camping place, and they saw nothing of the teams except when they were passing, nor did the teamster's track connect with the coach route, itself a bush track of the usual type, without any attempt at road-making or bridges. When bad washouts occurred on this route those using it would simply cut a fresh track with their wheels or horses' hoofs, and often one might see the traces of four or five roads that had been washed out.

The women's homestead was ten miles from the track taken by the coach, and to meet it this young girl would ride a horse over a goat-pad through the most impossible country. It passed the nearest point about eleven o'clock, and so she had to make this trip at night, never arriving home again before one in the morning. When there were stores to bring in she took a pack-horse, or perhaps two, and always carried a rifle in readiness for use, because this country was infested with the wild dogs bred between mastiff, blood-hound, and dingo, to which I have referred already.

I asked if the dogs ever showed fight, and she answered, with some surprise, "Ho, I don't know about 'fight', but I often have to shoot at them when the brutes won't get off the pad." And then she added, with some warmth, "I only wish I could get a lot of them, for the big cross-breeds are worth fifteen shillings a scalp."

So a score of years ago this lonely girl would shoot dogs and scalp them on the steep sides of the mountain, and always just before or after midnight, and her powder-puff sisters of to-day read their illustrated papers and nod to one another: "We modern women! Air machines! . . . Swimming! . . . Surfing! . . . Cricket! . . . Sport of all kinds! What surprises we could give the namby-pamby girls of long ago!"

Sometimes these women of the range were pestered by tramps. Not swaggies; I do not want the reader to confuse the swaggie with this class of man, because some of Australia's most eminent public men once carried Mathilda. Tramps are quite different. The mother told us of a tramp who happened at their place. After he had stayed two or three days she gave him tucker and told him he must go. He went, and in a couple of days turned up again, making the excuse that he must have started in the wrong direction that morning and had not noticed he was walking back.

"Well," said the mother, "now you know that this morning you walked in the wrong direction I advise you to put a stick across the track to-night, so you won't make any more mistakes, because when you show up again I will put a bullet over your head, and not so high that you won't hear it, and if you don't turn for that one you will turn on your back for the next."

So the girl got on her horse and saw that he did not camp within ten miles of the house that night. When he did camp he must have put the stick across the road, for he never came back.

"Yes," they said to us, "you can have some meat, but you will have to kill it for yourselves." Then, on a second thought, they asked if we had ever killed a goat. Dick got in first, and answer, "Fred has killed hundreds."

"That's fine," said the good woman; "only mind you don't smother the mutton with hairs!"

Then Dick assured her there would not be one hair on the mutton, and they both said, "We will believe it when we see it."

So we yarded the goats, and they pointed out a nice young wether. After its head was cut off I turned to Dick.

"How can you do this skinning job without getting hairs all over the carcass?"

Jim suddenly remembered that he had a puncture to mend, and Dick said, "I think I'll get my bike ready too."

They knew, of course, that this job of skinning a goat without spoiling the mutton with the hairs is very difficult, as even the experts find. So I thought of the pretty mess I should make of it.

Then I got a bright idea. I lit a fire with two logs laid three feet above it, and on them I put the goat. With a long stick I kept turning and rubbing it till all the hair was burnt off, and after skinning it I carried my mutton to the meat-house where they all came to inspect it, and not one hair could they find.

The women said it was the only time they had seen a goat skinned without hair being left on the mutton, and then the mother asked another question.

"What did you do with the skin?"

I answered that I had burned it, and she seemed troubled over that, saying, "Oh, we get two and sixpence for the skin."

Dick came to the rescue.

"Oh, that's all right," he said, "I told him to burn all the refuse."

So he paid for the ruined skin, but the women could not dismiss it from mind, and that night, while yarning by the fire, the mother again raised the question.

"I wish I had seen you skinning that goat," she remarked. "We often have to pack carcasses over to the mail, and the men always complain about the hairs."

Then I told her.

Next morning we went on the track again, leaving behind two very kind friends whose hospitality had been of the best, and they had given us five meals each. We left a pound note with a brief letter of thanks, promising to write and let them know how we got on. For a month or two we kept in touch, and then faded out, but now I think that they were worth remembering, and that their battling should take some place in the history of women pioneers.

I have forgotten their names—and I am sorry.

P. G. TAYLOR

CAPTAIN PATRICK GORDON TAYLOR, G.C., M.C., the well-known Australian pilot and air navigator, is remembered for his gallantry during the crossing of the Tasman Sea in the Southern Cross in 1935. The story of that flight and of sundry others is told in *Call to the Winds* (1939).

FOREST VALE

WE landed on a large area of open grassland and I decided to put the Gull under a tree with good shade and no rotten branches, build a fence round the machine to keep off inquisitive cattle, and tie her down to pegs driven into the ground.

Having once just avoided having my aeroplane eaten by camels at Wyndham, and having seen something of the attraction of aircraft for cattle, I had quite made up my mind that I would amuse myself for the rest of the day making a fence. There were plenty of good saplings about, and a fine sharp axe, and I had visions of making a really magnificent affair and at the same time not being an infernal nuisance to everybody else, who wanted to see the cattle.

I was not allowed to do this, however, and Mr White, the manager of Forest Vale, just walked into the saplings, flung an axe about, apparently without any effort, and in about twenty minutes the Gull was enclosed in an excellent fence of rails supported on crossed forks. It rather destroyed my illusion of the wonderful job I was going to make of it in perhaps four or five hours.

Aspiring business men taking correspondence courses in efficiency, and scientists concerned with the conservation of energy should see the manager of Forest Vale make a fence. It is most enlightening.

The whole management and life of this cattle station greatly impressed me on account of the stupendous amount of work which was done and the results achieved without any particular hurry, without wasted effort, and with a refreshingly humane treatment of the animals. The cattle had to suffer their various inevitable fates from time to time, such as branding, and other things which it is decreed shall be their lot, but it was all done with regard for the feelings of the wretched beasts, and previous impressions of breaking horses were shown to be based on methods unnecessarily cruel and unlikely to produce a horse disciplined but unbroken in spirit, which seems to be the right idea.

Perhaps there is something in the rather disarming question of the Chinese to the European who was so bent upon saving time, when he said, "And when you have saved all this time, what will you do with it?" Presumably save some more I suppose, so that there will be more time to save more time to be lost in saving time—which doesn't seem very good for air charter work and the aviation which is a business.

There is, however, a difference between rushing ineffectually and moving quickly. Or does this explanation still leave me vulnerable?

One of the great joys of flying is that there is no sense of rush, no straining after things, yet having flown somewhere there is, perhaps unreasonably, a pleasant sense of having done something satisfactory, of having fulfilled a purpose, which leaves you content to dwell in peace and dream of other things and of flying somewhere else.

Then, gradually, your dream becomes an urge, you wake, and are impelled to set out again.

Perhaps it is this habit which makes people undertake, usually without hope of material reward in the slightest measure commensurate with the risks and efforts of the undertaking, adventures which are often preceded by the hectic activity one tries to avoid in preparation, accompanied by much personal risk and agony of mind, and often followed by a great deal of disturbance, but a joyful elation which can hardly be acquired in another way.

Certainly many adventures with aeroplanes follow fairly closely to this specification, and though in flight there is no sense of disorderly rush, or any particular hurrying at all, one cannot escape some agony of mind whether with, or, as usually turns out to be the case, without cause.

First comes the idea. This is the period quite free from misgivings. There is just an impelling force and the attraction of flight. Then a seeking after the means of carrying out the idea, a tiresome and sometimes disillusioning affair. If the dreams have been vivid, and the idea one's own, it seems impossible that the necessity for its fruition cannot be understood by everybody. Once the thing becomes a firmly rooted ambition it calls so strongly to be done that no obstacle seems to justify delay.

Flight across the Indian Ocean has captured me in this way. Desire to do it has led me to seek out every good reason why it should be done; and there are many.

The Pacific was a dream for a very long time. Then the crossing with Smithy in the Lockheed Altair was an unimaginably satisfying reality. It was crazy with one engine and wheels, but it was a lead that has not yet been followed towards British development of this route.

Flight across this other ocean, with the right equipment, is crying out to be done—a proper air survey of this great air-route of the future. It will be done, of course, by somebody who can get the proper equipment to do it, or by somebody who is even crazier than Smithy and I, and who cares to sit on the westerly with one engine and wheels and fly non-stop five thousand miles from Port Elizabeth to Perth. I do not think this chance is good enough, but I do think the chance of making the islands on the northern route with a twin-engined flying boat that really will fly on one engine with normal load is very good indeed.

I have wandered a long way from Forest Vale. It is the peaceful seclusion of such places which encourages these dreams.

I enjoyed the few days there. They told me there was water in the Maranoa River. You could get it a foot under the sand. This intrigued me because the sand, of which the "river" apparently consisted, was white and dry and looked as though the river-bed would be just the sort of place to die of thirst. I went down to the bed of the Maranoa and dug, to satisfy my curiosity, and at exactly a foot water oozed through the sand; and when I dug another six inches it came so quickly that the hole immediately filled with water as I bailed it out.

Then there was a dog called "Pup". The name must have stuck to him from his very early doggy days because he was an enormous bull-terrier cattle-dog cross. He could round up a wild steer, or any beast too cunning or tenacious to be brought in with a horse, take him by the nose, pull him down, and intimidate him sufficiently to keep him there till somebody arrived and did something about it. He was a quiet, good-tempered fellow; and because of his prowess and good manners was allowed certain privileges about the house usually denied to working dogs.

He was covered with the scars of conflict, but his spirit was quite unaffected and he lay on the veranda with one eye asleep and one on watch for any movement which might suggest some possible adventure.

The method used for breaking in horses here was quite different to others I had seen. There was a circular yard about ten yards wide with rather soft sand surface, enclosed by a fence about eight feet high. A horse which had just been brought in from the hills, completely wild and full of high spirits, was manoeuvred into this yard and the gate closed on him. He was a real brumby, born and bred from wild horses, and had known only the touch of the winds and the trees in the hills where he had roamed.

He did not panic, but looked around him, shrewdly summing up the possibilities of escape, nervous and full of apprehension, but ready on the instant to seize an opportunity for a dash to freedom. Standing there with challenge in his eyes he did not seem to be a good subject for gentle, persuasive treatment. I was keen to see what would be the first move.

Wave White, who was going to break this horse for riding, climbed quietly into the ring, taking with him a thin stick about six feet long, with a handkerchief tied on the end. At first he made no move to handle or touch the horse, but merely occupied the yard, rather disinterestedly, with him. The brumby eyed him with suspicion, probably expecting some hostile act, ready to do battle, but slightly puzzled when nothing seemed to happen. Then White quietly reached out with the stick and let the handkerchief stroke across his back. The horse flinched and sprang against the side of the yard. This was something rather puzzling. Ready to attack in the face of direct hostility, but fundamentally not a rogue, he could not quite understand this sort of thing.

He ambled off, moving slowly round the yard, and wherever he went he felt this gentle touch on his back. He soon found this, in itself, was not intended to do him any actual harm, and so accepted it, still suspicious of his freedom.

Next the handkerchief travelled to his head, up and around his ears, and after a few leaps and nervous dashes he accepted this. Obviously puzzled, he moved around the ring wondering what it was all about, still, I think, merely waiting for the real attack. It was at this stage that White, having established some slight degree of confidence, having shown that at least so far he meant no particular harm, had to bring his personality to bear on this brumby really to start him on the way of faith in man, his master.

By absolutely firm, but sympathetic handling he got a bridle on the horse, led him round, pulled him up, set him off again, held him, stroked his mane and head and spoke to him in language he could somehow understand, and within half an hour of bringing him in, a wild, suspicious, hostile creature, he had the complete confidence of this horse, a confidence based, I imagine, on discovery of a friend where he had expected none, rather than any resignation to his future fate.

Getting a saddle on caused some trouble. He rebelled strongly about that, but sensing some new scheme of things in which anyhow he had found a friend, he accepted it, obviously with reservation. He might have clearly said: "Well, to avoid a lot of trouble which doesn't seem to get

me anywhere and because somebody about this place seems
to understand me, I'll take this saddle now, but that's no
guarantee that it can become a habit."

Wave White rode him in the yard within an hour, told
me he'd ride him again tomorrow and get him used to the
idea. This horse was no faint-hearted creature; nor was he
a rogue, but he was a fair sample of a young, high-spirited
animal with ideas of his own. Somebody told me you can tie
them down, beat them, haul them about and break their
spirit, but they're no good as horses afterwards, and it's not
necessary anyway. Once they get confidence in you they
enjoy their work and for that you need the horse on your
side.

We flew back from Forest Vale over the country south
of Mitchell where the white sands of the Maranoa River
wander down through the scrub, landed at Mick Kater's
place near Moree, lunched with them there, and came on to
Sydney over the track that passes a lot of good country that
way, over the edge of the Nandewar Range by Narrabri,
across the Liverpool Range, the Hunter River valley, and in
by the eastern fringes of the Blue Mountains.

M. BARNARD ELDERSHAW

M. BARNARD ELDERSHAW is the name under which Miss Marjorie Barnard and Miss Flora Eldershaw, both natives of New South Wales, have collaborated successfully in several notable novels. In *My Australia* (1939) they present the history and landscape of Australia in such a manner as to provide useful material for understanding the work of the creative writer.

SUNSET

THE sun goes down into the Indian Ocean over one of the oldest tracts of land on the globe, the north-west of Western Australia. South and east of this ancient shield is younger and more fertile territory, Swanland and the timber and gold country east of it. The natural line of division comes at the twenty-fifth parallel of latitude which cuts the coast of Carnarvon, a little north of the crab claws of Sharks Bay, and includes on the map the Gascoyne Division, North-West Division, and Kimberley Division. It is all generically the North-West. The southern portion of the state can be called for the traveller's purposes Swanland, though the name applies officially only to a part of it. In a population of some four hundred and fifty thousand in the whole state not more than five thousand live north of the twenty-fifth parallel.

1. The North-West

IF Eastern Australia has turned away from the sea to the bush, the North-West has its attention riveted on the Indian Ocean. It is a coast with a rind of life clinging to it. It looks outward for riches and danger. Behind it eternity beats a tom-tom on almost empty country.

From Carnarvon the coast bulges out, broken, sandy, low lying, melting into the sea. Back in the hinterland are ranges which pour rivers down to the coast, the Gascoyne, the Lyndon, the Ashburton, the Fortescue, the Yule, the De

Grey, then as it runs north along Eighty-Mile Beach to the promontory of Dampier's Land the map is blank, sans rivers, sans mountains, with a thin fringe of names on the seaboard only. Beyond Dampier's Land is the deep indentation of King's Sound, on which stands Yampi with its outcrop of pure iron, north and east to the Territory border is the jagged mass of the Kimberleys, matted with rivers, and cut off on the south by the King Leopold Ranges. From Carnarvon to Wyndham, the eastern port of the Kimberleys, is a very long way, 1600 miles, and it is a colourful coast in the sense as well of natural pigmentation as of the life which, if spread thin, is highly assorted, and of the tales and legends which encrust it as thick as the barnacles on an old hulk. But it does not conform to any conventional picture of tropical richness and luxuriance. The sea is rich and the land is poor. It is not romantic in any story-book sense. If adventure is man's daily bread, he eats it prosaically and off a deal table. Man has to struggle for existence in the inland, he has to fight for it on the north-west coast, and they are two very different battles. In the inland, the dry Centre, men are bound together in a far-flung brotherhood against the monotonous resistance of the land. It is the same life for all, there is only one division, Man against Nature. The empty distances leave their impress, they breed tenacity and solidarity and a slow movement of life. In the North-West life is highly competitive, men are divided by colour and interest, and by degrees of poverty and wealth. They have before them continually, as a model, the savage struggle for survival in the teeming seas. Here life is jagged and restless, a sort of hotch-potch in which man and nature have become inextricably mixed. This is the wider back-ground that must always be postulated behind the incidents, the rarities, the splashes of colour that seem in many accounts to make up the life of this fabulous coast. The printed page brings into close contact happenings and contrasts that in reality, are spaced out over distances and time. Live element tends to be forgotten or omitted, but it is there, emptiness behind the bright pattern.

Carnarvon is built at the point where the Gascoyne River

enters the sea, but that is a statement whose connotations need amplification. The truth is a little different from the picture the words automatically call to mind. For the Gascoyne is a river that runs only once in two or three years, its dry and sandy bed is the backyard of the town where camels are tethered and poultry run, the common, as it were. A flood is something abrupt, a wall of water travels down from the hills and Carnarvon is warned by telephone to remove her livestock. But water, though not visible, is there; the Gascoyne only uses its official bed in flood-time, the permanent river runs underground and is tapped by a forest of wind-mills. The sea is almost as disappointing—seven miles of shallows make it impossible for even the small coastal boats to get any nearer to Carnarvon and the exports —wool, fish, sandalwood, and pearls—have to be laboriously transhipped. The houses are of tin or a mixture of mud and shell-grit, but the streets are paved with pearl-shell. The population is of all colours, and white is the least of it— Chinese, Japanese, Arabs, Koepangers, Melville Islanders, Malays, Manila men. The hinterland is a treeless salt-bush plain (it is one of the local wheezes that the crows have to nest on the telegraph poles), sheep country fairly stable since it has artesian water, and the salt-bush can outlast most droughts. The holdings are huge and fenceless, the aspect of the country grey-green and desolate. On the other side of the sandy coast the sea teems with life and the first pearls of the coast are found, honey-coloured ones popular in the Orient, that are won by digging the ocean floor. The oysters are turned into pogey pots and left to ferment, then they are boiled and the pearls sink to the bottom. Pearl-shell which brings from £14 to £35 a ton is the secondary product, and the shell-grit industry gathers up the pieces.

All the notes of coastal life, that reach full chorus in Broome, eight hundred miles away, are struck in Carnarvon —the contrast between sea and hinterland, the mixed population, the teeming life of the Indian Ocean, the pearls, the eccentricities forced by circumstances on habits of living. Following the coast northwards, life and scenery take on

Q

stronger colours. When the line swings at North-West Cape,
its red sand-dunes and dark mangrove swamps get the
full force of the hurricanes—the cock-eye storms and willy-
willies. (Willy-willy is also a name for the dust spirals that
dance in the Centre. Australians are economical with their
words; the same words have different meanings in different
places. To find your way among them without a false step
is one of the secret signs of brotherhood.) They come from
the north accompanied by heavy electrical discharges. They
are unanswerable, everything in their path goes. The country
itself, so low and hard-bitten, can suffer little damage, but
the works of man do. In 1935 a pearling fleet of twenty luggers was lost at the Lacepede Islands off Dampier's Land.
The jetty at Port Hedland is swept away year after year, the
little town of Onslow has been razed nine times, Cossack
eleven times, Roebourne fifteen times, and perhaps these
figures are already out of date. In Roebourne the houses are
chained to the ground. With so much snuffing the towns
are small and struggling, some of them have been discouraged
almost out of existence. Roebourne, once thriving, is now a
ghost of itself, with its one claim to current fame, the possession of the only rickshaw in Australia. Cossack, once called
Tiensin (Tea and Sin), and with the most bloodstained
record on the coast, is fading, too, from its pristine vigour.

Ernestine Hill in her book, *The Great Australian Loneliness*, recounts a conversation she had with an old woman in
Cossack, whose poultry she had admired, which reduces the
"blows" to their domestic proportions. " 'I did have a decent
lot,' she told me, 'but they always blow away. The cow blew
over to the island. You can't keep anything in this country.
My husband blew away. He had a good contract for building the road to Roebourne and had it close on finished when
a blow came, and him and the road and the contract, they all
blew away together. He's down in Kalgoorlie now.' " The
height of the willy-willy season is at Christmas.

In Broome, and the seas about it, the life of the coast
reaches its zenith. It is the finest, the best kept of the North-
West ports, the centre of the pearling industry, the obser-

vation station of a marine wonderland. It began as a cable station in the sand-dunes lying between Roebuck Bay, where Dampier landed two hundred and fifty years ago, and a mangrove-smothered creek. Now it is quite a considerable place, layered as the northern seaports are. First on the beach come the huts of the pearlers, then the town proper, white buildings with green well-watered gardens, and a tramline, the whole having some of the smartness of well-cut white ducks, then the self-contained Japanese quarter, and on the outskirts the aboriginal camp of "wicky-ups", as fugitive and ramshackle as they sound. All shades of colour, white, yellow, black, are there, and all the rigid social castes. The highly paid labour is Japanese, the aboriginal is at the bottom of the scale.

A traveller who brought seeing eyes to Broome, describes, in his book, *Peter Lecky*, by Himself, his first impressions of the shore.

"Behold me then taking a walk. High in the wine of the vault circle three pompous, rose-breasted pelicans with clumsy pterodactyl-like wing-beasts. A schooner's snowy sails, beating north, relieve the aching blue of the bay. Dull, shining mangrove-green adorns a point near the wire-netting-walled bathing enclosure. Behind are the low, oxide cliffs, which, when one sights them from the sea, look like smears executed with red chalk. As I step out along the foreshore I come on fish weirs in use and in ruins. Dead fish discarded from the last catch lie about, with an occasional live one flopping in a diminishing pool as the tide recedes. Bald-headed, rusty-coated, fish eagles police the beach for these luckless loiterers. Along the sand one comes at times on the ribs of some wrecked and half-buried lugger which forms the back-bone and setting of a delightful marine garden, all green with weeds and bright with anemones, coral and delicate chrysanthemum-like worms that withdraw instantly at the vibration of one's footsteps into their tubed stems with a series of little 'clops' like living pop-guns. Here and there the sands are alive with crabs. Here and there, too, the waters are alive with irritable or skittish fishes. A turtle browses

dreamily, like a marine bullock, amid the weed meadows between two strips of coral reef. Gulls glide about the fringe
of the water on twinkling legs, like small white beads of
foam blown along by the lazy wind. Every little while they
turn sideways for a second in their gliding trot, just like
foam-clots on a stream, caught and deflected an instant by
some snag or cross current of wind. An ibis, or a spoonbill,
or an egret, heightens the tropical effect of the turquoise sea
surmounted by its heat-bleached horizon. A mile away some
tall blackfellows are fishing with spears among a cluster of
rocks."

From Broome the fleets of pearling luggers go out. The
honey-coloured pearl of Carnarvon has become the flawless
gem with a milky lustre, and the method of winning it is
quite different. Each lugger has its diver, generally a Japanese, who works under water in his diving-suit for as long
as nine hours a day, being brought to the surface every hour
or so with his bag of shells, prised off the sea floor. The
opener, generally the only white man aboard, addressed as
Mr Clerk, opens the shells and feels for pearls, "between
those slimy flounces". The diver who, with wages and commission, will earn about £600 a year, is in command of the
lugger and decides when, where and how the fishing shall
go. The opener watches the owner's interests and has the
pearls in custody. Only in the event of an outstanding find
can he order a return to port. He is paid £8 a month and
rations. The crew is always coloured and gets £2 a month,
rations and the discarded oysters, which they spear on wire,
dry and sell to China.

There are more things in the sea than pearls and pearl-
shell. Trochus, bêche-de-mer, whales, dugong—described by
Ernestine Hill as having "a face like a pair of boxing-gloves
and an internal organism like a fireman's hose"—crayfish,
kingfish, sardines and other fish yield their profit; but far
beyond their profit is the amazing variety of these fertile
seas. Myriads of bright fish hover and flicker through the
coral gardens bright with sea anemones, weeds and sponges.
There are diamond-fish with long poisonous spines, that can

rip a diver's dress and flesh so that he dies before he can be brought to the surface, venomous sea snakes, like lengths of striped or spotted ribbon, the sergeant-fish with his three stripes, the rooster-fish with bright red comb and what look like tail feathers, knight-fish with shining black eyes, the Spanish flag who bears green and yellow stripes on his dark body, monstrosities rarely seen, with scales as big as pennies and barnacles growing on their bodies, a white-fish with claws, sucker-fish who take free rides on the hulls of luggers and enjoy the refuse thrown overboard, sharks, ferocious rock-cod, more dangerous than sharks. It is the sea of death and resurrection. To quote *Peter Lecky* again:

"At times, all over the surface, literally for miles, schools can be seen leaping clear of the waves, either pursuing or pursued by other species. When, as again sometimes happens, the air is thick with sea birds, swooping upon the leaping fish and screaming over their prey, the magnificent ferocity of the holocaust stirs the imagination. . . . Keen, vivid, flashing beauty everywhere . . . everywhere fighting, everywhere spawning beneath the vigour-dispensing sun. Savage, ravenous, swift, efficient, and murderously beautiful children of Proteus! Even in the less crowded hours the universal destruction goes on. Often when peering into the hyaline waters, I could see some dead thing lying on the gleaming sand, its upturned belly hardly discernible from that gleam if it were not for the savage tugs and nudges administered to the bobbing corpse by its busy sextons, the flensing-clawed crabs and the tiny darting fishes like minute flaying knives, flashing out of the crannies in the coral."

It reminded him of the Druidic Circle of Abred, life eternally fed by death.

Inland from Broome it is another story—but there is death there, too. It is spinifex country, and here the grass comes to its highest perfection, exuding gum which makes it highly inflammable. The country is useless in its grip, but a new use has been found for it—it can be mixed into macadam roads, they are then everlasting. To the south is mineralized country, Marble Bar with its reef of jasper and an Australian record for summer temperatures, Moolyella where the aboriginals yandy for tin—that is, toss sand and gravel in a coolamon to separate them from the mineral—deposits of tantalite, silver, copper, lead, asbestos, gold—many small gold mines that flourished for a moment and then expired. There are many small mining towns deserted and forsaken in the spinifex. Most valuable of the minerals is the iron at Yampi Sound, across the Dampier's Land peninsula from Broome. It is a great mass of pure iron accessible from the water. As it is unexploited the surroundings are still dramatically beautiful—a narrow channel of pale green water fringed with dark mangroves and winding between steep hills of red and black.

King's Sound marks the beginning of the Kimberley district. Again the pattern changes. This northernmost part of Western Australia, held between a rugged coast and range of mountains, is cattle country so far as it is developed at all. Its area is about 116,000 square miles. It is, taken as a whole, a huge sandstone plateau, one to two thousand feet above sea-level, seamed with deep canyons which make transport at any time extremely difficult. Spinifex claims the southern Kimberleys, but the northern area is clothed with eucalypts, cypress pines and cabbage-tree palms. The baobab tree is to the Kimberleys what bamboo is to China. It supplies water, fodder for beasts, food for man, fibre for weaving, the flowers are distilled for liquor and for medicine, glue is made from the pollen, while the carved seed-pods sell as curios and a tree hollowed out makes a house. They live for centuries and they never forget; a name carved on their bark remains clear while the tree lives.

The Kimberleys have two cattle ports, Derby on the west, built on marshes and surrounded by mirages, and Wyndham on the east side of the promontory, two thousand miles from Perth. It is built on a strip of mangroves at the foot of Mount Albany. The permanent population is about seventy whites, but every April there is an influx of meat workers to the tune of three or four hundred, and the town comes to life. It is like the season at Ostend—only the reverse. The Chinese open their shops, there is a picture-show, cricket, refrigeration, social life. When the herds brought in have been dealt with Wyndham relaxes again into its tropic torpor. During the wet season, December to April, it is cut off from its hinterland. Its only connection with the world is the monthly ship, the *Koolinda*, from Perth. She gives and she takes away. They say that time is reckoned in wets and *Koolindas*. Transport inland is generally by donkey team. There is a passage in Ernestine Hill's book which perhaps illuminates the slang phrase, "not in donkey's years", meaning, not for a very long time. She writes: "Christmas is carried out to the far stations by donkey teams and, sometimes with the rivers in flood, arrives in March, the plum-pudding mouldy, the three-tiered cakes long stale, and all the cards and presents, and maybe the mailman, covered with tropic fungus. They hold Christmas when it comes."

There is a great deal that is picturesque in the telling about the Kimberleys—pictures of out-back stores where money is never seen and all trading is done in rough gold and dingo scalps, brilliant landscapes like the broken ochre slopes of Slattery's, "rising in prismatic cadences of colour, vivid rose and mauve and blue, a harlequin patchwork cut into the sky", and odd characters—Mrs Dead Finish, the haulage contractor, who made a fortune in a gold rush, charging £120 freight a ton; old Hot and Cold, the cook; Billy the Bull Tosser; the Galloping Thistle. . . . But it isn't happy country and it looks as if it never will be. It is unsuited, except for a few patches, to agriculture, there is no timber of value, minerals have proved consistently disappointing, the climate is hard on white men and they are easy prey to malaria, boils and other tropical disorders. Insect pests, never negligible in Australia, reach their height here. The flies are so bad that even the black men scoop themselves holes in the sand and cover their bodies to escape them. Ants, termites, scorpions, centipedes, ticks, carry on unceasingly the work of irritation. Willy-willies batter the coast. The country is only possible for cattle, and then only if the holdings are very large. They range from half a million to a million acres. The Victoria Downs Station is the largest in the world. The wet seasons bring on the feed; it grows to be eight feet high in places, but it does not last through the dry. The rivers are tidal, or dry up in the winter, when water becomes a problem. There is a small artesian supply. Cattle have much to contend with —poisonous shrubs, ticks, grass seeds, pastures which, being rank, are unsuitable. . . . The cattle tend to deteriorate and the stock has to be constantly renewed. Many big cattle stations have failed and been abandoned. Sydney Upton is of the opinion that the Kimberleys cannot carry more cattle than they already do, and that the industry is more likely to fall off than to improve. Hot, humid, barren, difficult, the Kimberleys are sullen country with all the disadvantages and few of the advantages of the tropics.

2. Swanland

LIKE South Australia the west is largely plain country, plains and plateaux on the north and a great central peneplain, which, starred though it is on the map with blue lakes, is arid and difficult. The lakes of this central region are dry salt-pans, no rivers, not even dry ones, appear, and all the place-names, few and far apart, with the exception of those attached to the intermittent ranges, which cross the plain in a central band to link up with the Petermanns and Macdonnells, refer to water—Joanna Spring, Helena Spring, Patience Well, Boundary Dam. . . . The history of this region has, for practical purposes, stopped short with exploration. The plain, extending the conditions of the Centre far into the western state, has thrust back fertility towards the coast. Western Australia's considerable riches are packed into a coastal belt, thin on the north-west and broadening out into a thick wedge in the south-west. Wheat and wool mottle the map, with cattle country farther out in the dry areas, vineyards in the valley of the Swan, timber, orchards and dairying on the coast, and gold-fields shaken like stars over the whole.

Thirty years ago Western Australia was importing flour, to-day wheat is her premier product. In 1905 when gold began to dwindle and prosperity with it, James Mitchell, the

Minister for Agriculture, saw the possibilities of wheat as a staple, and fostered the industry with all the strength of the state. It prospered exceedingly along unconventional lines. The wheat belt runs north to south for six hundred miles; Geraldton, Fremantle, Bunbury, Albany and Esperance are its ports. It is undulating country, and takes in many types of land and soils that would once have been thought impossible for wheat-forest, lightly timbered open bush land, mallee, heath and salt-pan. It is broken with outcrops of granite and patches of useless wodgil or laterite soils. It is all dry country, but the drought-resisting wheats thrive. On these broken plains that know fertility only in a big way, the traveller learns the meaning of distance. Fenced from the sea and the sandy coast by the ranges and bounded to the east and north-east by the arid inland, like eternity beyond time, the bronze-green wheat lands and the silver-brown sheep country which surrounds and penetrates it, are dry and clear, and of a spaciousness that belongs also to the sky and sea. The landscape is painted by light. Writing of the light on the plains just beyond the Stirling Ranges, Doctor Thomas Wood, the musician, says in his book, *Cobbers*:

"Light plays such tricks here. It brings mountains so close that you feel you could poke them with the end of a stick; but there is no solidity in them: no certainty, fantastic as it seems to say so, that they are there. The Antipodes again. The light is so hard and brilliant that even when the sky is clouded you have to screw up your eyes; but the word 'pale' jumps to the mind when you try to describe it. The reason must be the landscape. I know no other country which depends so much upon sunlight for its colouring; no other country as a whole repays the sun so little. The shading has the sombre hues of bleached grass, dark leaves, dun earth. It is a scheme in low values—violas and bassoons. The only relief is given by the bush flowers in spring and the silky sheen of the white gum, and all this under a radiant sky, clear as a sapphire dome. Put England in the same place and it would glow like the tropical east."

That is the bulk and the background of Swanland; but

there are also highlights in the picture, specialities of the country which embody its unique physical or social character —there is the city of Perth, timber, gold, the group settlements to which the national character seems to lend itself with genius, the wild flowers and other lesser wonders that cannot all appear.

Perth, the capital, is the most Australian of the big Australian cities. After the port of Fremantle, flat, sandy, desolate, dumb, with its artificial harbour, built where the sand was dredged from the mouth of the Swan River, its jangle of trams and total absence of greenery, the city is a very happy surprise. It is still obviously young, with open traces of a less sophisticated but not distant past. It grows while you watch, though it still retains some of that leisurely air which envelops a country town. It is a pale city, the greys and creams of reinforced concrete picking up from the bleached weatherboard. It is in a beautiful situation beside the wide Swan, and a bluff above the river, King's Park, has been kept as a natural reserve. Here in a setting of wild flowers and bush, are the statues to city fathers dead and gone, the memorial grove to keep evergreen the memory of men who fell in the War, and an avenue of gum trees that, when they are in full bloom, are one of the most famous sights in Australia. Each tree becomes a mass of foaming blossom and the colours range from pink to scarlet through seventeen shades. The grace of the trees, the colour and mass of the flowers, so vivid and generous, the birds and bees that swarm about them portray a beauty essentially Australian, aromatic, a little fierce, a little strange, neither tropical nor temperate.

Beyond King's Park is the university, another speciality of the west. It was brought into being by a Royal Commission and began life in temporary premises, a collection of weatherboard shacks lined with asbestos and roofed with corrugated iron, to which were added a miscellany of outbuildings as expansion demanded them. It had no income, for it was the first free university in the Empire. Entrance was, and is, by scholarship alone. What with drought and war, Government could spare it little. But learning is not dependent on Gothic architecture, cloisters, pleasances. It kept alight for seventeen years without them. In 1916 Sir Winthrop Hackett, who had been chairman of the Commission, died, and the university became his residuary legatee. At first, it appeared as if there would be no residuum; but under careful management by the trustees the estate, which included the newspaper *West Australian*, appreciated, and when years later the university realized its share, it amounted to four hundred and twenty-five thousand pounds. A further bequest of sixty thousand pounds from the will of R. J. Gleddon, in 1927, set the former Cinderella on her feet. The university rose, not in the traditional Gothic, but in a style more adjusted to the climate and traditions of the new world, its great hall, the Hackett Hall, decorated in vermilion, black and gold, with aboriginal designs. The students co-operated, digging the artificial lake which mirrors the hall. The Western Australian educational system can claim to be the most enlightened, the most democratic, in Australia, and the University of Perth, at its apex, achieves a closer connection with national life than is, alas, usual in the academic world.

Another speciality of the city—at the other end of the scale from the university—is the night Trots, open-air trotting races held at night. The vast oval race-course is situated on a reclaimed swamp, the races, in which the horses are harnessed to light gigs, called spiders, and disqualified if they break out of a trot, take place under floodlights. It is a brilliant and curiously artificial scene, a sport of the people, which is attended *en masse*. A totalizator, Australian invention of Sir George Julius, "as big as a town hall", handles the betting, and the maximum stake is five shillings. It is quite possible to lose a lot of money nevertheless, but it takes more application. The sap of the community flows towards the Trots. They know nothing of depressions.

The most dramatic pages in Western Australian history are written in gold. The whole State is sown with it, gold in the spinifex, gold in the plains and the ranges. Reading the map, the names give an impression of water and gold, water because it is scarce, and where it occurs draws to it all the possible settlement, gold because it is plentiful. It is often the only quick of life in the ancient weathered rock, and can only be won with great energy and endurance. Often there is too high a price on it, even for gold. Often it petered out and a deserted ghost town slowly perished in the spinifex, the bleaching and crumbling memorial to hope. But other fields became world famous. In 1892 Arthur Bayley and John Ford discovered Coolgardie on the salt lake plain nearly four hundred miles east of Perth. It was rich, but a year later a man named Hannan was prospecting to the north when his horse kicked over a stone. It shone. He dismounted to look at it, and found it to be a mass of pure gold. He and his mate, Flannigan, found themselves on Tom Tiddler's ground. They walked about the bush picking up nuggets. Then they pulled themselves together, went back to Coolgardie and made official application for their claims. It was the Kalgoorlie goldfield, and soon eclipsed every Australian record. The gold on the surface was only an earnest of the gold veining the rocks beneath it. A rush began, beaten back again and again by the waterless bush. Water cost more than beer. The Government took a hand when it was obvious that this field was not going to peter out in disappointment. In March 1896 the railway from Perth to Coolgardie was completed, greatly expediting the arrival of stores, and in the same year the Kalgoorlie water scheme was undertaken. It was conceived by Sir John Forrest, the Premier of the State, himself an explorer, and carried out by C. Y. O'Connor. A reservoir in the Darling Ranges, twenty miles east of Perth, in the heart of a state forest, was built. It was the nearest satisfactory catchment area. From it the water was pumped to Kalgoorlie, three hundred and fifty miles away, through a series of three-foot pipes. It is capable of delivering five million gallons of water a day. Kalgoorlie, with water and gold, was made. The tremendous and costly engineering feat justified itself at once. To-day the richest mining centre in Australia (though past its pristine glory) is a square red-brick town, dominated by a clock tower, standing on a tan-coloured plain. There is not a tree to be seen except one luxuriant pepperina, which has its own water supply and is the town's memorial to Hannan. From the "Dirty Half Acre" which supports seven public houses, to Boulder, stretches the Golden Mile, where the richest lodes lie. No one would imagine it to look at the place. It is given up utterly to ugliness. The plain is stripped, torn and ravaged. To the eye it presents a confusion of shafts, dumps, sheds, chimneys, slag-heaps and poppet-heads. The only hill is a pyramid of grey mullock, more imposing than the pyramid at Waterloo. The air throbs with batteries continually at work, and a pall of smoke hangs over the plain. The gilding that the mines have brought the world is not to be found in Kalgoorlie. Specks of gold can still be found in the gutters, or in any handful of earth taken up at random, but the days of the prospector are gone; big companies with costly plants work the claims. Far out in the sand among the dry salt lakes in endless spinifex country, the lonely fossickers are still following Jack o' Lantern gold. They can generally make their tucker. It is a life that becomes an anodyne and an obsession, and more than one life has been ended by thirst beside some chimerical lost reef.

When Perth was in her infancy in the thirties of last century and things were going very badly, the timber of the south-west coast saved the situation. It provided the first export, twelve months after the foundation of the colony. The magnificent hardwoods are still one of the glories of the State. They grow principally in the sandy country between Cape Naturaliste and Cape Leeuwin, that snout-like promontory in the extreme south-west, up in the Darling Ranges and along the south coast—banksia, cypress, jamwood, red ebony, red gum, salmon gum, sandalwood (but that's in the north), she oak, tuart, York gum . . . but the greatest are jarrah and karri. Jarrah is a rough-barked eucalypt which grows at its best to a height of one hundred and fifty feet, a clean bole of sixty feet or so. It loves a granite soil, and its wood is hard, reddish, and works beautifully. There are thirteen million acres of jarrah, but the best of it grows in a two and a half million acre belt from Mundaring in the north to Manjimup in the south. The great bush timber yards of Yaloop are its centre, and here railway sleepers, paving blocks and weather-boarding for the world lie seasoning within sound of the shrieking sawpits. The air is heavy with the smell of resin and sap, the night glows with burning sawdust dumps, in the ranges above the timber is being felled and the sticks drawn to the railway by horse teams. It is a world of experts, of virtuosity; as far as the industry goes it is self-contained—and the Forestry Department looks after the future.

Karri is also a eucalypt, smooth-trunked, harder and taller —at its perfection it measures from two hundred to two hundred and fifty feet in height—and stronger than jarrah. It grows without scrub in areas of higher rainfall. It requires even greater effort and skill from the getters, and bullock teams instead of horses to drag it. Dr Thomas Wood, quoted before, describes Pemberton, a typical town in the karri district, and catches, I think, the essential flavour of it:

"Pemberton runs up and down a hill, and has gutters big enough to hold a cart-horse. There are lots of dogs, all friendly, a tinkle of cow-bells, rows of square boxes where the bachelors live, some scattered houses set among flowering shrubs, one or two hotels, gaunt-shouldered saw-mills, acres of woodyards, a network of railway lines, a chimney stabbing the sky, and over all, night and day, the haze and smell of burning wood from a sawdust dump."

Not beautiful perhaps, these little timber towns, but with a sort of functional rightness about them, an ingenuous singleness of outlook that forbids extraneous pretention. The work's the thing, social life groups round it, giving these places a sort of spiritual cohesion.

There is something else in Western Australia, not a natural product, that deserves special mention, and that is what appears to be a special social aptitude for communal action. A history in which there has been much struggle, a rich but difficult terrain, a democratic system of education have all co-operated to foster a community spirit, and some very interesting experiments along these lines are being carried out with success. In the south-west the Government has been for a number of years now planting out group settlements. A group consists of twenty families; to each family a block of Crown land of about—it varies according to locality—a hundred and sixty acres is made available. The blocks are distributed among the settlers by ballot. Then for two or three years all the intending settlers work clearing and developing the land, not each man on his own place, but systematically preparing the whole for occupation and receiving a living wage from the Government. When the whole is ready each family retires to its own block. The Government assists with stocking, and allows a sustenance allowance of ten shillings a day to each family for three months. At the end of that time they can usually support themselves. This means a big outlay for Government and no visible returns, but it does produce the most valuable type of settler, the independent small farmer, free from debt and accustomed to co-operating with his fellows. It is an experiment in something more than economics.

There are two other communities in Western Australia that, though not in any way connected with the Government group scheme, are interesting in this connection. One is the Fairbridge Farm School, the other New Norcia. The Farm School was founded by a Rhodes scholar, Kingsley Fairbridge, one of the few, despite the hopes of the founder, who have done significant work for the Empire. The scheme brings out as emigrants from the slums of England boys of eight for whom in the ordinary course of events there would be no future except poverty; the School trains them to the land and finds them work upon it. By bringing the boys out in childhood the problem of adjustment, often so acute for older emigrants, and the reason of their failure, is done away with. The School is a farm, the farm-house built in the Dutch style (possibly in imitation of Shur Groote) by Fairbridge for his own home, is used for reception purposes only, and the boys, in groups of fifteen, under the care of a matron, live in jarrah cottages scattered over the estate. The houses are named after national heroes—Shakes-

peare, Clive, etc.—and the energy of the boys is stimulated
by keen competition between the houses, possibly, in the
light of modern educational theory, a regrettable feature.

Another famous colony in Western Australia, again very
different, is New Norcia, on the Swan to the north of Perth.
A hundred years ago a Spanish Benedictine monk, Father
Salvado, arrived in the bush with a bullock-cart, five goats,
two fowls, a dog, a cat and an axe. He called the place New
Norcia, after the monastery in Italy where he had served his
novitiate. He was joined by other Spanish fathers, and the
colony in the wilderness grew. They cultivated the vine and
they built with their own hands, making the little community self-supporting. To-day New Norcia has a cathedral,
three schools, a hostel of Byzantine architecture with a
marble staircase. It is Spain in Australia, a tradition and a
purpose steadily maintained and forced upon one small patch
of alien soil.

Our fifth arbitrary highlight of the west is the wild
flowers. There are four thousand different plant species in
Western Australia, and her native flowers in their profusion,
their beauty and their strangeness are one of the miracles of
the world. A difficult and unwelcoming country, sandy, arid,
often barren, with outcrops of ancient sterile rock, with
broken ranges and great plains, it seems as if all the sweetness that would be diffused through a more gentle landscape
is here concentrated in the flowers. Hard conditions have,
as it were, reduced them to an essence. The life of the bush,
banked down to resistance, flares up suddenly in them. Their
scent is stronger—you can smell the wild flowers twenty
miles out at sea in their season, when the wind is off the
land—their colours brighter because they have to force their
way in a difficult world; they are strange because to survive
they found a way of adapting themselves to almost impossible conditions. Most of the four thousand different plants
are xerophytic. They resist the natural aridity in one way
or another. In some the roots go deep down into the subsoil
after water, others store it like the baobab tree in their trunks
or in swollen roots, or underground stems or in their leaves

like the mesembryanthemum, the succulent parakelia, others guard what they have by giving away the minimum in evaporation—their leaves are reduced to needles as in the hakeas, or they hang vertically as on the eucalypts, so that the sun shines only on their edges, or they are hairy like Kangaroo Paws, or frosted like salt-bush, or waxy, or the young shoots are shiny, coated with a substance containing caoutchouc, like the red tips of the eucalypts in spring, out of which children make whistles, blowing between the thin envelope and the leaf, or hard metallic leaves like the banksia; or they do without leaves at all, like some of the wattles, showing instead phyllodia or flattened stems, or the whole plant is of a dry paperiness, like the everlastings. It is vegetation under siege, and it has found its own perfection within the rules that the climate and the soil lay down for it.

. . . There is one plant of the bush, which though not a flower, should have mention here, the Black Boy or Grass Tree. It is as ancient looking as the Banksia, but far more human. Standing from two to ten feet high in the grass or bracken of the plain, he is not, from a distance, unlike an aboriginal, a rough thick stringy trunk without branches, crowned by a mass of grass-like fibre, resembling a tangled and unruly crop of hair. Out of it rise, like spears carried over the shoulder, two long bulrushes or, rather, growths that resemble them. The Black Boy inhabits the plains. His ancestors are far beneath in the coal seams. He hasn't changed in a thousand years. His trunk is packed with resin and can be sliced in shiny layers. It burns like fireworks. Looking at Black Boy you feel that as he possessed the world before we came, so he may well possess it after we have gone.

The flowers in their seasons paint the country-side. They are the only high notes of colour. In the spring the wattles can turn a whole landscape golden and, as they fade, bronze. Gum blossoms make a torrent of colour through the green. In open bushland the Mock Sarsaparilla, the small purple flower of a little twining plant, can in its masses colour the whole ground. The Everlastings can turn the dry plains to a

R

sea of crackling flowers, pink, white and yellow. The Desert Pea, its red and black fused to a colour nearer purple, makes a brave showing over the wide open level plains. Unlike the eastern, the western flowers have landscape value; they come in tides and tidal waves. Some of them are malign because poisonous to stock, but they are part of a world in which no sheep or cattle browsed, they are the barbaric mantle of an earth still barbaric and wrapped away into its own concerns, the world of the Black Boy, in which we are only ephemera.

MALCOLM UREN

MALCOLM UREN, editor of the *Western Mail*, Perth, has in the course of his travels gained an intimate knowledge of Western Australia. *Sailormen's Ghosts* (1940) is a vivid account of a sojourn on Houtman Abrolhos, containing much of historical and topical interest.

THE ABROLHOS

THE length of Pelsart Island is such that it has come to be known as Long Island. Measured on a chart its length is probably eight or nine miles, but fully to realize the distance between its northern and southern extremities it is necessary to walk it or attempt to walk it as our party did on the sixth day of our sojourn there.

By that time we had become reasonably familiar with the southern portion of the island; we had even been accepted as guests by the terns. The reef had revealed most of its wonders and the land had discovered to us many new things of interest. So much had been disclosed on the southern limits that we expected a number of new experiences on a northern walk.

With about twenty miles to cover—or so we planned—we made an early start, Bruce striding out in the van impelled on by his unquenchable enthusiasm and his eagerness to see all he could in the time available. He led the way along the western shore made familiar by our first ramble and made a courtesy call on the osprey chickens he had found on our first walk on the island. They were thriving but their smell was no less.

As he left the low bush where the ospreys lived, Bruce disturbed two young gulls, who, had they kept still, would have remained unobserved, so completely protective was their dark, mottled downy colouring while they remained in the shadow of the bush.

These two young things were on an adventure. They were

bound for the water. The elder walked perkily ahead to show that he knew the way and had been there before. The fluffy younger was very uncertain if he should go. Mother and Father Gull might not approve. They had warned him that if he stayed in the bushes the naughty sea eagle, that giant bogey man that descended from the sky and snatched young gulls up in his great claws and took them to his nest, there to eat them, could not see him. On the open beach he was taking a risk.

Finally he risked it and hurried off to join his playmate, the two of them standing irresolutely on the shore within a few feet of the water. Soon they hurried back to the bushes presumably to talk excitedly on the risk they had run and how they felt and what they saw. Later we saw scores of young gulls getting used to the water and learning to feed themselves from its many tasty offerings.

Near the remains of a fence leading into the sea—a fence, we thought, that had something to do with the restraining of horses used on the tramways when the island was being worked for guano—Bruce made the first discovery of the day—starfish.

He had been walking along in the shallows when he saw a colony of these creatures in the water. Whether it is usual for them to colonize in this manner we knew not, but our experience on Pelsart Island was that they were most numerous in this one spot and that elsewhere they were rare.

Starfish fascinated Bruce. On several later occasions he made a pilgrimage to this starfish colony to pick up specimens and included among his Pelsart Island "treasures" was a box crammed tight with these extraordinary fish.

For they are extraordinary creatures! There are probably several species; but we encountered mostly a brownish-red variety varying from six inches to one foot across. In the water they look like a piece of red cardboard cut inexpertly in a star pattern ready to decorate the fancy dress of some giant reveller. When you pick them up the points turn up or down in a plaintive gesture of helplessness. Their tube feet, which give them their tedious means of locomotion, can be seen; but the remainder of their organisms are indistinguishable except for an orifice in a central disk which looks something like a mouth.

We had heard that starfish prey on oysters. To look at these frail and brittle starfish and at the oysters safely ensconced in their protective valve, the statement seemed ludicrous; but it appears that these tube feet possessed by starfish have extraordinary power in them. They fasten on to the edges of the oyster valve and exert a pressure sufficient to force open the mouth of the valve. Even that strong muscle of the oyster that can resist some of man's efforts to force open the shell, succumbs to the steady pressure from the starfish's feet. Then the starfish's stomach does the rest!

It is certainly an accomplished stomach. When its owner faces up to a feed of oysters or anything else beyond the capacity of the owner's mouth, the stomach obliges by emerging through the starfish's mouth and enveloping the food, digesting it before retiring again inside its owner.

There seems no limit to Nature's adaptability, and it might have been this extraordinary ability of the starfish that so completely earned Bruce's respect for the species.

For about a mile beyond the rusted fence we followed the westward shore. This was easy going, too easy for John and Malcolm, who moved across to the eastward shore and began to make their precarious way over rough lumped coral. Wiser, Bruce and Reginald kept to the beach where only limestone outcrops interfered with comfortable walking.

Although on opposite sides of the island neither pair was out of sight of the other, and conversation could be carried on by talking a little louder than customary. This was the narrowest part of the island and in places was only about thirty yards across.

On this narrow neck we saw what appeared to be a small look-out. It stood between five and six feet from the ground and was composed of all manner of flotsam and jetsam, some of not inconsiderable size. As we approached it a sea eagle flew from the top and circled in silent protest above us.

Here was the home of the pirate of the island—the sea rover who caused such consternation when he flew over the tern flat in search of food. This was the home that the Bird Bloke had raided—the lair of a bird pirate sacked by a human freebooter. That thought gave us quite a new outlook on the character of the Bird Bloke.

When we looked at the bird and looked at the nest it seemed impossible that he, or she, could have erected such a huge structure; but a closer scrutiny of the nest showed that it had been in the course of construction for some time. Probably it was the old home handed down through generations of sea eagles, each of whom in the first flush of possession had added its bit to its newly acquired heritage.

Among the things added long ago enough to have reached a ripe condition were the bodies of smaller sea birds upon which the eagle had preyed. When curiosity had been overcome by nausea at the smell, we moved hurriedly on.

A rough highway seemed to have been raised along the centre of the island, probably while the island was being worked for guano, and along it were what appeared to be cart tracks, although how any horse managed to walk those rocking, clinking pieces of coral was beyond the comprehension of John and Malcolm, each of whom was picking a very painful way northwards.

In the elbow of a neck of land a mile or so farther on, we came upon a guano pan surrounded by mangroves. The mangroves were studded with nesting terns sitting in a crazy swaying manner in primitive nests in the forks of the very forked mangroves. These were of a different species of tern from those on Tern Flat at the back of Trigg's Hut, and we thought that these might be the noddy tern.

The raising of a family to a noddy tern must be something in the nature of a gamble. They seem to be born gamblers, taking risks from the very start. In the first place their nests seem to possess little comfort and less security. If they succeed in depositing the egg in the nest without its falling to the ground, they probably pride themselves on a preliminary accomplishment. Then, if the nest is not blown to the ground, egg and all, by the strong westerlies that never seem to cease, they must regard the nesting season as a distinctly lucky one. If the young tern survives the adventures of its nesting period its parents can feel safe in the thought that they have done their duty in teaching their hatchling to live chancily.

Despite these undesirable features, from the human viewpoint, of their habitat, all the noddies seemed very comfortable. All were turned the one way into the wind and were barely disturbed by the entry of humans into the ornithological maternity ward.

The guano pan was lined with a very green weed and the water in it was pastel blue. To the eye this was the prettiest spot of land we had yet seen on the island; but if it pleased the eye it offended the nostril, and we left the terns to their job.

In the centre of the narrow neck there was an extraordinary hole. About twenty yards wide and fifty long it was bounded by overhanging rocks beneath which four large fish raced above beds of green and brown weeds. Only about four feet deep in the deepest part the water in the hole was crystal clear and pale green and blue in those places where the light illuminated it. In some way the hole was connected with the ocean, we thought, for at one end there was a slight bubbling as if some upward pressure of water was forcing its way to the surface. It was one of those pools which, while beautiful to look at, gave the impression that all sorts of sinister creatures lurked in the shadows of the overhanging ledges. There, in the darkness of the rock, were places fitting for the home of some sea monster, cruel and powerful.

No one felt like swimming in it; but Reginald and John tried to entice the fish to a bait, and Malcolm took photographs of the fishermen forming a frieze against the skyline. Bruce dangled a tentative leg into the water at one spot and threw bits of coral at the four fish, who obviously despised the bait so temptingly offered to them.

With a shudder Bruce got up. "Come on," he said, "I don't like that place. It gives me the creeps, I wouldn't eat the fish if you caught them."

None needed a second bidding, so forbidding an air pervaded the hole.

Where the island widened out again the shoreline took a long sweep towards the reef, hesitated as if it had been too venturesome, and then turned eastward again into the shelter of a quiet lagoon. Near a large grove of mangroves a halt was called for lunch, and from a bag were produced the bare necessities to sustain us, Bruce being prone to regard one bottle of beer among the four of us as a very bare necessity.

This was a pretty spot, too, for the Artist who painted the ocean had been in a sportive mood with his blues and greens. He had splashed down on one spot a large daub of dark blue which had lightened in colour as it spread, and then the rest of the canvas had been filled in with light greens and light blues in a score of nuances. A blotch of dingy brown marking a coral outcrop served not to spoil the general effect but rather to make the bright colours gayer by comparison. The pea-green of the mangroves, lolling along the shoreline and sending their suckers marching down below high-water mark like a dwarf army entering the sea, provided an edging in complete harmony.

We tarried there longer than we should. John and Malcolm took off their boots and bathed their feet, which had been under punishment from the merciless coral. Reginald and Bruce lay on their backs and smoked contentedly. It was a place of contentment, isolated and beautiful.

Bruce, of course, was first astir. He reminded us that we were bound for the northern end of the island and that end was still a long way off. For his part he had no wish to tramp back in the dark, and it was his purpose to sleep that night in his one-man flat, not under the stars elsewhere on the island.

It was well said and all very convincing, so we moved on.

Malcolm again lured John to the eastern shore, for along there he expected to find all that remained of a ship. Once the barrier of broken heaped-up coral had been clambered over and the foreshore gained, walking was much easier than it had been, so much easier that the whole party was called over, and in Indian file purposeful progress was made north-wards. The rocky shore was plentifully bespattered with wreckage, including several crayfish crates, large affairs in which captured crayfish were kept awaiting marketing. These had probably broken loose from their moorings at Dongarra or Port Denison and been cast up on Pelsart Island compara-tively recently.

Rounding a little point, Malcolm stopped. A hundred yards or so from the shore, where the surf began to break, there were standing up a few ribs of a ship, the many spaces being eloquent of how the sea had done this vessel to death. ... There are few more dismal sights than that of a stricken ship, and we moved on northwards, relief being provided in the form of an outcrop of oysters in remarkable numbers. They lined the shore, crowded together like onlookers at a football match, the outcrop extending for about three-quarters of a mile northwards.

They positively leered in their luxuriance. We took the leer off their faces to the extent of a dozen or so each and then Reginald, whom no amount of oysters can satisfy, in-sisted upon gathering others for later use. In quick time we collected sufficient to fill half a chaff bag and Reginald reverently laid the bag well above high-water mark, taking great care to flag the position so that the oysters could not be overlooked on the return march.

An hour later a conference was called. The end of the island was still shrouded in the murk, and the boots of the party were very full of feet. The sun was tiring in its daily run and was slipping down the heavens to its rest in the sea and, while the enthusiasm of the party to reach the northern end was no less, energies had considerably dwindled.

The retreat was sounded.

It would be an over-statement to say that the retreat was made reluctantly. There might have been a mental reluctance —there probably was—but the physical gratitude was com-plete.

The trek homeward was a quiet affair, each man con-cerned with the very considerable job of dragging feet mashed by broken coral in the direction of the hut, which, because the island is so flat, beckoned invitingly on the distant horizon.

On the way we stopped for a while at a little bay, a harbour in miniature with all the attractions of colourings of deeps and shallows that are characteristics of these waters. Here a home could be erected and have an ever-changing but always dependable interest for artists and lesser people.

In daylight we made the hut and in the few rays of sunshine that remained Reginald opened sufficient oysters for his purpose, which was the making of an oyster stew.

Oh, you who know not the Abrolhos, can you conceive of so many oysters that they stud the stew in even greater profusion than meat in the common man's stew?

. . . Although we were the only humans on Pelsart Island we were by no means the only inhabitants. There were lizards in their hundreds and the daily migration of birds to the island could only have been counted in tens of thousands. When an eagle passed over the bird flat at the back of the hut, the sea birds rose shrieking their fear and indignation at the intruder and the air was black with them.

Into this bird domain we intruded one morning and it was a rich experience. We could not take an unconsidered step. Terns were sitting on the ground everywhere and under the ground the place was stiff with mutton birds. None of the nesting birds seemed to have any fear of us—large though we were, we were not in the shape of their traditional enemy, the hook-billed sea eagle. They found us disturbing—but by no means frightening.

The mutton bird is a shy person. He dresses in rusty dark brown, permitting himself only one dash of brightness—the red on his hooked bill. The shyness of generations of mutton birds has led them to burrow into the earth for their nests, and there in the privacy of darkness and dirt new mutton birds are hatched in surroundings inculcating the first principles of the retiring habits so firmly fixed in later years.

But Nature planned wisely. If the mutton birds, the terns

and the gulls had arrived at Pelsart Island simultaneously to go about the business of nesting, there must have been such an over-crowding as would have inevitably led to fights; but Nature arranged things much better than that. The mutton birds occupied the basement, one sort of tern and most of the gulls the ground floor, and other sorts of terns the upper floor.

Those people who create chaos by quarrelling over territorial rights could learn a valuable lesson from the small birds, who have sense enough not to interfere by fighting with the important business of procreating their species.

Instead of disputing, the birds organize their arrivals and departures so as not to clash. The terns all get home to their nests before sunset and the mutton birds land after dark, depending upon a remarkable sense of locality to take them to their personal burrow. Ornithologists tell us that if the mutton birds are arriving for the first time that season, they usually see and generally find the nesting burrow of last season, spring-clean it, mate and settle down to the routine of domesticity.

On several occasions we must have seriously disturbed the routine. For instance, Reginald was chopping wood outside the hut one night when there was a muffled complaint from below the wood; the earth opened up and a mutton bird hurriedly emerged. Innocently, Reginald had been chopping over the nest and his energetic swing had broken through the shallow covering. Reginald was nearly as surprised as the mutton bird.

Mutton birds are edible—although it was probably a particularly vivid imagination that connected their oily flesh with that of the sheep. We never tried them on our menu; they were friends of ours, trusting friends.

The terns that nest on the ground believe in simplicity. They go to very little bother in making a nest—a few wisps of seaweed seem to be enough. In some instances these nests are in the shelter of a shrub; but in many more they are in quite an exposed position. The nests always seemed to be occupied, one of the pair keeping the single egg warm while the other went to sea foraging. So intent on its job was the sitting tern that he—or she,—declined to move at the approach of humans.

So far as they were concerned you could make a detour; they had work, important work, to do and did not want to be disturbed.

Romantic balladry has a very positive place in the courtship of the birds. The words, in bird language, must be particularly lover-like and compelling, because the tune, judged by human standards, is distressingly morbid. A wail we eventually traced to the mutton bird sounded like the howl of some departed spirit lost in the labyrinths of an unknown, frightening new world.

Bruce claimed all the credit for tracing the wail to the subterranean lover's bower of the mutton bird. The discovery, he claims, cost him three sleepless nights.

Your tern is a much more vivacious lover. He has something of the complex of the crooner, "hotted" up a little. Reginald declared a noddy tern croaked like a frog; but compared with a mutton bird's cry the tern's love call was the acme of vivacity.

Nearly on the other side of the island there was a flat which seemed to be a playing area for the sea birds. Here gulls, in stiff white shirt-fronts and grey close-fitting habits, made playful darts at each other, screaming like children at boisterous play. Here terns circled dizzily into the wind and landed with graceful ease. Half a dozen larger gulls strode the edge as if impatient that there should be anyone who wanted to play. There was a collection of birds at one end darting hither and thither and at the other end a giant assembly like elders in conference all facing the one way as if listening seriously to the harangue of some leader.

It must have been a broadcast address, for none faced the assembly.

Members of the assembly cast sidelong glances at us as we approached, and portion of the conference adjourned while the strangers passed across the flat, reassembling immediately following our passage. Bruce sat down on the flat and the birds sat down near him as if they rather enjoyed his company. He certainly enjoyed theirs.

If we had only had the Bird Bloke with us he could have identified for us all the birds, told us of their habits and where they went when they left these islands.

The extent of our ignorance depressed us, and we circled back to the hut. Almost every day we paid our visit, individually or as a party, to our bird friends.

That afternoon Reginald and John decided to take advantage of the fact that the south-westerly wind had dropped for the first time since our arrival at the island and had been replaced by a light easterly blowing offshore, to set out north along the western shore in the dinghy.

The idea was to scull the dinghy along the shallows collecting trophies, fishing a little, and perhaps gathering a few oysters. Here is John's entry in our log made immediately upon his return:

"Right from the start the trip was packed with interest. With the smooth water, the bottom of the lagoon was spread out like a giant garden brightened by great plants of coral in every shade of the rainbow.

"Just opposite the hut a large purple growth of coral was fished up with the gaff and another larger one was marked for collection with heavier gear. These were intended as a gift to the skipper [Malcolm] who on the first day of his arrival on the island had stated his intention of gathering sufficient coral to build himself a coral rock garden at home and had daily been actively carrying out that intention.

"Slowly the dinghy drifted northward assisted by the set of the current, and a landing was made about two miles north of the hut. In few places is the island more than a hundred yards wide—in many places it is not more than fifty yards—and here it was only a few steps across to where the breakers rolled in against the coral terraces of the eastern shore.

"Reginald was in search of oysters; but the rock terraces yielded only a few, and it was decided to push on north-

ward to the point reached in our previous expedition northward on foot.

"From the point where the landing was made the course
lay directly across a long shallow bay, and this proved to
be the most interesting part of the journey. Here and there
in the shallows were turquoise blue patches, deep holes
bounded by sheer cliffs of coral which could be seen to
a great depth in the crystal clear water as the dinghy glided
across. Half-way across the bay half-a-dozen turtles were
seen in the shallows, apparently returning from or about
to nest on the beach near the grove of green mangroves.
They lay submerged in the water like dark patches of weed
until disturbed by the dinghy, when they shot away with
incredible speed, swimming with a peculiar breast-stroke
movement of the flippers. Now and then one would thrust
its head above the surface to breathe, then disappear in an
instant.

"Far out on the lagoon was a black speck at first thought
to be a fishing boat. As we approached closer it was seen
that the specks—a closer view separated the original one into
several—were seals sunning themselves on a barely submerged
rock.

"It was about four miles across the bay, and when at
last the distant point was reached, the dinghy was run ashore,
and we set out for the oyster patch, which was still a mile
to the northward. The course lay around the beach of the
placid blue land-locked lagoon where we had lunched on
our previous expedition, then across the island and north
along the eastern shore. At last the oyster beds were reached,
and in the space of twenty minutes a sugar-bag was filled
with oysters larger and more luscious than any others on the
island. When we had as many as we could carry, we started
opening them and Reginald filled a pickle bottle with oysters
ready for the stomach.

"Then was evolved a system which reduced oyster-eating
to a mere business. One man knocked the lids off the shells
while the other came behind, scooped them out with a knife
and swallowed them. By this means it was possible to swallow

a dozen in a matter of seconds. After three or four dozen even Reginald began to feel that he did not care much about oysters, and shouldering the bag, we set off for the dinghy.

"The long voyage home was a laborious affair, more particularly as the south-westerly had set in again and it was a head wind. About two miles from home Bruce and Malcolm were sighted on a distant point. They had come in search of the long overdue voyagers and assisted in towing home in the dinghy the tired travellers.

"On the way back across the bay a school of large silvery fish were seen feeding on a reef, their tails, which were nearly one foot across, flapping out of the water. John stood poised in the bow with a line as Reginald edged the dinghy towards them; but as the reef was approached, they shot away to another reef and finally disappeared."

ION L. IDRIESS

NO traveller's name is more familiar to the Australian reader than that of Ion L. Idriess, whose books reveal an extraordinarily wide acquaintance with the northern and central parts of the continent. *The Great Boomerang* (1941), from which the following passage is taken, is not only a travel book. It is also an impassioned plea for a grand plan which, he believes, would bring water and prosperous activity to the desert lands of Australia.

THE LAST OF THE STRZELECKI

AND now we cross the last border, and the dry old rivers cross it too. The Cooper near Innamincka, the Diamantina just below Birdsville, the Georgina a little farther west—all going the way we are going, to vanish in the final section of the Plan, the Great Salt Lakes system. Surely such futility was not meant. After those countless centuries of work, after making that vast network of channels designed to collect water from thousands of miles of country, the old rivers in their full strength now enter the Dead Heart—and vanish.

A weird area of Australia this, a ghost land brooding of things that have been. South-east of the centre of the continent it stretches from the southern boundary of the Simpson Desert and the south-west corner of Queensland straight down south almost to Port Augusta. Nearly the eastern half of South Australia, this arid area. With a north portion desert, it is in part a series of gigantic chains of dry salt lakes.

A chain of many scores of lakes runs from west to east, right along the desert border into south-west Queensland where another "arm" of lakes turns north-east. The main chain stretches from the desert border down through Lake Eyre to Lake Torrens, a distance of 400-odd miles. The eastern chain runs parallel between the main chain and the New South Wales border.

This is the country of a thousand lakes. A thousand lakes,

and yet the driest area in Australia! A thousand lakes, all dry; and yet they are below sea level. Why then do not the inland rains flow down and fill this vast hollow?

Surely in any other country in the world water would flow downhill and fill these thousand lakes, transforming this desolate area into a smiling countryside, with prosperous towns. But here it is not so. Our Dead Heart remains.

As we gradually learn the facts about this contradictory country we begin to feel that this particular area is fighting against the very laws of nature. We have already followed big rivers into this vast dry hollow—and it still remains dry.

Stand with me a moment in the bed of Lake Eyre, the distant shores a fantasy of haze and mirage bathed in heat and loneliness and desolation. We are now thirty-eight feet below the level of the sea. If that shallow rim of higher coastal ground towards Port Augusta, 300 miles south, were to break away the sea would come rolling in here. Neither rain waters nor river waters come rolling in. Yet twenty miles across on the western shores of this dead lake are the broken mouths of age-old rivers. To the east, within that haze of sandhills, are the harsh, barren watercourses of the three rivers. Yet there is no water here.

Another thing we learn. Although large areas here are barren in the extreme, the earth is good earth. Under the shimmering haze it stretches bare and grey, or sun-scorched and red. Yet in that earth slumbers the power to clothe it-self in wildflowers and herbage. Ages ago the rivers were designed to flow into this rotting core of the continent, so that it would ever be a garden. But the rivers have ceased to flow, and the core, formed long ago, has grown and spread rapidly within the few years of the white man's occupation. Truly a mystery.

It was a fierce day under a cloudless sky. Mile upon mile of white sand-ridges, their crested ends on fire. High up there appeared tiny puffs of vapour, on some, a little spiral of white "smoke" feverishly active. Air currents these, drawing up fine sand in tremulous "feathers of smoke". It was midday,

s

and we squatted there, spelling the camels. The grey earth between the sand-ridges was baked almost hard as rock.

Something hit the rim of my hat sharply. Then a large raindrop hit the back of my hand. In amazement I gazed at the sky—then smiled. A dozen drops of rain in the middle of a blazing day may be only one of the queer things that happen out there. A drop fell solidly between my feet. Sitting there smoking I gazed down, for the sound was quite loud and anyway there wasn't anything else to do.

But something was happening. Where the raindrop had fallen there presently appeared a mysterious movement, a tiny, slow writhing, a weird movement suggestive of a determined struggle to awaken from sleep. That movement was so vague, yet so definite; it would have been unnoticeable unless a man had been sitting there just staring down, awaiting the time to move off with the camels. The movement drew itself into a contortion slowly gaining strength, a wriggling determined to accomplish some certain thing. I stared down to see what actually was this sleeper awakening.

A grass seed!

It was boring in, wriggling, struggling to stand up; fiercely it battled to up-end itself so that the point could bore into the hard earth. Its tiny point was sharp as a needle, shaped exactly like an arrowhead. Again it wriggled, twisted. Ah! it was in, just the needle-point was *in*. Lopsided, like a long spear quivering at a slant in the ground, it rested for another effort. I saw then that up from its arrowhead it was more than an inch in length. Half an inch was coiled like a tiny, delicate spring, shaped just like a corkscrew. To the end of the corkscrew was a long feathery tail, now gently pulsing. Now its entire length wriggled gently and the head began to bore in, then slowly to bore around and around. Exactly as we put the point of a corkscrew into a cork, then twist it deeper in, so was the grass seed boring with its screw and its tail was helping it, lifting it slowly upright as the needlehead bored in.

Now that it had a firmer grip, it paused for breath, the tail gently pulsing, constantly straining towards the perpendicular. And now it went at it energetically again, the screw pushing round and round with the tail reaching up towards the sky. The arrowhead completely disappeared and with a mighty effort the tail lifted the entire length right up straight. Rapidly the screw unwound, pushing the arrowhead straight down, deep. Slowly now the corkscrew straightened right out, the tail stood right up, the grass seed was firmly anchored.

The tail was the leaf.

I realized that the firmly embedded arrowhead, having done its first job, was even now starting on its second—to split up and grow, grow roots.

Thus will one raindrop start a cycle of life.

South Australia's good lands hug the narrow strip of her south-eastern coast. Two hundred miles inland her arid country begins and it follows up the New South Wales border right to the Queensland and Territory border, our "corner" country. The land within the salt lakes system varies little. It is practically all low, flat country, sombre with its dry lakes, and its sandhills and sand-ridges towards the north. Before erosion and the creeping sands came the country around the lakes was cattle and horse country, although great areas were needed to support the stock. In good seasons the land grew sweet grasses and shrubs, but with the sanding up of the creeks and waterholes numbers of stations have been abandoned—for nothing can live without water.

Some large areas are gibber plains, such as the Great Stony Desert which stretches right up and across the border into south-western Queensland. A huge expanse of level country this, covered with chocolate brown, polished ironstones which are a mirage of dancing water under the heat. It is the seasonal winds with their screeching sands that have polished these brown stones smooth as fresh-made chocolates. Some acres again are of what was once good country under saltbush and bluebush, with mulga forests here and there. But man and bush-fires have wiped out great stretches of this precious mulga. The watercourses, mostly dry, were lined with coolabah and gum, as were the then permanent waterholes. Farther north there is more and more sand country, until a very Sahara merges into the desolation of the Lake Eyre basin. This in turn merges into the southern boundary of the Simpson Desert. The lakes themselves, whether to north or south, are desolate expanses of glistening gypsum or salt or dried mud, probably floured with creeping sand.

Very different the picture must have been ages ago. The mighty bones of extinct animals, birds, and reptiles dug up in Lake Callabonna, for instance, tell us that. Now enclosed by sand-dunes drab with samphire bushes, this lake is a vast expanse of white salt, windswept and desolate. Out in the haze a yellow-brown island shows mistily. An utterly desolate spot—yet, miracle of miracles, life is here. A few little chats wearing orange-coloured waistcoats—very pleased with themselves, for they must know of a hidden drop of water somewhere, and of something in the larder. Here also mallow grows thickly. It is a drab plant that can be highly useful to man, for from the bark and clean white fibres the aborigines in my boyhood days used to make strong cord. This cord they fashioned into big nets which caught and held the powerful emu and kangaroo no matter how they kicked and struggled. Surely we could cultivate and make use of this rank plant which produces such strong fibre and grows in profusion under the harshest of conditions?

Lake Callabonna in ages past was a haunt of the diprotodon, a lumbersome giant of prehistoric times. He had character-istics in common with the kangaroo; yet he was more like a wombat. On short, thick legs, his body looked like that of a fat, medium-sized elephant; yet his head and bovine face were more like those of a hippopotamus. He was an unwieldy, slow-witted bulk of flesh and bone, weighing tons. A grass eater we know, because of his teeth and because petrified masticated vegetable matter has been found among his bones. This story in stone consists of small twigs of salt-bush, bluebush, cotton bush and samphire, large ancestors of the plants that precariously exist in the salt lakes district to-day.

Years ago, the experts of the Adelaide Museum dug up from the wastes of Lake Callabonna many petrified portions and several complete petrified skeletons of the diprotodon. The Museum has reconstructed in minute detail one of these huge brutes from his own petrified skeleton. Thus we can see the type of beast that once roamed those lands so barren to-day.

From the extreme north right down through the State to Port Augusta the lakes are all connected by dried-up channels. Thus, ages ago, the overflow from lake after lake would flow from near the centre of the continent right down to the sea—and from much farther still, for the lakes actually start away up in south-west Queensland. There is a chain of lakes in north-west New South Wales too. Those were the days when our continent smiled under its inland sea of fresh water. What a different picture to-day!

And now let us drift back again to the few hardy people who carve out a living from this area. From the corner of New South Wales leave the shadow of Sturt gazing in despair for his "great inland sea". We cross the Queensland border with the Cooper and are immediately at Innamincka station, right where Burke and Wills perished. From Innamincka the old river course vanishes far away, to be swallowed by the sandhills towards Lake Eyre.

The roofs of Innamincka homestead gleam above the big old coolabahs of the river, a welcome sight above the box-trees of a big flat. A little settlement in isolation this, for apart from the big station homestead there are only a bush hotel a mile or so away, a tiny police station, and an A.I.M. nursing home. A startling place, for there are no less than six white women here. There used to be a little white boy, too; but now he sleeps up on a stony hill. The women here are fortunate in having their own company, but they have a long way to go to make a telephone call—to Cloncurry in Queensland, about five hundred miles away. In one direction there is no habitation for 220 miles. To

Farina in South Australia stretch 280 miles of gibber plains and sand. Broken Hill in New South Wales lies three hundred miles away, the boundary rider's hut at Mount Hopeless in South Australia over a hundred miles, with Murnpeowie homestead about sixty miles farther on. The first fence to the north is eighty miles away at the Cordillo Downs boundary; the first fence is 150 awful miles south near Mount Hopeless; to the north-west the nearest fence—I don't know of any. But white people can live there contentedly. It is only after a succession of dry seasons that trouble comes. For the waterholes begin to dry up and when the water gets very low gastric troubles come.

Those are beautiful waterholes on the Cooper, the larger ones a few miles long and up to eighty feet deep. Neither stock nor humans could exist without them in that country. But the good earth is good indeed—as can be seen from the gardens of the tiny settlement.

Many tens of thousands of cattle and horses have been bred on Innamincka station. But with the drying up of the old rivers, with erosion and sand and eating out of the grasses, every area of all this country produces far less stock than it did fifty years ago. Our object is to make it produce ten times more stock than it did fifty years ago. But first see what we are up against.

Take a trip south-west down the Strzelecki to where it runs into Lake Blanche 130 miles away. This little trip explains much; it is really the secret of the Dead Heart. Its present-day desolation explains just what happened ages ago. It explains too what is more slowly yet surely happening over all the very great area of country we have already travelled over. It is grim warning also that the Dead Heart is growing, spreading ever farther east, south-east, south towards our good lands. It is a present-day warning unknown and unheeded by all except the very few who know, yet can do nothing.

The Strzelecki was once a river. The explorers and pioneers called it a large creek, for thus it was in their time. Then, it contained not only waterholes but running water when, after an exceptionally good season, the Cooper spilled its overflow into it. Now it is not even a creek; it has been swallowed by the creeping sands.

The Cooper, when in heavy flood, used to overflow into the Strzelecki near Innamincka. Now there is rarely sufficient water to make the Cooper flow, let alone the Strzelecki— even if it could.

We travel down the Strzelecki a hundred miles, across clay flats baked hard by the sun. It is difficult to realize that a once huge creek bed ran here, for it is now silted up. To right and left gleam line upon line of red sandhills that will turn white as we penetrate deeper into the bad lands. Already a red haze is drifting across the sky, feathers of sand are whirling across the claypans. There is a desolate stillness here, no sign of life, only camel bones along what was once a track.

You stare at the broken fragments of what once was a track. Two broad, broken ribbons of rock-hard earth stand one foot above the level of the ground—earth compressed by coach wheels, wagon wheels, horses' hooves that travelled this road in years gone by. But now, since overstocking, droughts, bush-fires have killed the binding vegetation, the fierce winds have torn away the soil and left the compressed wheel tracks standing high above the earth. And here stands a dead tree, balanced upon stilts that are its roots. The wind has torn the earth from its base. The surface of the earth here has actually been torn away to a depth of three feet; the precious layer of good soil has been blown away, leaving behind the hard, bare clay which will grow nothing.

Now stunted bushes cover the flats, the road tracks disappear. Those bushes have bound the soil and held it against the wind; and wherever the bushes survive the track vanishes. Later on a broken fragment reappears, scoured out by the wind. Then it vanishes where creeping sand has covered it.

Here is an area where vegetation has disappeared utterly and the loosened sand is creeping, creeping on. Hot wind comes, hisses past in puffs, grows into a screeching whistle that scurries sand like demon will-o'-the-wisps on ahead and far away. The sky is one moving red haze through which the sun glows like molten copper.

Ghostly by the vanished track there loom the ruins of a homestead, smothered by the sand. Like miles of a great grey ghost there looms the dreaded Cobbler, a giant sandhill. The Cobbler must be crossed.

Years ago, this enormous sandhill was one hill. But stock ate its few binding grasses. Hooves of horses, cattle, camels, ploughed its sides and surfaces, loosening the sand, making it the play-toy of the winds. Man made a track through it. Then the giant sandhill, like some sleeping monster, began to react, it actually began to *move*.

It has divided now into a hundred sandhills—of creeping sands. Slowly, inexorably it began to swallow the man-made track. It did so, easily. Its creeping sands swallow, swallow, swallow. Not a man now in two years crosses the Cobbler.

. . . Through the scuds of the storm we flounder into a mighty snow-drift. No, sand-drift. Here it had covered a homestead fence, had crept on, crept on up the kitchen walls, then up to the roof. Its weight had broken down the roof. Next season, reinforced, it had crept on, crept on towards the house. It was now deep over the veranda, had crept deep into the rooms. Ghostly doors do not bang in this storm— the sand holds them fast.

And so the ghost track vanishes on, to the haze of Lake Blanche—into which the waters of the Strzelecki shall never flow again.

Unless the Plan can bring it about.

The desolation of the Strzelecki in part explains why those great chains of dry lakes way down in Australia's hollow are waterless. No water flows into them because numbers of the old river channels have become silted and sanded up. That smothered track was years ago a road and mail route of considerable importance connecting Farina in South Australia with Cordillo Downs in south-west Queensland. But now the track and homesteads along it are dead. So much can happen in our time.

ELYNE MITCHELL

ELYNE MITCHELL, Australian ski champion who has won inter-
national fame, has an intimate knowledge of the topography of the
Alps that are her home. *Australia's Alps* (1942) paints a fascinating
picture of the majesty of these mountains.

"OUT ON THE TOPS"

As soon as the morning light began to slide its long
lissom fingers into the Crackenback Valley, I awoke
and dressed quickly, determined to get some distance
up the ridge above the hut, to orient myself with the country
which seemed in some subtle way to have melted with the
snow to a different form.

I sped up the path, through wet, impeding snow-gum
suckers, for about 600 feet till the ridge top suddenly flattened out. There the trees grew sparse and there were clumps
of monolith rocks. Ahead were two mountain tops, pile
upon pile of rock raised one upon another skywards. The
easternmost peak was what I have always reckoned as the
South Ram's Head. But opinions vary. There is endless argument about the identity of these Ram's Heads, as about several
other peaks, and as many of them have two if not three
names, it is highly confusing.

Later we rode up this ridge. Just past the rocks we came
out of the dead snow-gums, across a little swamp, and went
into a maze of living trees, a fantasy-forest of weird-shaped,
stunted snow-gums growing over and amongst huge granite
rocks, their twisted roots emerging from minute crevices
and clinging tenaciously to the rough rock surface. There
was a purple shade through the smooth bark of the trees,
and green and brown; the dark green leaves were glossy,
and purple seemed the colour of the rocks. Over the stony
ground grew the silencing snow-grass and black-green
heather bush. We were like Lilliputians riding through a
weird rock garden.

This forest was enclosed by a wall of rock, the South Ram's Head forming one wing of it. We rode through the centre of this amphitheatre till we rose up on to the grassy tops behind, and then out on to a ridge point overlooking the Leatherbarrel and Groggin. From there we turned towards Kosciusko and twisted in and out through a maze of rocky peaks, each one of which was acclaimed to be a different member of the Ram's Head family—if it wasn't the South Ram's Head or the Ram's Head itself, then perhaps it was the Government Ram's Head. The white pillar cumulus clouds in a brilliant blue sky framed these grotesque tors or hung suspended on the skyline of a pass. Underfoot wild flowers were prodigally dusted through the grey-green grass. There was a little vivid-green moss with a white flower like a flattened-out bell, a beautiful small lily, pale mauve-white with purple veins, some mauve flower like a nemesia, the blue mountain aster, yellow and white daisies and the rustling everlastings. Sometimes there were carpets of silver leaves— regal pathways for our horses' hooves—and starring over the leaves were big white daisies.

Only one dust-blotched patch of snow hung where the Great Cootapatamba Drift usually is, bearing testimony to the dryness of the previous winter and the heat of the summer. The lake itself, couched below Kosciusko, looked chill and sombre.

The summit of Kosciusko is not an inspiring one; perhaps that is the reason why I had never previously been on it. We could canter our horses up its grassy flank almost to the very top, and the view gives no real idea of the majestic drop to the two rivers, the Indi and the Swampy; it looks down the length of the Main Range only, like looking over a beautifully groomed green park, right past Tate to the Rolling Grounds, or out to the Murray Valley far beyond Corryong.

A few heavier clouds rolled up intermittently, collecting to hide the sun and then dispersing. We rode down the stockman's path that is cut over miles of these mountain "runs", going on and on over the hills. As we rode into that cleft whose sides are Lee and Northcote and the Townsend Spur, a misty haze hung over Geehi and the Murray, so faint that it seemed as if swirls of fine green tulle, shot with pink, were hanging in the gorges. Geehi had relapsed into its mysterious silence again. Opposite was the red-scar landslide, remote-looking, as if it had already forgotten our intrusion, our passing meaning no more than the light touch of a mountain breeze. We were in that austere land of rock gorges and canyons where the ridges that we had slept beneath in Geehi hurl themselves suicidally to the foaming river below. Long arms of ridge shut us off from the world, leaving one window opening on to the Geehi and the Murray, the window that looks out from the Northcote Canyon. Below us, the ragged-outlined Lake Albina lay in the hanging valley floor before the abrupt drop into the Northcote Canyon itself. I could remember this as a snow landscape, coloured vividly by the thrill of a ski race down Townsend's steep sides.

Over Carruther's Peak and down, beyond the junction of several ridges, we followed the track to the Blue Lake, and there, at its lower end, we boiled the billy for lunch. Opposite us the rock walls of this glacier lake rose up jaggedly to a crown of great white clouds and bright blue sky. The water was deep green, still and cold. One could hardly believe that, in winter, it takes nearly ten minutes to ski across its smooth white surface and that the area is about seventy acres. . .

Lunch was a cheerful meal. My hopes of this trip had been realized one hundredfold and many of my fears sent fleeing. I had found possible a system of mental acceptance and rejection, and realized that if I sought something in the hills I could still find it, though I was not alone or with Tom, hitherto always my companion. Is it perhaps true that each member of a large party feels something quite different as the spirit of the days spent together, altered by what each one puts into it, what one sets value on and appreciates? I feel that this must be so. For me at any rate, there was something else behind all those days, a background of memories

and experiences shared; not only a discovery of something
new, but a previous knowledge, some understanding, a longing for more and more; and a new feeling, a wish to sink my
mind into everything I saw and did and to absorb it all, a
feeling perhaps conceived in enforced days and months of
lying contemplating the mountains to which I could not
climb.

I wondered if love of the mountains had been awakened
in any of these young Australians, born so close to the hills.
Would any one of them take up the mountain tradition and
carry it on?

The clouds dispersed as the day wore on and it was a
lovely evening. Our long cavalcade cantered steadily home-
wards along the motor road that leads to the summit of
Kosciusko. Suddenly someone turned back and cried:
"Look!" We turned to see long flurries of dank grey mist
sneaking over the ridge behind us. We hurried on. Mist on
this grey-green tundra is a strong-armed opponent. Presently
a mutter of thunder sounded close at hand and, as we turned
towards the Ram's Head Range at the Snowy Crossing, hail-
stones came battering down. But our armour that day was
the chain mail of happiness, and the persistence of the hail-
storm with the thunder and rain found no flaw in its strength.

All the night before I had been disturbed by the recurring
thought, like a dream, that I should see a particular view of
the South Ram's Head from near the hut; now, as we rode
the ridge down which we had skied on that first visit, that
view, snowless but identical, suddenly flashed at me through
the darkening night. With a jolt my mental map came into
place and the soft wings of memory brushed against my
eyes.

Night came and with it a thick rain-mist. Outside the
hut the stockmen had lit a huge log fire and we stood there
in the intermittent showers yarning, glad of its companionable glow. My conversation with Leo Byett was of the skiing
days at Kiandra when it was a gold-mining centre, and the
eerie figures of the others, illumined by the glow made
ethereal by the mist, could have been the ghosts of those for-

gotten days when, even near by on the Crackenback, gold was feverishly sought. . . .

The mist was still there when we woke in the morning, making the day gone by seem like a dream. But the sun suddenly blazed through soon after breakfast; so after the packhorses were saddled and loaded, we set off for Groggin again via the Cascades—the little-known home of the wild buckeens. . . .

The Cascades gets its name from the huge waterfall that empties out of it to drop nearly 2500 feet into the river below. It is a fairly open green valley with hills blocking off all views—a secretive place with some strange attraction. It is like a basin, sunk below the higher Alps, whose outside rim hides the sudden fall to the Indi at its feet. A creek winds down the centre of it and on one side, raised up on a little hill, is a slab-and-bark hut. From a nebulous situation on the map, painted around with romantic stories of wild horses, the Cascades had become something real with a magnetic force of its own. What would it look like in winter, covered in snow, with a long narrow ski-track winding up the valley floor to Purgatory, the mountain at its head?

We had heard much about the steepness of the ride out from the Cascades, and the stories had not been exaggerated. We went out through the yards and down gently till the ridge seemed almost to turn under, and we began to drop like stones cast from the top of a cliff, down through the high majesty of the mountain-ash, down and down and down, with never a let up for 2350 feet, till we reached the swift, keen waters of the Indi where the Cascade Creek hurtles into the stream. One can look up and see, through the trees, the endless stream of water that is the Cascade itself.

The "road" along the Indi is not cut into the bank like the "River Road" to Geehi. It is an erratic track high up along the red shingle of the banks and through the blacksoil of the pocket flats; trees overhang it; a track I should not like to ride at night when a slip or a stumble could mean a long drop into the rock-broken water.

It was five o'clock when we reached Groggin, so strangely

civilized with its buildings and orchard. We put up our tent with all possible speed and ran down in the sunset to the river for a swim.

The last two days had been long ones, but the next was longer still. Four of us rode out to Pinnabar. On the principle of barter I had purloined some onions for Mr Nankervis's breakfast (over whose land and snow leases we had been riding) on condition that he would take us. . . .

We struck our trouble early with half-burnt scrub, which was almost impenetrable. In the struggle the horses grew tired and thirsty and we found no water all the way. Here again we rode through many wild flowers and I saw for the first time the Trigger Plant, a small, puce-coloured flower, growing on a stalk like a bush orchid. When it is pressed behind the throat it ejects a little trigger in protest.

On the top of our second ridge we found, stretching out in front of us, a knife-edge, rising and falling in little knobs of granite talus and ever gaining height, sometimes steeply sometimes gently, till it opened out on to a broad ridge of Pinnabar. It was bad to ride along, with precipices on either side and rough rock scrambles. As we rode up the broader section of it leading towards the summit, I realized that it was, after all, the ridge we had once skied down, and I saw again the same corner of Groggin as we had seen then.

The sky was mostly overcast and it was cold and grey on the top by the last gnarled snow-gums. We could see no water and I was fairly certain that we should only find it below the great south slope, in one of the innumerable gullies. This south slope was thick with snow-grass, too steep and too slippery to ride down, so we led our horses. Suddenly we saw water ahead, just a tiny soak at the head of a scrub-choked gully. . . .

We boiled our quartpots a little lower down the gully and lay back on the soft snow-grass, munching cheese and biscuits and plum-cake with that divine content born of something achieved and enjoyed. Ahead of us still was the return to Groggin, and the lowering clouds repudiated any promise of moonlight. For twenty minutes only, we stopped there. For a short time I became merged, once again, in that strong remoteness and spirit of the wilderness that is Pinnabar's; but my memories of that day are mostly of tense, unrelenting effort, as we strove up the steep spurs with only rotten soil, leaves, bark and bracken and rolling stones underfoot, and above and around us the tenacious scrub, burnt so that its tops had curled into a Herculean weave, one with another; then that long knife-ridge on which our horses seemed to balance uneasily, and the clouds sliding over the sky. Ahead of us and later behind us, massive Pinnabar rose from its wilderness like a king of a wild and formidable army that guarded its ramparts well—an army of steep ridges, trees and scrub and bracken.

We returned down a different ridge, one that would lead us more directly to the floor of the Omeo Creek. The ridge dropped fairly fast through open mountain-ash forest; when we looked back we could see the overpowering, immense wave of the summit, curling like a "dumper" to break and hurl itself down on us.

Another ridge took us down to the creek, dropping at a tremendous angle and going through the same twisted, woven scrub. Great fallen tree-trunks lay this way and that, but the actual ground underfoot was less rotten. We had to lead our horses over the worst of the grade and the biggest logs, but for the most part we simply rode and hoped; and the ridge went on and on for an inconceivable length. We reached the Omeo Creek as dusk and dark clouds were softening the daylight. The valley was full of a thick mat of bracken and logs, and tall tree-ferns interlaced their branches over the banks of the winding creek.

It took us about two hours to Groggin from the foot of our spur, continually crossing and recrossing the creek. Eventually we found a cattle-pad and pushed along fairly fast until I felt that if I jumped one more log I must surely fall off.

Rain started and darkness closed in around us just as we reached the first slip-rails. We pulled on our oilers and set off for home. Mr Nankervis led the way, waving a three-pronged stick he pulled from a bush. The first steeplechase could not have looked much stranger than we did as we cantered through the rain and darkness, jumping log after log and laughing and shouting, with our oilers flapping —and always the Mephistophelian pitchfork ahead, wildly cheering us on. . . .

The next day was a very necessary "off day", with only swimming and lazy thought. Then came the long ride home, from Groggin all the way to Towong, thirty long miles. We started getting the horses packed and everything ready for the road before the moon and the stars had gone completely from the sky. I spent most of the day on my own and loved the ride through the bush, with time to smell the scents of it, hear the silence and the sounds of it; to watch the birds and the flowers and to think back on all these days, the questions that had found their answers, and the uncertainties that had been stilled. I had learnt, as I had never learnt before, that the summer mountains could hold me in thrall with a subtle attraction of their own, an offering of knowledge and experience. I know now that the mountains, bare and blue or covered with snow, summer or winter, spring or fall, have gifts of strength and joy for those who go into their highways with unstinted energy, giving all their understanding to the many voices of the hills.

FREE GIFTS FROM FOCUS

More and more smokers are taking advantage of The FOCUS Collection. It's an exciting range of stylish free gifts and experiences.

You can obtain your gifts FREE in exchange for FOCUS Points which are available in all packs of Embassy and Regal sealed with a gold tear tape.

For your personal copy of The FOCUS Collection telephone **0787 881666** or write to: **The Focus Collection, P.O. Box 1020, Sudbury, Suffolk CO10 6FX** and include the words 'I am a smoker aged 18 years or over' together with your signature.

Please also tell us if you do not wish to receive future updated catalogues or other tobacco offers. The Focus offer is only open to smokers aged 18 years or over, resident in the U.K.

Issued by Imperial Tobacco Limited, WF

ADVICE BY H.M. GOVERNMENT
If you do smoke cigarettes
Leave a long stub. Remove from mouth between puffs. Inhale less. Take fewer puffs.